About this book: The art of Joseph Cornell has been a source of fascination since he first began constructing boxes and collages in the 1930s, initially under the influnce of European Surrealism. In this book, by drawing on the widest range possible of primary material – virtually all Cornell's scrapbooks and source files, as well as correspondence and diaries – supplemented by further details gathered during more than fifty interviews undertaken with the artist's family and acquaintances, including Robert Motherwell and Susan Sontag, Lindsay Blair gives us the most detailed picture yet of an artist who hid so much of his life from the world. What emerges is Cornell the obsessive notetaker, collator, joiner, editor, archivist, curator – an artist in fact whose boxes were built up from a mass of intensely felt personal yearnings, attachments, fears and disappointments. *Joseph Cornell's Vision of Spiritual Order* offers a wealth of insights into how it is these works succeed in entangling the beholder in the rich strands of allusion, association and reverie that are so akin to those that forced their genesis. And her conclusion, wholly convincing in the light of the evidence she provides, is that Cornell's ultimate subject was the mind itself.

About the author: Lindsay Blair received her doctorate on Joseph Cornell from the University of Essex, having spent several years living in New York while researching it, and was later Associate Producer of 'Joseph Cornell: Worlds in a Box', a BBC TV *Omnibus* programme first transmitted in Britain in 1991. She now lives in the Scottish Highlands.

ESSAYS IN ART AND CULTURE

The Landscape Vision of Paul Nash
by Roger Cardinal

Looking at the Overlooked: Four Essays on Still Life Painting
by Norman Bryson

Charles Sheeler and the Cult of the Machine
by Karen Lucic

Portraiture
by Richard Brilliant

C. R. Mackintosh: The Poetics of Workmanship
by David Brett

Image on the Edge: The Margins of Medieval Art
by Michael Camille

Illustration
by J. Hillis Miller

Francis Bacon and the Loss of Self
by Ernst van Alphen

Paul Delvaux: Surrealizing the Nude
by David Scott

Manet's Silence and the Poetics of Bouquets
by James H. Rubin

The Symptom of Beauty
by Francette Pacteau

Figuring Jasper Johns
by Fred Orton

Political Landscape
by Martin Warnke

Visionary Experience in the Golden Age of Spanish Art
by Victor I. Stoichita

The Double-Screen: Medium and Representation in Chinese Painting
by Wu Hung

Painting the Soul: Icons, Death Masks and Shrouds
by Robin Cormack

A Short History of the Shadow
by Victor I. Stoichita

Peter Greenaway: Museums and Moving Images
by David Pascoe

Terminal Architecture
by Martin Pawley

Joseph Cornell's Vision of Spiritual Order

Lindsay Blair

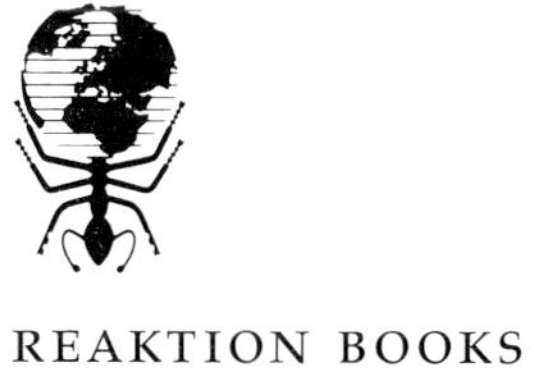

REAKTION BOOKS

A Dhomhnuill, le mo ghaol

Published by Reaktion Books Ltd
11 Rathbone Place
London W1P 1DE, UK

First published 1998

Series design by Hu..nphrey Stone

Printed and bound in Great Britain by
BAS Printers Ltd, Over Wallop, Hampshire

British Library Cataloguing in Publication Data

Blair, Lindsay
Joseph Cornell's vision of spiritual order
1. Cornell, Joseph – Criticism and interpretation 2. Art, American
3. Art, Modern – 20th century – United States
I. Title
709.2
ISBN 0 948462 49 3

Contents

Acknowledgements

Warm thanks to Richard M. Ader, Dawn Ades, Anthology Film Archives (New York), Archives of American Art (Smithsonian Institution, Washington, D.C.), John Ashbery, Dore Ashton, Edward Batcheller, Helen Cornell Batcheller, Lindy Bergman, James Blair, Rudy Burckhardt, the late Nicholas Calas, Roger Cardinal, C&M Arts (New York), Mary Ann Caws, Robert and Rhett Delford-Brown, the late Teeny Duchamp, Richard Feigen, Charles Henri Ford, Betsy von Furstenburg, David Hare, Denise Hare, Lynda Roscoe Hartigan, Howard Hussey, the late Ray Johnson, Allegra Kent, Kathryn Kuh, Jean Levy, David Mann, Duane Michals, the late Robert Motherwell, John Bernard Myers, Hans Namuth, The Pace Gallery (New York), Eve Propp, Harry Roseman, Carolee Schneeman, Linda Scott, P. Adams Sitney, Barbara Somers, Susan Sontag, Sandra Leonard Starr, Allan Stone, May Tabak, Dorothea Tanning, Dickran Tashjian, Gwen Thomas, John Willenbecher, Donald Windham, Trevor Winkfield, and Steve Wood.

My special thanks to Elizabeth Cornell Benton and Leila Hadley for their great inspiration, and also to the staff at Reaktion for their patience and help. Thankyou to my parents, my brother and my sons for their love and support. My greatest debt is to my husband, Donald, for his vision and insight, for his help in preparing the manuscript for publication, and for always being there. This book is dedicated to him.

Chronology

1903 Cornell is born on 24 December in Nyack, New York, the first of four children of Joseph and Helen Cornell. His father is a prosperous textiles designer.

1905 Elizabeth Cornell born.

1906 Helen Cornell born.

1910 Robert Cornell born. At one year old he is discovered to be suffering from cerebral palsy.

1917 Cornell's father dies and the devastated family is faced with a collapse in their way of life. Cornell is sent to Phillips Academy, Andover, Massachusetts, where he studies science and Romance languages.

1918 Helen Cornell rents a house in Douglaston, Queens, for herself and the family.

1919 The Cornell family moves to Bayside in Queens.

1921 Cornell leaves Phillips Academy, and, after a brief spell working in a textiles mill in Massachusetts, finds employment in Manhattan as a travelling salesman for the William Whitman Company, selling woollen goods. Thus begin his 'wandering' and 'exploring' habits in New York, with Cornell often stopping to gaze through the windows into art galleries, and at other times acquiring precious fragments and memorabilia. He also begins to attend the opera, ballet, and movie theatres.

1925 After experiencing a healing, Cornell converts to Christian Science, joining the Mother Church in Boston and the First Church of Christ, Scientist, in Great Neck, New York.

1929 Cornell, along with his mother, sisters and Robert, moves to 3708 Utopia Parkway, Flushing, where he remains until his death in 1972. In June his sister Helen marries and leaves the family home.

1931 Loses his job as a salesman for the William Whitman Company. He makes his first artwork, a collage/montage, after watching Julien Levy in his New York gallery unpack some Surrealist pieces by Max Ernst that had just arrived from Europe. In August his sister Elizabeth (Betty) marries and moves away.

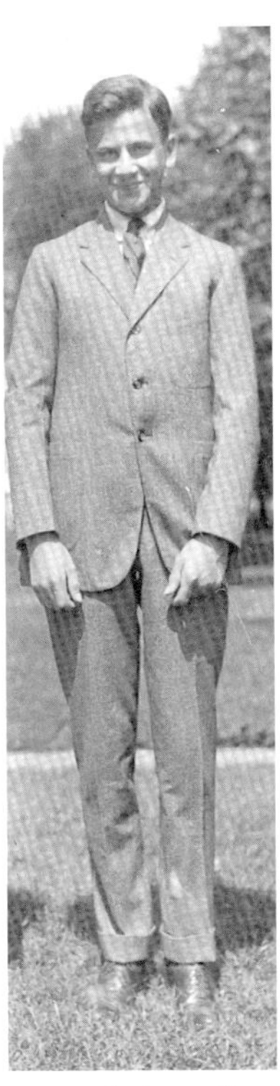

1 Joseph Cornell: the schoolboy at Andover.

1932 Has his first one-man exhibition at the Julien Levy Gallery, and remains affiliated with this Gallery until its closure in 1939. Begins experiments with various containers for his artworks.

1933 Writes a film scenario, *Monsieur Phot*, which he dedicates to Marcel Duchamp.

1934 Is hired by Traphagen Commercial Textile Studio as a designer, and continues with this company for the next six years.

1936 Makes his first film, *Rose Hobart*, in collage format, and continues to be fascinated by film-making throughout his career. Makes his first box construction, which becomes part of an installation piece for the hugely successful exhibition held at the Museum of Modern Art in this year – 'Fantastic Art, Dada, Surrealism'.

1940 His employment with Traphagen ends, but during the 1940s he consolidates the box format and pushes further his ideas for installations. During the 1940s he also develops works in series, and establishes his dossier system (these dossiers are expanding folders that hold Cornell's notes, clippings and paper ephemera, each spun around an obsessive point).

1941 Begins freelance work for various magazines, including *House and Garden*, *Vogue* and *Dance Index*. At home in Utopia Parkway, he organizes a studio space in the cellar in which to work.

1942 Meets Robert Motherwell and Matta Echaurren. Peggy Guggenheim includes work by Cornell in the inaugural show held at her Art of This Century Gallery. Meets Max Ernst.

1943 Produces his special issue of *View* magazine, Charles Henri Ford's review, in January.

1944 For several months this summer he works in a garden centre in Flushing that is owned by a Christian Science Practitioner. This is an inspirational and spiritual period of great significance in his life.

1946 At his 'Romantic Museum (Portraits of Women)' exhibition held at the Hugo Gallery in New York, Cornell exhibits dossiers and portfolios alongside box constructions.

1948 The exhibition 'Objects by Joseph Cornell' is held at Copley Galleries, Beverly Hills, California.

1949 In New York, 'La Lanterne Magique du Ballet Romantique of Joseph Cornell' is shown at the Hugo Gallery, and '"Aviary" by Joseph Cornell' at Egan Gallery.

1950 By this year Cornell is becoming oppressed by an increasing need to organize his notations and his collections of objects, and throughout the 1950s continues his never-ending 'voyaging' in dime-stores, bookshops and cafeterias as well as making return visits to favourite Manhattan haunts like the Bowery and Grand Central Station.

1951 Meets Willem De Kooning and Mark Rothko.

1955 Cornell's 'Winter Nights Series' exhibition is held at the Stable Gallery in New York.

1960 Begins to direct his efforts towards collages. During the 1960s he makes few new boxes, but he does refurbish a number made in previous years. He also hires assistants to scout for materials, to organize these materials in the dossiers and source boxes kept in the studio basement, and to run domestic errands and help with chores.

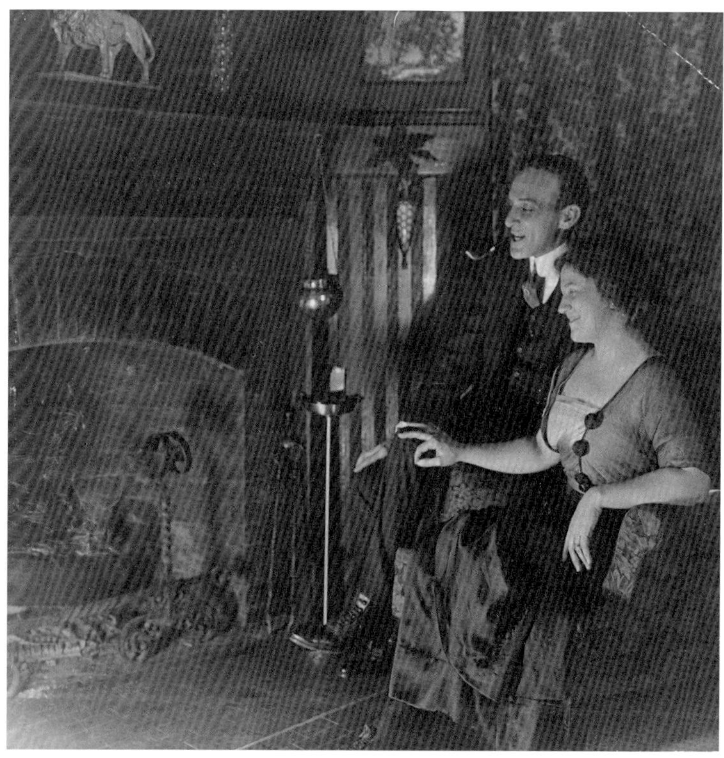

2 Joseph Cornell's parents at home, Nyack, New York.

1961 Works by Cornell are included in 'The Art of Assemblage' show held at The Museum of Modern Art, along with examples by Marcel Duchamp and Kurt Schwitters.

1962 Meets Joyce Hunter, a teenager who works in a New York coffee shop.

1963 Charles Henri Ford takes Robert Indiana, James Rosenquist and Andy Warhol to visit Cornell at home at Utopia Parkway.

1964 Joyce Hunter and friends are arrested for stealing boxes from Cornell's garage, but he refuses to prosecute. Later this year Joyce is stabbed to death in New York, an event that severely shakes Cornell.

1965 In February Robert dies at the home in Westhampton, Long Island, of his sister Betty. Cornell, overwhelmed with love and sadness, makes collages in memory of his brother.

1966 Cornell's mother dies in October at Betty's in Westhampton.

1967 Major exhibitions of works by Cornell are held at the Pasadena Museum of Art, California, and at the Guggenheim Museum in New York.

1972 Cornell undergoes prostate surgery in June, which leaves him much weakened, and he stays at Betty's in Westhampton to recover. In November he returns home to Utopia Parkway, but on 29 December dies of heart failure.

1980 A major exhibition of Cornell's work opens at The Museum of Modern Art in New York, after which it tours in Europe.

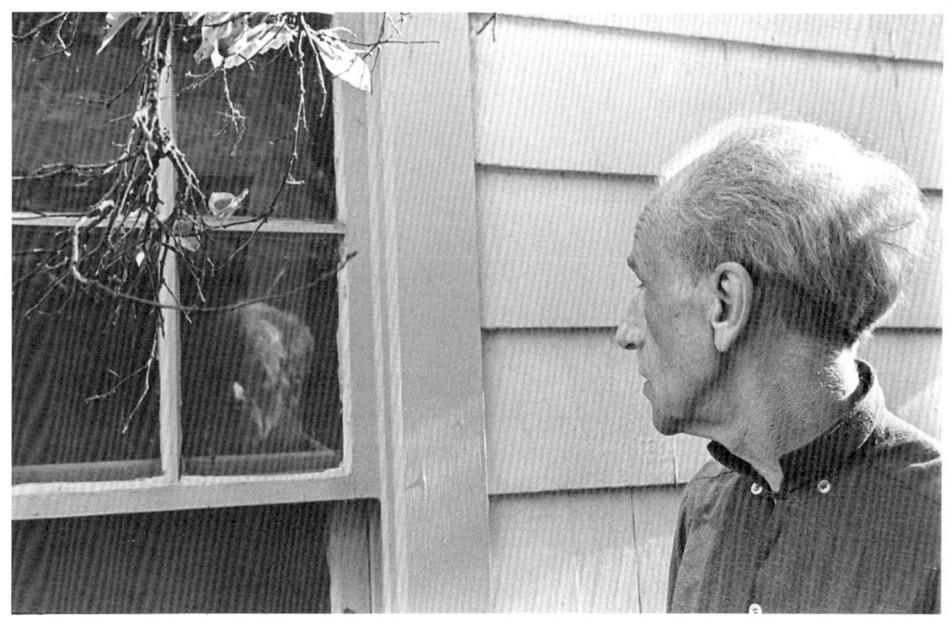

3 Hans Namuth, *Joseph Cornell*, 1970, a window reflection photographed at 3708 Utopia Parkway.

Introduction

One of the most distinctive features of Joseph Cornell's working method is the all pervading self-scrutiny that accompanied his every move. He kept a record of everything he thought, saw or felt in his dossiers, those files that he meticulously stored, classified and returned to throughout his career. This intense scrutiny of his own working method from the moment of inspiration onwards shows that Cornell identified the creative mind as his ultimate subject. We should not be surprised, therefore, that on looking into the boxes he constructed we discover such strong reflections of their maker.

Cornell was born in 1903 in Nyack, a small town in New York state on the Hudson river. His father, also a Joseph, was a textiles designer; his mother, Helen Ten Broeck Storms, taught at a local nursery school. Both were of Dutch descent. Cornell had two younger sisters, Betty (Elizabeth) and Helen, and a younger brother, Robert, who suffered from birth with cerebral palsy. Nyack, which lies 29 miles north of the city of New York, was a comfortable middle-class community during the time Cornell was growing up there, and his family's way of life had a graciousness and an ease about it. His father's business prospered, and the Cornells lived in a large house with servants at 137 South Broadway (illus. 4), with grandparents and an extended family not too far distant.[1] They holidayed regularly at Ashbury Park, in the Adirondacks, and at Lake Mooselookmeguntic in Maine.

The comfortable financial situation the Cornells enjoyed at that time enabled them to indulge in various cultural pursuits, not least music and amateur dramatics, and there were frequent trips to New York. Cornell's sister Betty has recalled in detail many Wordsworthian 'spots of time' from their shared childhood years: the young Cornell sucking shards of ice as he sat on the fold-down step of the ice wagon that toured the streets; as the fireflies buzzed around them in the garden, watching tadpoles swimming in glass jars; special treats when they were allowed to sleep out together on the porch with mosquito nets draped over their beds; standing

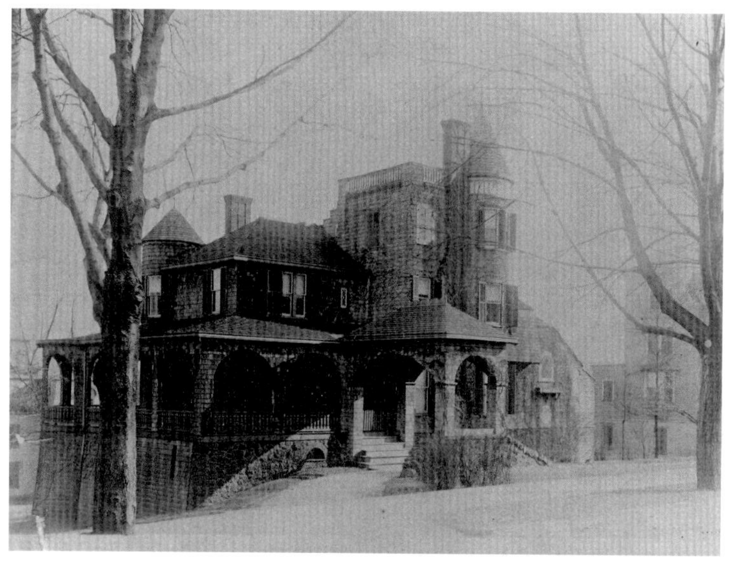

4 The Cornell family house at 137 South Broadway, Nyack, New York.

on the roof of the big house at Nyack while gazing at a strangely lit balloon as it floated down the Hudson river.[2] She also retains vivid images of their parents, for example father playing 'Dick-Dead-Eye' and doing the soft-shoe-shuffle while mother accompanied him on the piano, the music drifting up to the children huddled together at the top of the stairs. She remembers her grandfather tying small white paper bags around the clusters of grapes in the arbour, and her grandmother opening the top of the piano at Christmas-time to reveal the cache of home-made jams, pickles and preserves prepared for the new year. Christmas was very special, being a double celebration, for Cornell's own birthday was Christmas Eve ('I am peculiarly prone to Christmas, from childhood, in the context of New York, snow, magical store windows. . .'.) It is clear that one reason his art remained so self-concerned was because he sought always to recreate the remembered qualities of this childhood.

The idyll ended abruptly in 1917 when Cornell's father died. The first thing to follow from this disastrous event was that Cornell was sent away to school, to Phillips Academy, Andover, Massachusetts, where he remained until 1921. The financial position the bereaved family suddenly found itself in meant a considerable change of circumstances. Cornell's mother was obliged to work part-time baking cakes and knitting jumpers, and the family had to move – first to rented accommodation in Douglaston, then to a small house in Bayside in 1919, and finally in 1929 to 3708 Utopia Parkway, Flushing, which lies in suburban Queens, one of the two boroughs on the western edge of Long Island that form part of the city of New York. And although in time both sisters married, Cornell continued to live with his mother and Robert. His role within the household was that of the main provider, though he also had to help provide care for his brother. Cornell's respect for Robert was enormous: the latter's well-being made up a large part of Cornell's daily concerns.

By the time the family moved to Utopia Parkway in 1929, Cornell had been working as a travelling salesman for eight years. He suffered much from depression during this period, and in an attempt to combat this he began reading *Science and Health, with Key to the Scriptures*, the revelations of Mary Baker Eddy (1821–1910), founder of the First Church of Christ, Scientist. He went on to join the Mother Church that Eddy had established in Boston and also a First Church of Christ, Scientist, nearer to home at Great Neck, New York, in 1925. He was to remain a devout Christian Scientist for the rest of his life. He lost his job as a salesman in 1931, but was

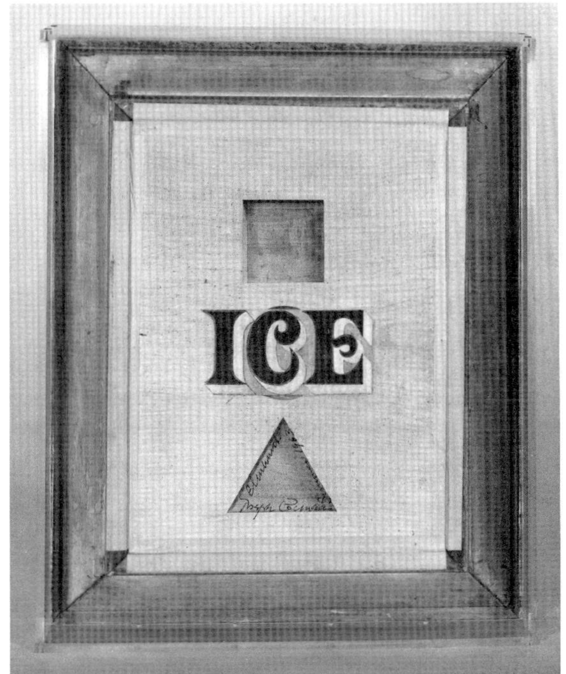

5 Verso of *Untitled (Ice)*, 1963, collage.

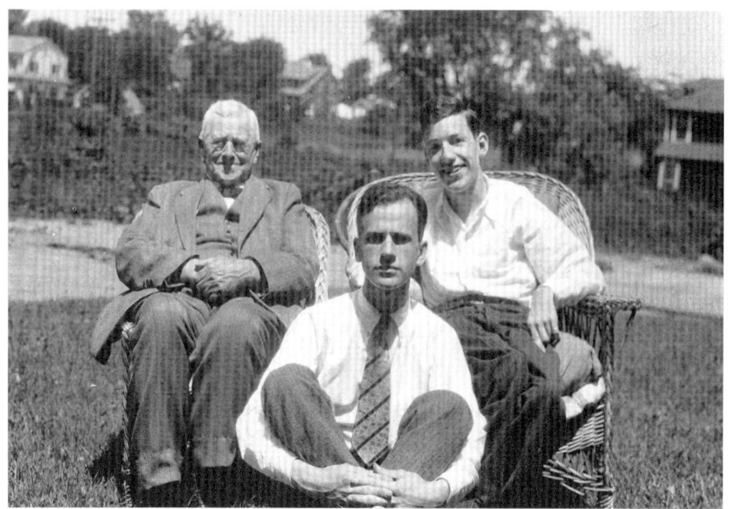

6 Joseph Cornell and brother Robert with their maternal grandfather, late 1920s.

employed as a textiles designer from 1934 to 1940, and later undertook freelance design work for various magazines, including *Vogue* and *House and Garden*. For a brief time he also worked on an assembly line, and in 1944 spent an important few months working at a garden centre. In 1965 his brother died, as did his mother the following year. From then on, domestic and studio assistants were to stay at Utopia Parkway. Cornell himself died at the house as a result of heart failure on 29 December 1972.

Cornell's assemblage art went through various stages of development, as did the recording process that accompanied it. In 1931 he made his first artwork after watching Julien Levy unpacking some Surrealist pieces that had just arrived from Europe.[3] In 1936 he built his first box construction, created his first installation, and it was in this same period that he began keeping a diary. In the 1940s he consolidated the box format, pushed further the installation idea with two shows, 'Romantic Museum (Portraits of Women)' and 'Aviary', and developed his dossier system. In the following decade he developed his series. Cornell's work at this time was becoming sparer, more architectural, more involved in textures, openly focused on signs of process, erosion or weathering. He integrated collage within the box interior, and in this period he also began to collaborate with film-makers. In the 1960s he made numerous collages using colour magazines, but produced fewer pieces.

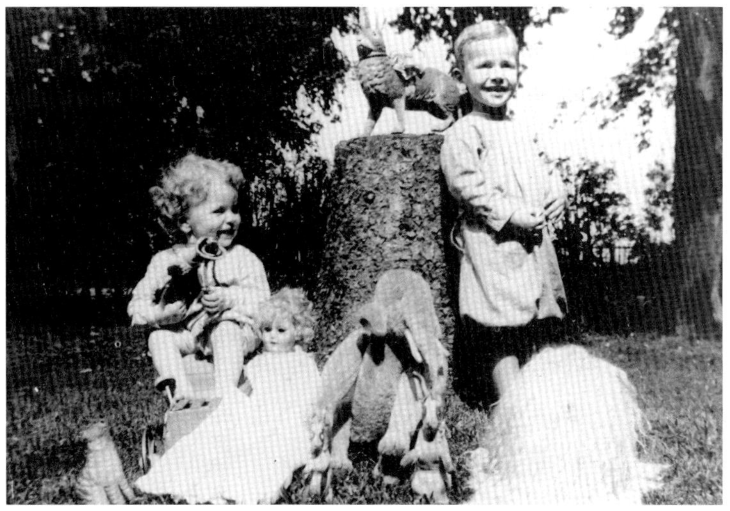

7 Joseph Cornell and sister Betty, Nyack, *c.* 1907.

Surrealism is the single most important art context to consider in relation to Cornell's work.[4] When Cornell was emerging as an artist, Surrealism was establishing itself as a phenomenon in the USA. By the early 1940s many European Surrealists were there in person, having fled a war-torn continent. Cornell was there to see the new Surrealist art arriving at the Julien Levy Gallery (and subsequently at other establishments), and gradually he began to become acquainted with the artists responsible. Looking back on this exciting period, Cornell wrote of it as the 'revelation world of Surrealism – a golden age, one of white magic without which I don't know where I'd be today.'[5]

The first Surrealist show reached America in 1931 at the Wadsworth Atheneum in Hartford, Connecticut, and, with some changes, was transferred two months later to the Julien Levy Gallery in New York. Cornell had his first one-man show at the same Gallery in 1932, and in it were several works labelled as 'Jouets Surrealists'. Cornell came to know several of the Surrealists, and some of his works, especially collages and works from the 1930s and 1940s, are clearly influenced by them. Apart, however, from the specific debts in terms of imagery that he owed to Surrealism, it is important to consider the iconoclastic perspective of the Surrealists and to see how that affected him.

André Breton, in his first Surrealist manifesto of 1924, wrote that Surrealism was

> Psychic automism in its pure state, by which one purposes to express – verbally, by means of the written word, or in any other manner – the actual functioning of thought, in the absence of any control exercised by reason, exempt from any aesthetic or moral concern. / Encyclopedia. Philosophy. Surrealism is based on the belief in the superior reality of certain forms of previously neglected associations, in the omnipotence of dream, in the disinterested play of thought.[6]

As can be seen from this celebrated definition, the emphasis is on process, and a process that resembles the free association of psychoanalysis rather than anything that has to do with conventional creativity or craft. Within this overall approach, the function of art is very much to reveal to the creator (as much as to anyone else) the actual workings of the mental and creative processes. From here it is easy to see why collage was so much a favoured form for the Surrealists and for Cornell with his associative obsessions, for it stimulated almost limitless groupings of diverse objects, a process very like the encouragement of free association in Freudian therapy.

But Cornell, like most Americans who were associated at one time or another with the Surrealists, always kept his distance. Those in the Surrealist movement itself were dangerously charged with inconsistencies and tensions: while advocating freedom of thought some were strict adherents to Marxist dogma; while advocating democracy others practised a nationalistic (i.e., French) elitism; and while ridiculing religion there were those who insisted on placing their faith in occultism and numerology. Cornell's connection with the movement is difficult to define with any real precision, but it is not something that can be ignored. As Dawn Ades has put it, 'Cornell remains a paradoxical figure on so many levels. He was never committed to Surrealism, and yet his connection with it was not simply reflective of its being the strongest and most vital movement around at the time. He was attracted to visual Surrealism, yet he was probably closer in sensibility to the American Transcendentalist tradition.'[7]

Cornell's work was part of a continuing struggle to come to terms with consciousness, but he was also caught up in the American spiritual quest. This is most specifically evident in relation to Christian Science. *Science and Health* was a hugely

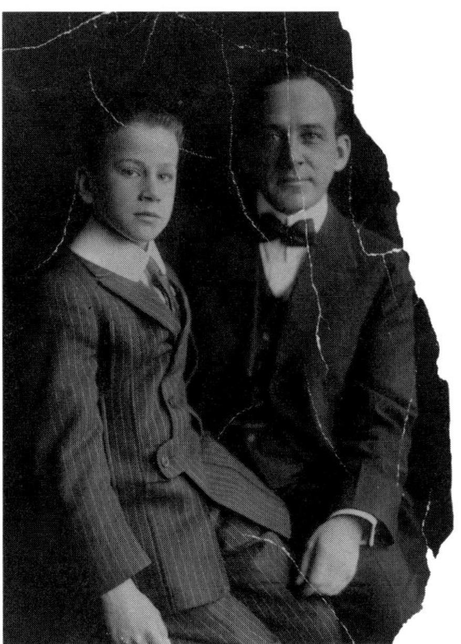

8 Joseph Cornell with his father, *c*. 1915.

influential text, and quickly passed through over one thousand editions. It exerted a compelling fascination on Cornell, completely validating his researches into the self. Christian Science insists on explaining all cause and effect as mental, not physical. It denies any reality whatsoever to matter: disease, for example, is regarded as unreal. No kind of Christian theologian other than a Christian Scientist has ever accepted the view that matter is unreal in the sense that the phrase was used by Mary Baker Eddy. She utterly denied the reality of an objective universe. This approach, which elevated the status of the inner quest to that of being the only quest, was all that Cornell's own selfconscious inclinations could have desired. Nothing, after all, could be more selfconscious than an obsessive habit of noting, hoarding and storing the history of one's own mind.

Cornell's obsessive relationship with his own boxes is usefully illustrated by a conversation he once had with the gallery owner David Mann. According to Mann,

> I once praised a new group of things that he was working on and he said, I'm glad you find them beautiful and then he became very sort of depressed. I said well that's a funny way to take a compliment and he said you don't know how terrible it is to be locked into boxes all your life, you have no idea what a terrible thing it is.[8]

Cornell was an eccentric bachelor artist who was able to use his private and isolated situation to focus on the state of his mind. His geographical position on the edge of Manhattan – in suburbia, as opposed to living in the heart of things alongside his fellow artists – meant that he could have more independence of movement and thought. (Robert Motherwell has explained that he often suggested to Cornell that he move from suburban Flushing into Manhattan.) It was also very significant in that this situation was the physical sign of Cornell's detachment: although he sought for the self relentlessly, this self was something that had always to be protected by a web of symbolism and complex crosscultural borrowings. It would be a mistake to see Cornell as having been openly confessional. As Deborah Soloman suggests in her recent biography of Cornell: 'It is often said of artists that they live in fear of being misunderstood. Cornell, by contrast, lived in fear of being understood.'[9] Later in his life, in his letters, diaries and collages, he was to reveal a chronically repressed sexuality. Innocence and desire were both frequently evident in his work, and it is the conflict between these two forces that so often created the dynamic ambiguities of his art.

In *Joseph Cornell's Vision of Spiritual Order* I examine the scope of Cornell's journey in his search for the self. His dossiers are the first subjects that have to be unravelled, for they reveal the extensive and continuous self-analysis that marked his every creative step. 'GC 44' especially, his largest dossier, yet one that has received little notice, displays the neurosis that threatened to envelop him as he strove to create a system of classification that would make some order out of the relentless tide of associations that flooded his mind.

As might be guessed, and Cornell's critics were quick to notice this, it was to childhood that Cornell was most persistently drawn. He was for ever searching for a new angle, an unexpected detail, perhaps, that he or someone in his family had remembered, or photographs, or books, or an insight received from children's books or tomes on child psychology – anything in fact that might provide him with a clue to his own selfhood. Though the field has already been scoured somewhat, the range of strategies Cornell employed to recover his sense of childhood has yet to be fully understood.

The search for the self required more, however, than an unreflecting gleam of childhood. Cornell needed the reflection of others in order more fully to realize his own image. Thus Lauren Bacall, Susan Sontag and Leila Hadley become parallels for him. With regard to his fascinations or obsessions, his portraits reveal much more about the artist than they do about his subjects, and in this sense they are more properly self-portraits than they are portraits.

Finally, Cornell had to orientate the self: he had to find a place for that self in a created universe. He wanted to invent, recreate a miniature universe – this we see most acutely in his Soap Bubble Sets, where the widest range into space exists, suggesting immensity and yet at the same time compression. In the Soap Bubble Sets, either timelessness exists, or all times do. This created universe he imagined may have been one characterized by elements of synechdoche, anecdote and soap bubbles rather than by stringent scientific analysis, but his approach was quite consistent with his search for the self. His science was of the Victorian kitchen-table variety, for it referred to the memory of his own childhood fascination with scientific experiments about the house. It was this spirit that, essentially, he tried to recover in his boxes.

In the very early Church, confession was public, made to God and a group of other believers, as Augustine of Hippo's

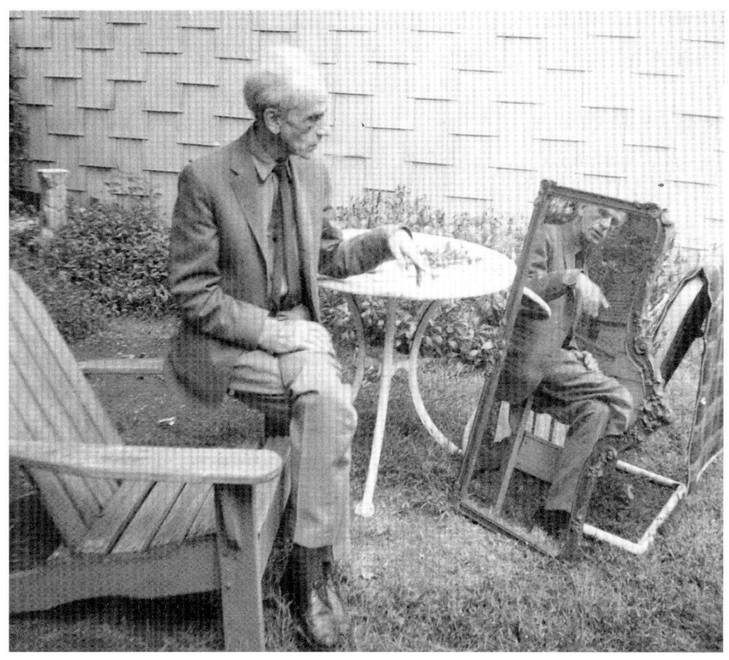

9 Cornell with a looking-glass in the garden, Utopia Parkway, 1960s.

'Catching sight of the mirror portrait of oneself, as though seeing oneself as a portrait done by a master.'

late fourth-century *Confessions* indicate.[10] In Northern Europe, however, confessional boxes were being installed in churches in the early seventeenth century, and so the confessor found himself (or herself) conversing with an unseen presence, a voice. In the same way, the psychoanalyst's voice encourages a dialogue that is similar to the confessional in its emphasis on self-knowledge. When, in his diaries and dossiers, he addressed the unseen reader, or, in his letters, the unseen but known recipient, Cornell was using a similar technique of confessional search. When examining his writings and art works, one experiences an inescapable sense of something private being overheard, something not intended for public consumption. And yet the artist's urge towards self-revelation is everywhere apparent. A relentless process of self-examination, at once confessional and secretive, underlies all Cornell's box constructions. It has resulted in an art with layers and layers of meaning that seep out over time.

Visual communication with the self is dependent on the mirror: the mirror is the primary agent through which we glean knowledge of our appearance, and as such it is a symbol of the reflexive element within our natures. The appeal that the mirror has for the imaginative child and for the artist is very evident in Cornell's art. He selected a reproduction of a self-portrait by the young Dürer for several of his collages (illus. 10), a drawing Dürer had made at the age of

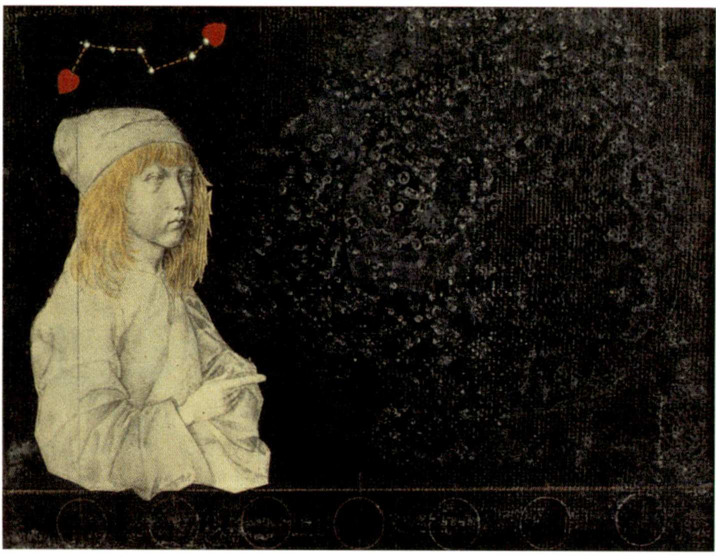

10 *Dürer*, 1965–6, collage.

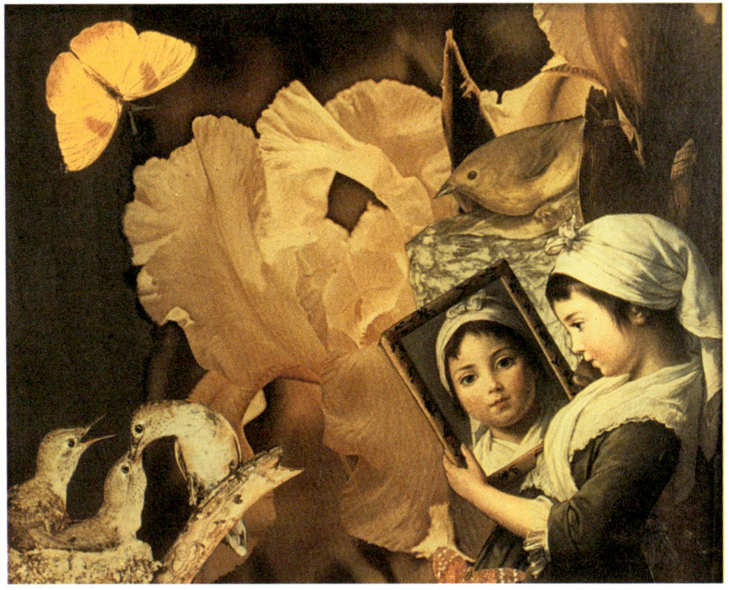

11 *Portrait of the Artist's Daughter by Vigée Lebrun*, c. 1960, collage.

thirteen (it is inscribed 'I drew myself out of the mirror in the year 1484 when I was still a child'). Cornell was also fascinated by the still-lifes of Juan Gris, who always worked with a mirror in front of him, despite the fact that his subject-matter was not overtly the self. Several other references in Cornell's art indicate his interest in artists who were preoccupied by the mirror. And portrait photos of Cornell by Duane Michals, Hans Namuth and Eve Propp feature him engaged with his own reflection (illus. 3, 9). One of the areas in twentieth-century art in which Cornell broke new ground is his recurring and innovative use of the mirror in his art (illus. 11). Numerous boxes feature them, or else a reflecting screen. Where, for the visual artist, the mirror leads to self-portraiture and unremitting self scrutiny, confessional writings in the form of diaries and dossiers lead to the interior world. Vision and voice merge in Cornell's art. His work is always a dialogue with – as well as a projection of – the self.

WORKING METHOD

To understand Cornell's aims and working method we must examine two essential stages in his artistic process: the 'voyaging' stage – his search for materials as recorded in the diaries, correspondence and dossiers – and the business of ordering, classifying and constructing the fruits of these voyages.

Rarely has a visual artist worked so consistently with a paperwork system: the artist and the archivist were as one. Cornell saw the world afresh, and responded poetically, yet at the same time he ordered and catalogued his responses in an elaborate system of dossiers, a system he maintained throughout his life. As he noted in his diary: 'the prospect of cluttered cellar – / creative filing / creative arranging / as poetics / as technique / as joyous creation'.[11]

The dossiers were made available to the public after Cornell's death in 1972. Since then they have been referred to in a number of critical essays, but their full richness is only now being recognized for what they tell us about the boxes

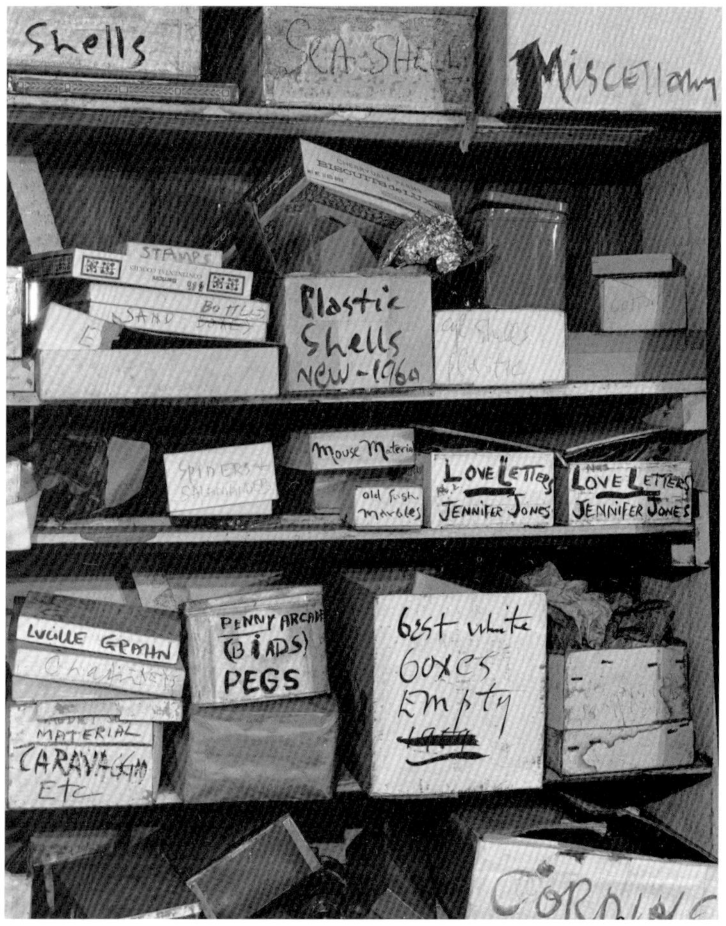

12 Hans Namuth, *The Cellar Workshop at 3708 Utopia Parkway*, 1969, photograph.

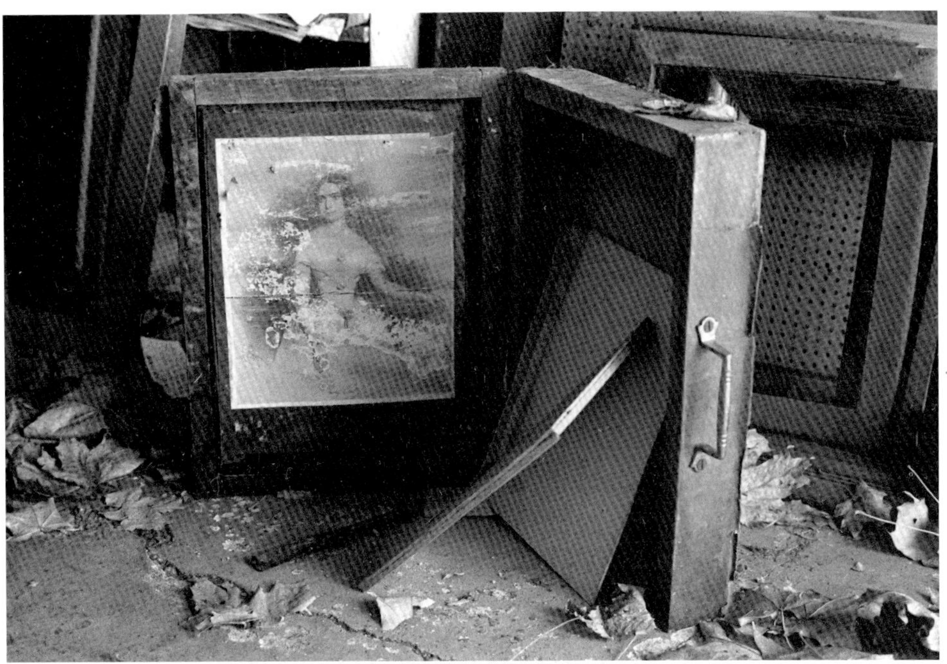

13 Harry Roseman, *Ballerina in a Box*; a discarded box in Cornell's garage, photographed in 1970.

and Cornell's working method. They are, of course, of great intrinsic interest too. The range and scale of these dossiers is immense: there are at least 162 of them that served as source-material files (also used at the source stage were diaries, celebrity files, correspondence files, personal files and files containing writings by others).[12]

The source-material files comprise an astonishing range of topics – Americana, Ballet, Astronomy, Birds, the Circus, Dutch–Flemish, Envelope Fragments, Mathematics, Maps, Fashion, Paperweights, the Grasshopper, Rabbits, and many others. Some files are dedicated to individual composers, ballet-dancers, film-stars, artists and writers, for example Mozart, Fanny Cerrito, Joan Collins, Picasso, Hans Christian Andersen. Others contain a fragmented, intense network of personal notations – subjective associations bound together, as it were, within the covers of the dossier. There are also more purely functional files – places with labels so that references can be easily traced, such as 'Dance Publications', 'Sheet Music', clippings from *The New York Times*. Some files are simply storehouses for pictures (sunsets, nudes, children's illustrations) or for correspondence with Robert Motherwell, Tony Curtis and others. There are, too, the files that are merely seeds, the embryonic beginnings of a work, such as 'The Bird with the Shoe Button Eyes', a piece dedicated to the French Romantic writer Gérard de Nerval.

The dossiers reveal an almost bewildering eclecticism and rampant associationism, so personal and complicated was the nature of the connections Cornell made. We can see that his decision to work with dossiers – some of which comprise only a few pages, while others run to more than 1,000 pages ('GC 44', for example) – was an attempt to control, categorize and label the wealth of material that flooded in.

Cornell's ultimate quarry was the source of inspiration itself, and the dossiers were part of his idiosyncratic attempt to pursue and define the shaping force that lay behind his art. Among the earliest are the stamp albums he began when a child. 'He loved that stamp collection', Betty remembered, 'you know he had thousands of stamps, he had duplicates of some, it must have been twenty or twenty-five of the same stamp'.[13] Stamps, in fact, remained valuable source-material, and Cornell included them in boxes and collages up until the late 1960s. At school he also compiled scrapbook albums, but the one he began on the Spanish ballad-singer Raquel Meller in the 1920s is typical of the method of working with dossiers he devised as an adult. His box construction extracted from this material was not assembled until 1950, which shows that this dossier remained 'active' for nearly 30 years. Most of the dossiers he repeatedly returned to, although some had dormant periods: the 'Celestial Theater', for example, lay so for fourteen years. Other dossiers might be constantly referred to, yet still fail to provide the necessary dynamic for an artwork to emerge. Some of the dossiers were added to after the artwork they inspired had been executed; this suggests that the dossiers had an independent existence.

Cornell's dossiers can be linked to the artworks in a variety of ways, from a one-to-one relationship to a non-specific, tangential one, to the point where what is art and what is dossier can no longer be determined. This shifting relationship between the two is underlined by the ways Cornell identified the purpose of each of his dossiers. Here is a selection of the labels he pasted on them: 'Journey Album'; 'Museum Without Walls'; 'Tower of Visions'; 'Scrapbook'; 'Metaphysique d'Ephemera'; 'Portrait Encasement'; 'Center of a Labyrinth'; 'A "Method"'; 'Repository'; 'Sanctuary'; 'Heritage'; 'Diary';

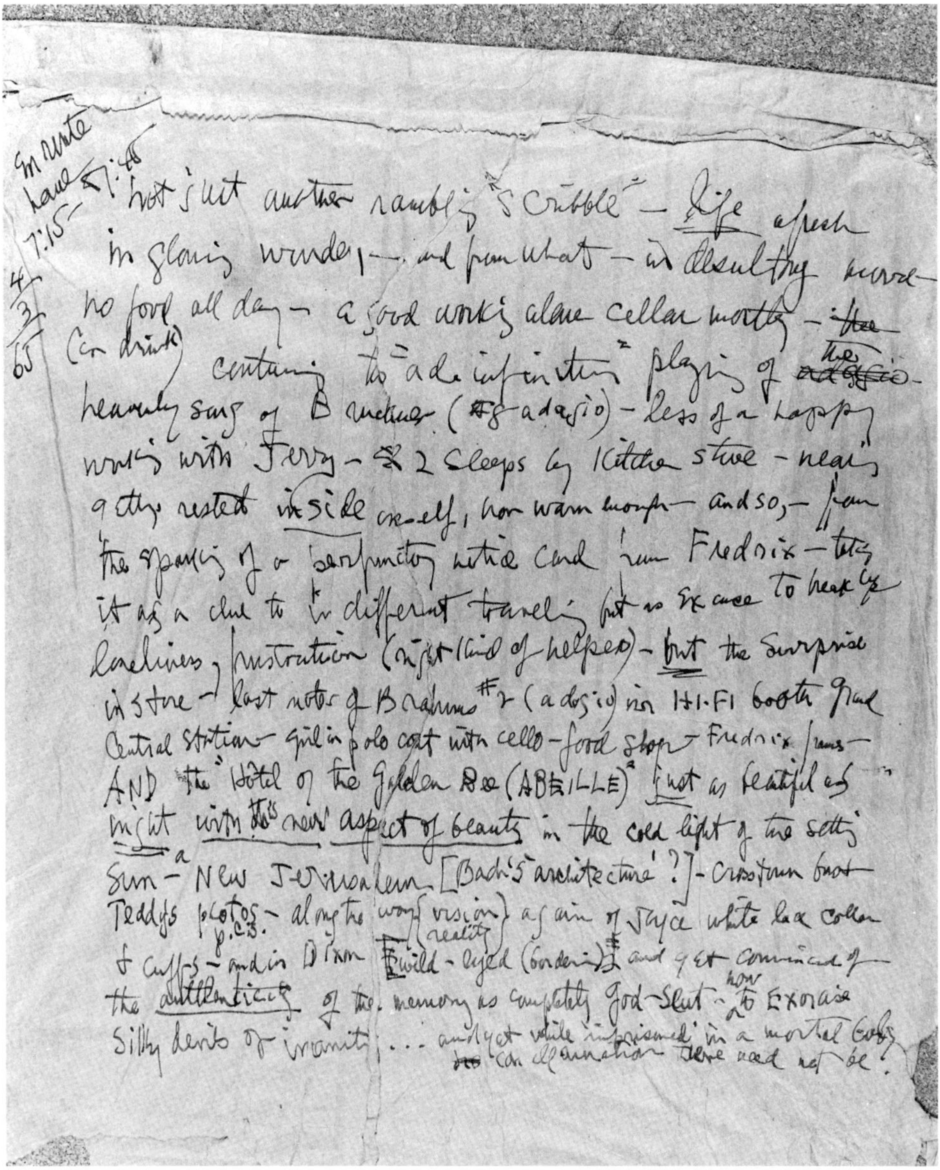

14 An example of Cornell's notes written on brown paper bags, 1965.

'Childhood Regained'; 'Poetic Exploration'; 'Feuilleton'; 'Keepsake'; 'Watershed'.[14] The fact that Cornell did not define the precise contents or subject in many cases – 'Museum Without Walls',[15] for example, or 'Scrapbook' or 'Poetic Exploration' – gives us some idea of the problems his method of collecting and storing raised. The changes in state or status of the dossiers signals the dilemma: Cornell knew that much

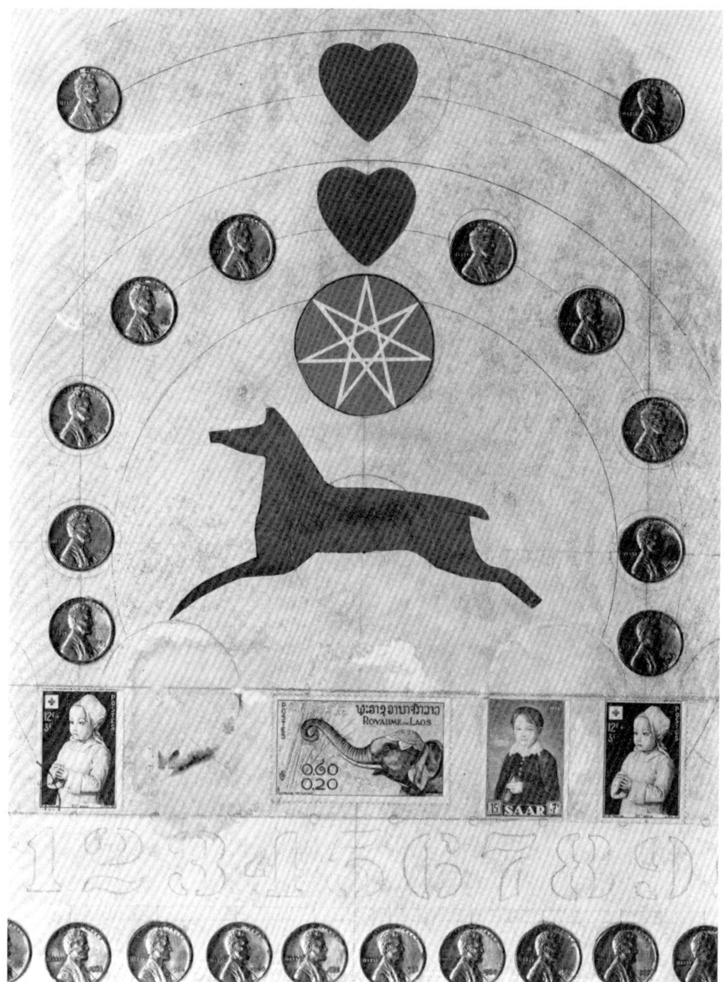

15 *Untitled (Silhouetted Horse Series, Penny Arcade Family)*, *c.* 1965, collage of photomechanical reproductions, coins and paper, with pencil and paint, mounted on fibreboard.

of each dossier concerned himself, yet, unable to accept without question that his own mind was the primary subject, he constantly searched for the theme or title that would suggest the moral or aesthetic aim. He also felt that his self-centredness revealed an error in thinking, for his religion dictated that personality be eliminated in favour of higher principles. He nurtured a conception of himself as a modest and reticent man who made things from the 'warp and woof of daily life', yet his dossiers reveal that he was obsessively absorbed with his own interior reality and with the possibilities of higher, spiritual states.

A one-man exhibition of Cornell's works, 'Romantic

Museum', shown in 1946 at the Hugo Gallery, New York, included several dossiers arranged alongside box constructions; the dossier 'Portrait of Ondine' was twice put on show in his lifetime (illus. 16); and Cornell showed some of his dossiers to certain individuals within the privacy of his workroom/studio; but these exposures amount to very little when we consider the vast quantity of written, clipped and collected material that exists. Even from beyond the grave Cornell planned to control the leakage of material to the public: several dossiers were labelled 'Destroy in Toto' or 'Destroy All' or 'Not to be opened until 10 years after my death'.[16]

When we turn to Cornell's public art, there is a great body of works that can be classified as existing somewhere between the dossier and the box construction, revealing that not everything reached a single, final, fixed form. His approach meant that it was very difficult to stop things flooding in once the process had been set in motion. Everything was fluent, fluid and contingent – part of the process. Even the box constructions themselves are rarely single works, more usually they are items in a series, for example the Soap Bubble Sets, Medici Slot Machines, Dovecotes, Pink Palaces, or they have variants, as are *Toward the Blue Peninsula* (1951–2) and *The Ellipsian* (1966). The uniquely individual viewpoint captured and frozen as a moment in time was not always possible, given Cornell's way of working. Certainly, a quality of stillness is apparent

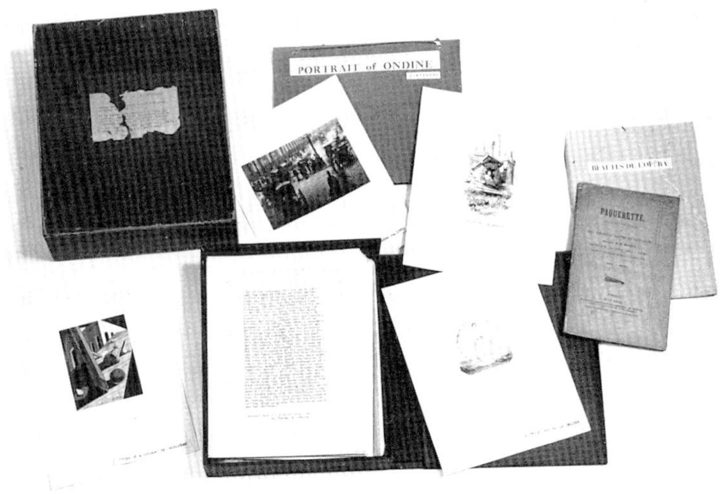

16 'Portrait of Ondine', 1940s–50s, box file with materials.

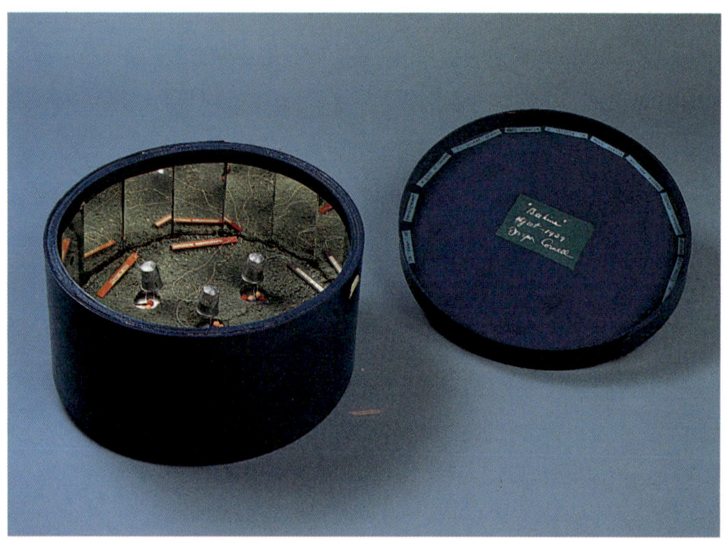

17 *Beehive*, 1939, construction.

in much of his work, even in moving pictures and in his use of stills, but this was only one side of the artist and his method, for there is constant movement too. Some boxes contain parts that move: they spring into action at the pull of a stopper; others sit within the palm of the hand and can gently tilt, making a thimble forest shimmer and shake, or sands shift across the incised ridges at the base. Some boxes do not even require to be picked up to initiate movement within. Vibrations caused by walking across a floor are enough to make the coiled watch-spring move in *Bleriot #2* (illus. 18) or the red lobsters dance in *A Pantry Ballet (for Jacques Offenbach)*, made in the summer of 1942. Within Cornell's valise works, which are among those that are halfway between dossier and box, a travelling suitcase is opened and has to be unpacked for the loosely piled imagery and small objects to be seen and for the process of associationism to begin.

Aspects of Cornell's working method that further confirm his uncertainty regarding one particular viewpoint include his reluctance to title or date works, his habit of occasionally dating works over a period of years, and his way of allowing imagery and connections to flow over and out of the actual box space onto the sides and verso of his constructions.

In describing one of his visits to Cornell's workshop, the writer John Bernard Myers supplies a fascinating glimpse of Cornell's method of composition:

I asked him how he managed to do the compass sets. He said 'Well, I was walking along Bleeker Street and I saw these boxes and I went in and bought them. I didn't know what I would do with these boxes but I kept walking along the same street and then I saw a man was selling compasses so I bought a whole bunch of those. I was looking for compasses and I was looking at these boxes and I thought now that really goes with that.' He composed that

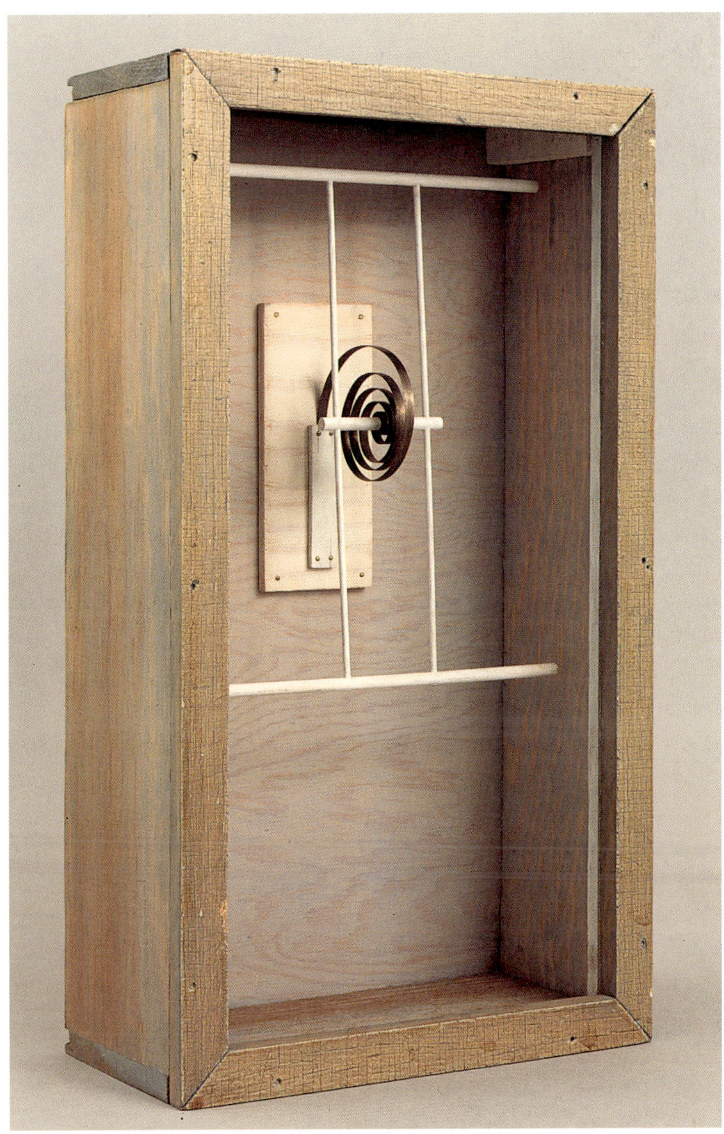

18 *Bleriot #2*, c. 1956, box construction.

> way. That's why he had everything on the wall, and all the boxes on the shelves. The way Mondrian composed.
>
> Joseph did it very much the same way. In Mondrian's cold white flat, he would have a big white wall space and he had the squares and he kept shifting them and shifting them and shifting them. And the *Broadway Boogie Woogie* was shifted thousands of times. So Joseph would be working on some of them, changing a marble here, something there, shift this around, shift that around, he'd have several of them going at once. He would say things like 'Well I would like to sell a box to Miss Garbo, but I have to get a variant before I can sell it.'[17]

Reworking and rearranging was almost like a principle within Cornell's method of working; even after boxes had been sold or bound over to friends and family for many years he would not hesitate to send a messenger to collect a box in order to make revisions or alterations.

One example of the way in which he would not allow one box to speak for his artistic vision is represented in the negotiations he entered into in 1936 with the Museum of Modern Art when he was asked to contribute to the exhibition 'Fantastic Art, Dada, Surrealism'. Initially he proposed a Soap Bubble Set, but in the end he supplied an installation, *Elements of Natural Philosophy* (1936), which comprised 87 pieces, including the *Soap Bubble Set*. The contribution did not stop here, for elements from this *Soap Bubble Set* were removed from the box, re-arranged yet again, further elements were added, and then this fresh assembly was photographed by George Platt Lynes.

Classification was a subject that Cornell himself was most concerned about. This was demonstrated at the time of the 'Fantastic Art, Dada, Surrealism' exhibition, when Cornell, though happy to participate in a Surrealist show, made a point of writing to the organizer, Alfred Barr, to explain that he wanted to be called an 'American Constructivist', not a Surrealist.[18] The exhibition raised for the first time the question of how Cornell saw himself in relation to major movements in modern art. Galleries and museums have had problems classifying and categorizing his art from almost his first exhibition. (Motherwell commented on how, in his day, Cornell was often left out of shows because the museums couldn't decide

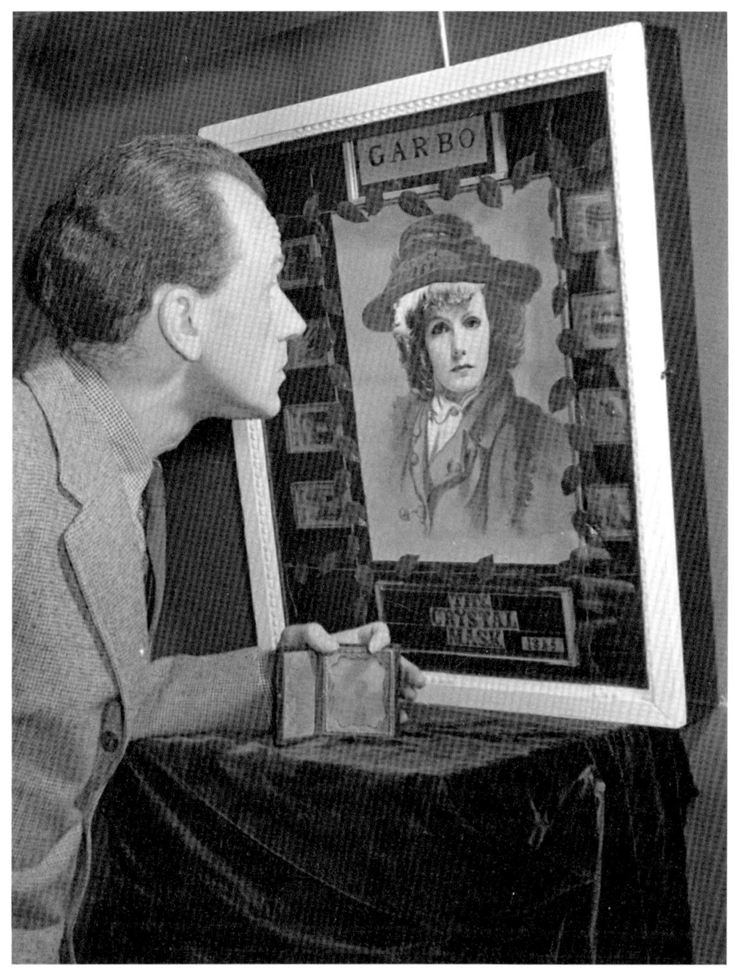

19 Cornell and *The Crystal Mask – Garbo*, c. 1939–40, construction. Destroyed by the artist.

'The story was that she didn't like it, so he destroyed it' (Betty Benton, 1982).

how to 'place' him.) This is not just a problem for institutions. Art historians too have widely differing opinions as to how he should be situated. Dore Ashton has traced the nineteenth-century American and European influences on his thought and work; Dawn Ades places him within the context of Surrealism, and Carter Ratcliff within the picturesque tradition. Lynda Hartigan takes a biographical approach and emphasizes the everydayness, the down-to-earth, the commonplace as Cornell's starting-point. Sandra Starr sees Cornell as a metaphysical scientist and religious thinker. David Porter has compared Cornell to Emily Dickinson; Anne d'Harnoncourt has looked at Cornell's affinity with Juan Gris; and Dickran Tashjian has examined Cornell's work as gifts for others. People who knew the artist personally also had widely differing views. That one thought of him as an 'authentic Surrealist' and another as 'priest-like' suggests that Cornell, like his art, was far from easy to classify. To make him into a consistent and exclusive mystic or to streamline his art into one particular group or to certain tenets or traditions is to ignore the obvious oppositions within him. Some of his concerns belong to the nineteenth century and to European culture, while others are charged with the excitement of Modernism, the twentieth century and American culture. He was part nineteenth-century poet – a visionary, a thinker, a moralist who was reserved, reticent and disinclined to reveal his private life – and part twentieth-century artist, one fully conversant with the latest developments within the art world and acquainted with a wide range of people, from ballerinas to waitresses, from movie-stars to drug addicts.

A table of some of Cornell's concerns reveals the apparent oppositions:

Nostalgia	Modernism
Nineteenth-century interests	Twentieth-century awareness
The poetic	The homemade/home industry
Erudite/would-be-intellectual	Non-intellectual/distrust of the intellectual
Mystic	Craftsman/mechanic
European – a fascination with Aestheticism	Americana – a fascination with science
The exotic	The local
Rare fragments	The toy
High culture: Maria Malibran, Vermeer, Fanny Cerrito, Mallarmé, Debussy	Low/popular culture: Barbie dolls, goods signs, Houdini, automats, slot-machine arcades
Understanding of symbolic, essential forms	Interest in design, theatrical effects, window display, sleight-of-hand, optical illusions, mechanistic inventions
A custodian – interest in preservation of nature/together art/tradition	Anarchic way in which he cut up Old Masters and put them with plastic spiders, children's games
A desperate need to contain/frame the flow of reality	Art as process, part of a continuum

If we try to tie Cornell too closely into a movement or school we inevitably simplify or distort the antithetical forces that shaped so much of his art. What may be assumed to be Surrealist, for example, may in fact be the result of quite other influences.

The construction/ordering stage of Cornell's artistic process itself underwent a process of development. During the 1930s and 1940s he experimented widely with different media: he began by making collages, he adapted tiny pill-boxes, toys, antique chests, Shaker boxes and small glass domes containing Roman Catholic iconography.[19] He incorporated objects within bottles and books and he assembled text packages and one free-standing object of a book and ball. He directed films, made a film montage and wrote a film script/scenario. He contributed historical essays to a dance magazine and poetic essays to an avant-garde arts magazine. His commercial ventures included designs for fabrics, batiks, Christmas cards, covers for home and fashion magazines, a fashion layout incorporating shadow boxes for reproduction within the magazine, a collage for clothes patterns and a whole installation of bridal traditions for a large commercial company.

The source material can be grouped within categories: Rare Objects include photographs, books, films, prints, nineteenth-century toys and unique or valuable objects; Household or Everyday Objects include newspapers, school-books, glasses, thimbles, corks, pencil-sharpeners, dolls, bric-à-brac; Natural Objects include grasses, twigs, driftwood, sand, shells, butterfly wings, eroded or corroded objects or fragments from the beach; Personal/Fetish Objects include net and tinsel from ballerinas' dresses, or a Victorian doll from his great-aunt's attic; Mathematical/Science Objects include maps, diagrams, compasses, watch springs, laboratory lenses, brass rods, rings; Working Materials include blue velvet, gesso, oatmeal paper, glues, paper, paint, inks (of a restricted colour range), wire mesh, glass sheeting; and Containers include museum chests, pill-boxes, oriental boxes, Shaker boxes, paperboard boxes and music-boxes.

The places Cornell went to in order to find objects and imagery can also be broadly categorized: in New York he frequented libraries, magazine and film-studio offices, the stores in and around 14th Street and Times Square, theatres, magazine- and newspaper-stands. In cafés and diners he sought chance meetings. At Westhampton he would scour the beach and woodland areas; in Flushing he haunted Main Street, but he also rode out on his bicycle to the locality's rural environs. The actual business of travelling to and fro was also of use: he used 'El'-trains and buses extensively, hoping to catch glimpses or snapshot images he could use. But it is important here to understand that I do not mean to give the impression that Cornell wandered aimlessly, haphazardly. He was driven always by a sense of purpose. In her excellent account of the influences on Cornell and the forces that shaped his life and work, Diane Waldman concludes that 'Cornell's dreams, locked within glass-panelled boxes are deeply personal and ultimately elusive. Mystery is the essence and substance of his work.'[20] In this book I explore some of the strategies behind the mystery.

Cornell's eclecticism has been viewed as a sign, the material equivalent of his eager appetite for knowledge, sights and impressions, but when we view eclecticism as a strategy rather than as a natural or intuitive form of behaviour it takes on a different aspect. As suggested above, Cornell pursued the glimpse; he actively encouraged the fleeting moment and the likelihood of the chance encounter while in transit. There is an undeniable sense of the voyeuristic in Cornell's relationship with the world. One of the most telling observations in Mary Ann Caws's Introduction to her published selection of Cornell's diaries, letters and 'files' (dossiers) is where she notes Cornell's sense of the primacy of the subject over the object: 'If he was often obsessed with what he saw, the desire seems to have been, in the long run, for the sightings themselves'.[21] That he was aware of pursuing a method is illustrated in his dossiers. Writing about his use of pictures, Cornell added that 'the pictures unconsciously became the basis of something else . . . the nucleus of further journeys developed from the technique evolved through their formation'.[22] Many of the people I have interviewed commented on how distracted Cornell was during conversations. His singular sense of himself, his tendency to speak in monologues and his determination to continue his own stream of associations indicate an active encouragement of this facility within himself.

Michel Foucault's comments on the behaviour of aphasiacs

when trying to group assembled objects are illuminating in the light of what we know of Cornell's own life:

> no sooner have they been adumbrated than all these groupings dissolve again, for the field of identity that sustains them, however limited it may be, is still too wide not to be unstable; and so the sick mind continues to infinity, creating groups then dispersing them again, heaping up diverse similarities, destroying those that seem clearest, splitting up things that are identical, superimposing different criteria, frenziedly beginning all over again, becoming more and more disturbed, and teetering finally on the brink of anxiety.[23]

Cornell's writings in 'GC 44' show all the signs of anxiety and obsessive behaviour that Foucault describes. Coexistent with the Cornell that can be recognized in this passage is one that is more selfconscious, deliberately excavating associations and resemblances from his long-term memory for the purpose of his work. Diaries, letters and miscellaneous paraphernalia (jottings on stacks of old record-sleeves) reveal his pleasure in word-games, puns and rhymes, making shapes out of words; his dossiers reveal a consciousness of the principles of similarity and opposition in the workings of association. It is difficult to marry the selfconscious observer of the mental process with the totally *un*selfconscious vehicle through whom the associations flow.

What is so distinctive about all of Cornell's exploratory voyaging in search of material is the selfconsciousness of it – the mind watching itself watching. Traces of the American Transcendentalist tradition can be discerned in Cornell's own trains of thought, and his dossiers certainly indicate, if not adherence to, at least a familiarity with Transcendentalist ideas. This nineteenth-century New England movement of writers and philosophers loosely bound together in their shared faith in an idealistic system of thought acknowledged the essential unity of all creation, the innate goodness of man, and – most importantly for Cornell – the supremacy of insight over logic and experience for the revelation of the deepest truths. He borrowed from the Transcendentalists a belief in a subjectivism in which the individual loses his sense of self to become, in effect, a transparent eyeball: this is a most unusual kind of subjectivism, one in which the individual personality and consciousness of the artist is subjugated to a spiritual force that flows through him.[24] It is subjective in the way that it allows the mind access to ultimate truth, but it is impersonal in the way that the mind submits itself to the spiritual force controlling it.

THE SURREALIST CONTEXT

The New York sculptor David Hare was editor from 1940 of the Surrealist magazine *VVV*, and he knew Cornell at the time. Hare's own definition of Surrealism still has a raw honest energy about it:

> Surrealism really had nothing whatsoever to do with painting and not very much to do with literature, it had to do with an attitude of mind. And the attitude of mind was supposedly an open attitude towards new ideas. The name of course comes from the psychiatry which was new at the beginning of it. The internal reality which was much more real than the external. In other words anything which destroyed your sense of right and wrong.[25]

Hare and Cornell were identified by Duchamp as the only two authentic American Surrealists, and Hare has insisted that 'Cornell's things are certainly Surrealist'. Cornell's relationship with the Surrealists has been the subject of much speculation and research, but Hare has indicated here an area that is of interest. According to him, there is a preferable reality beyond ideas of right and wrong and that this reality is internal. The notion of a higher order of reality would have appealed not only to the subjectivist position extolled in Cornell's Christian Science beliefs but would also have freed Cornell from any sense of guilt that might have accompanied his suppressed sexuality. Another fascinating point made by Hare is his description of the effect of Surrealism – how few people were affected, and the way that they were affected:

> the few American intellectuals, artists or creative people suddenly came across a real live creature who lived and thought the way they had heard about in school, about the Left Bank kind-of-thing. All of a sudden it becomes alive.

The behaviour and the attitudes of the Surrealists were, according to Hare, totally foreign to the Americans:

> That was a very curious time in America. It was the very beginning of Abstract Expressionism. Abstract Expressionism was a chauvinistic movement. This was the American take-off to culture and the arts. The Surrealists were always against abstraction. The Americans really had very little understanding of what Surrealism meant.

Hare also commented on Breton's attitude to America and its culture:

> The French point of view, Breton's point of view, was that he was in a foreign country, he did not speak English, he didn't have very much respect, or interest in American culture . . . He was interested in things that happened here that didn't happen in Europe, attitudes and so on, in the sort of Americana. He wasn't interested in America as a cultural centre in any sense.

And Hare summed it up by pointing out that 'although there was interest, there was antagonism on both sides'.

Robert Motherwell thought it peculiar that Cornell never really became part of the Surrealist circle, but was quite clear about the essential differences: 'Cornell's somebody in their direction who was neglected'.[26] He said that politically, for example, Breton and Cornell were worlds apart. However, Motherwell did see that Cornell connected with the Europeans in some respects:

> The native American desire is to be a good guy, to be democratic, in a sense everybody having his turn – a desire to be loved. Joseph was so self-absorbed that he was oblivious to the American social contract. I think it was only in Europe that I encountered somebody as individual. They simply are what they are: Ionesco, Beckett, Picasso. Americans tend to be more like Henry Moore in their aspirations to be very decent, civil. He was oblivious to other people. There was no interaction to a very marked degree; he was eccentric – and more so than any artist of any consequence I've ever known. Very pervasive in America is the idea of 'norms', so that makes the American very nervous, maybe that's why I quit seeing him.

There are many specific links between Cornell and the Surrealists. Juxtaposition rather than association is the word most commonly used to describe the Surrealists' attempts to bring together unlikely images . The Surrealists liked to meet life head-on, to arrest its codes and practices. Collage and its potential for disjunction had an obvious attraction for them. A scrap, or fragment cut, reassembled and pasted had the capacity to disturb order and suggest almost limitless and totally arbitrary possibilities. In *Dime-Store Alchemy: The Art of Joseph Cornell*, Charles Simic considers Cornell's debt to Surrealism: 'What he liked, no one was interested in. Surrealism provided him with a way of being more than just an eccentric collector of sundry oddities . . . His is a practice of divination. Dada and Surrealism gave him a precedent and a freedom.'[27]

Photography deals in fragments, and cinema, as an extension of photography, deals in fragments that are pieced together by mechanical means. The Surrealists and Cornell were fascinated by both. Duchamp, as inventor of the Ready-Made, brought the found object into the Surrealist arena. *Cit-Git Giorgio de Chirico* (1928) by Aragon and Breton was one of the early assemblages of objects – a box construction like a miniature stage-set containing a leaning Tower of Pisa and a tiny sewing-machine.[28] The Surrealists freed the artist from

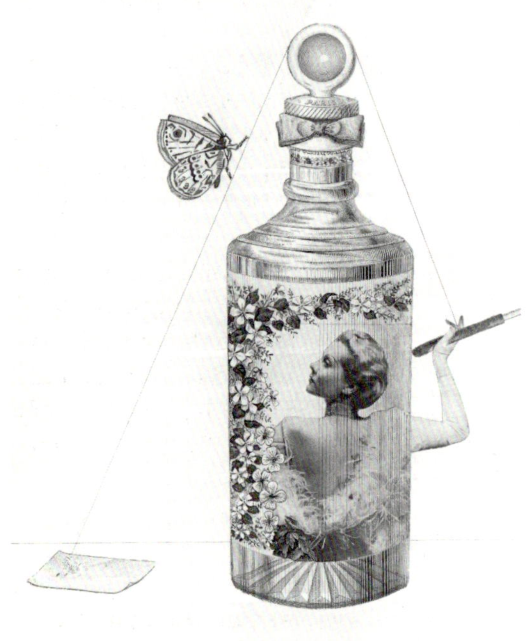

20 *Poetry of Surrealism*, c. 1935–8 and 1940, collage.

the brush. Not just this, but the fact that that they broke up reality in order to piece it together using collage, objects, photography and cinema meant that they were able to penetrate mental life and reach towards an understanding of the associative mechanism and the unconscious.

The particular bearing that Duchamp and Max Ernst have on Cornell needs brief explanation. Cornell's first collages were influenced by Ernst's collage novel *La Femme 100 Têtes* (1929). He would have responded to the imagery not only for the extraordinary juxtapositions and free association contained within the pictures but also because of the source-material – nineteenth-century engravings. Cornell was a great collector of these sorts of images; he was a plunderer of bric-à-brac and secondhand stores, which together furnished him with an archive of such material.

When Ernst was asked about the origins of his collage novels he responded by saying that 'they are reminiscences of my first books – a resurgence of childhood'.[29] Cornell also contrived throughout his life to keep his childhood in sight. A continuing fascination with the child's view of the world is a feature of pictorial and poetic Surrealism as well as of Cornell's work. One other formal link between Ernst and Cornell is the image-cycle or series – the single distilled image gives way to a series of frames.

Cornell was also influenced by Duchamp, not just formally but conceptually too.[30] Especially important here is the portable museum Duchamp constructed, the *Boîte en Valise* (1936–41), which he originally made in order to carry reproductions of his work across the French border during the Nazi occupation of France. It had the appearance of a salesman's sample case, for Duchamp disguised himself as a cheese merchant for his journey. Once opened, it revealed a miniature world, with items packed, displayed and compartmentalized together. The *Boîte en Valise* is technically immaculate, and the placing of things was fastidiously worked out. Later in the 1940s in America, Duchamp reproduced 200 copies of his portable museum.

Cornell's interest in Duchamp's portable museum was such that he actually worked on it with Jacqueline Monnier in order to help produce the 200 copies. He would have been attracted to the history behind the piece, including its escape from occupied Europe. He would have been especially attracted to its disguise as a salesman's sample case; Cornell had worked as a travelling salesman and would have carried something similar. He would also have been intrigued by the museum-like format of the *Boîte en Valise* once opened. The importance of the museum to Cornell has been underestimated: he was not only a dedicated museum-goer, he also developed a museum series, contrived the installation 'Romantic Museum' (1946), and returned again and again to the theme of museums. But the museum was also significant in that it gave him a structure for remembering. He was not just hoarding, he was classifying and making connections.

Besides devizing their own museums, Duchamp and Cornell both responded to the existent 'cultural framework' in differing ways. Duchamp made statements that deflected serious attempts by art historians and critics to make him define 'art'; he remained deliberately enigmatic about his position. He said he liked 'breathing better than working', and encouraged the rumour that from 1923 he had ceased to 'make things' and was concentrating on chess. Over the years Cornell also developed an equally enigmatic and powerful myth about himself. The number of descriptions of Cornell as

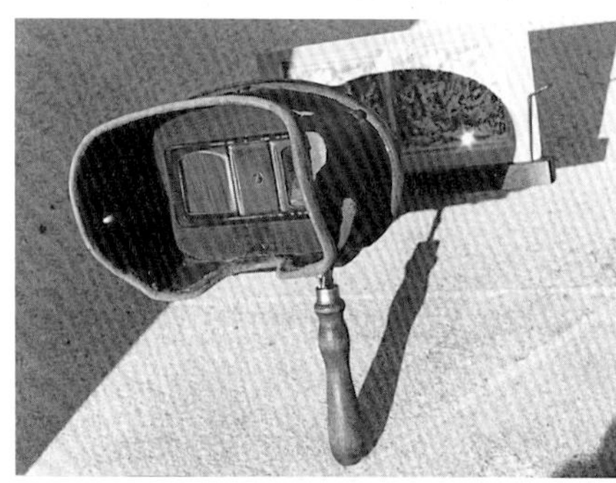

21 Cornell's own late-nineteenth-century stereoscope.

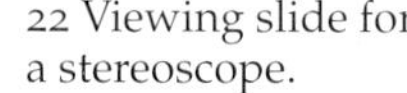

22 Viewing slide for a stereoscope.

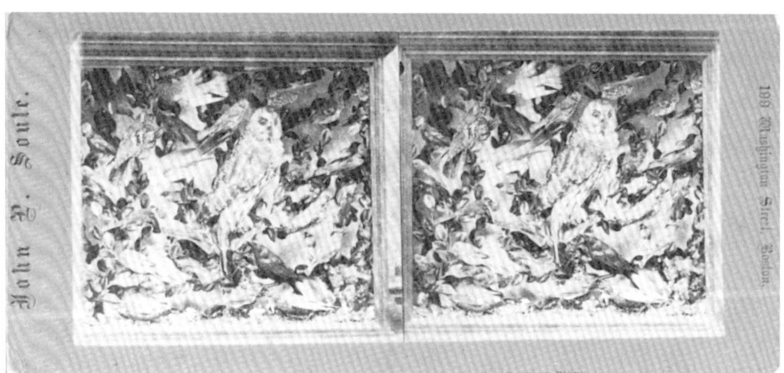

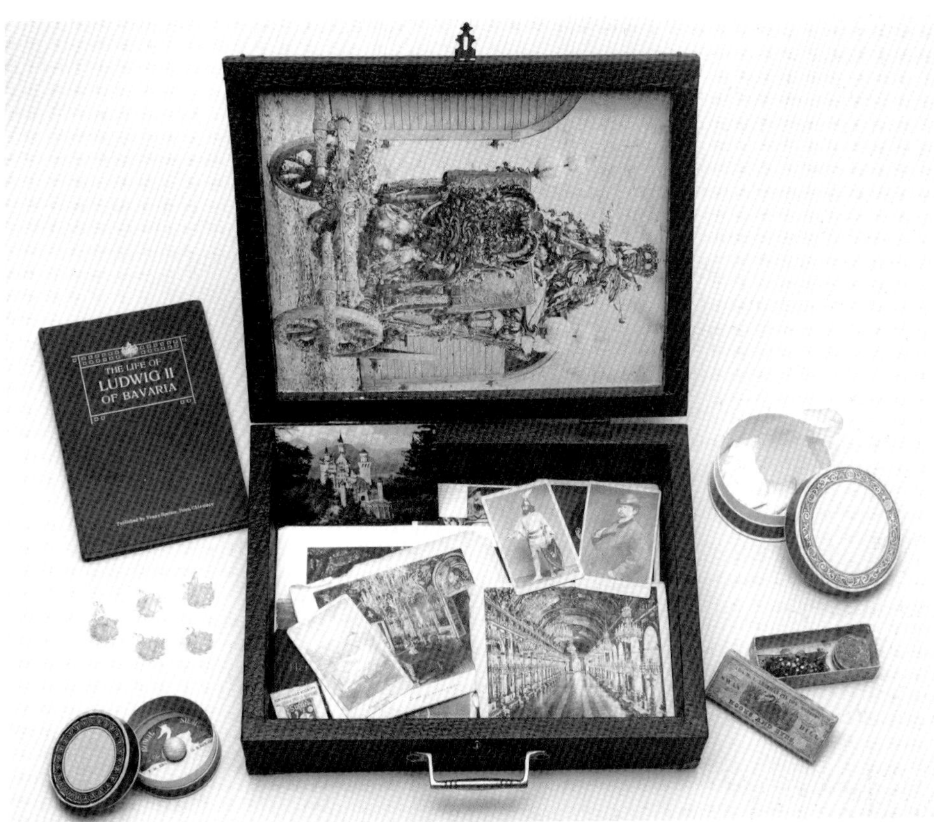

23 *Untitled (Ludwig II of Bavaria)*, c.1940–55, boxed dossier: a hinged wooden valise covered in faux leather paper with brass fittings and sepia-toned photograph mounted inside the lid.

an eccentric artist testify to the power of the myth surrounding him. He kept the art world at arm's length. He eluded categorization for his art and labels for himself; he refused to date, or often to sign, works; he was elusive regarding interviews; and he did not like to be photographed or have his voice taped, and appeared only twice, fleetingly, on film.

In 1934 Duchamp produced his first public edition of notes relating to artworks: 300 Green Box notes. This is a cardboard box covered in green suede containing facsimiles of the notes and drawings related to the planning and execution of his major work *The Large Glass* (1915–23); the contents of the notes date from 1911–15. Cornell may well have been influenced by this: the division between working notes and art works and the shifting of boundaries between the two became a central preoccupation of his.

A further link between Duchamp and Cornell is the

reflexive element – the focus on the creative process itself. While preoccupied with *The Large Glass* Duchamp was clearly fascinated by the process of working on glass rather than simply applying paint to canvas. At times he stated that it was the technical element – how to fix the paint, retain its brilliance, incorporate other materials – that really interested him. It took eight years to complete the work. At one point the work spent several months lying on the floor of his studio gathering dust. Duchamp fixed the dust in some areas – on the sieves of the glass, for example – with glue. He called his piece a 'delay in glass', and in his notes from *The Green Box* he refers to 'glass transparent juice'. Cornell, likewise, worked on his materials to achieve weathered effects, and just as Duchamp conceived of *The Large Glass* as a 'delay in glass', so too did Cornell see many of his constructions as parts of a process. As he noted in his diary: 'A sailor's box – an uncompleted cabinet brought up from the cellar, was covered in the most perfect application of mildew imaginable – like a frosting acquired in cold storage and yellow kind of dust on top cover resembling pollen – glue content was responsible for this.'[31]

Cornell responded to individual Surrealists rather than to the movement as a whole. He was influenced by others

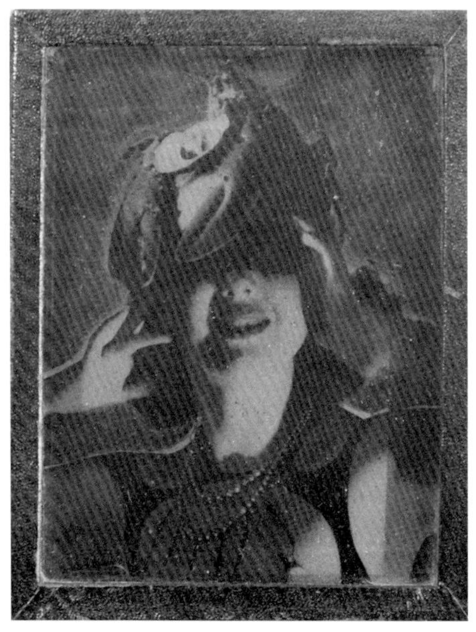

24 *Untitled (Object)*, c. 1933, box construction.

besides Ernst and Duchamp: De Chirico, Dalí, Magritte, and two artists more loosely tied to Surrealism, Pierre Roy and Dorothea Tanning. Cornell responded to a particular quality in these Surrealist artists: the mystery in the precision of their works. He shared with them a vocabulary and continued their use of towers (De Chirico), lobsters (Dalí) and trains (Magritte), for example. With the Surrealists in general, Cornell shared a love of some of the nineteenth-century Symbolist writers, such as Bertrand, Nerval and Rimbaud. On this point Motherwell says that 'the Surrealists had a very strong feeling for poetry, and from that point of view I looked at Cornell as a poet'.[32]

While he exhibited wholeheartedly with the group through the 1930s and the early 1940s, Cornell was, from the very beginning, only half-avowed in his affinities with the Surrealists. Publicly he made statements shunning direct connection with the group, shying away particularly from their theories. For Motherwell, Cornell did seem to stand out from his American contemporaries:

> To a degree he reassured me that an American was capable of making a work as sophisticated as anything in Europe. He was an intellectual with a narrow range, a specialist in nineteenth-century French artistic manifestations. My admiration for him was in seeing him as an individual, and for his total commitment, and total realization of his work. From one point of view he maybe got closer than any of the others did. Our immediate struggle was against America, and here was an American who could embrace Europe.[33]

1 The Self Observed

'GC 44' AND THE DOSSIER

'GC 44' is Cornell's most highly personal and most important working dossier, one of the 'high tides of inspiration'.[34] Its title is an abbeviation for 'Garden Center 1944', for the dossier is built around Cornell's thoughts and observations while he was working in the summer of 1944 at a garden centre in Flushing run by a Christian Science Practitioner. An important issue at this time was the work that the Practitioner was doing with Joseph's younger brother. (Both Robert and Betty were also Christian Scientists.) The Practitioner and Robert were studying hard together to achieve a healing, and according to Betty, Robert was free from epileptic fits that year. The spate of good health Robert enjoyed, and the brothers' shared enthusiasm for Christian Science, naturally affected Cornell's frame of mind in that year.

The background to 'GC 44' is of relevance here. Cornell had given up working for Traphagen Commercial Textile Studio in 1940, and in 'GC 44' he looks back to those days when he worked as a travelling salesman as a 'miserable phase' of 'business routine'.[35] He recognized that, in August 1944, he was now able to enjoy what previously he had been forced to save up for weekends (his 'weekendy' feeling was a 'strong anticipatory pleasure associated with departure to the country to new places'[36]). He loved to be working nearer to home and travelling to and fro on a bicycle, getting to know the rural routes and quiet passageways. In addition, since 1941 he had his own workroom/studio in the cellar beneath the family home, a place in which he could work in private and store his materials. (It had previously been a point of contention that Cornell was taking over the house with his bits and pieces, for when his mother wished to organize tea for visitors she had always to deal with his ephemera piled on the dining-room table.) Thus there was a sense of new-found freedom in the summer of 1944, a spiritual resurgence, and a third element (not yet fully brought out) – his revitalized feeling for nature. 'GC 44' is Cornell's tribute to

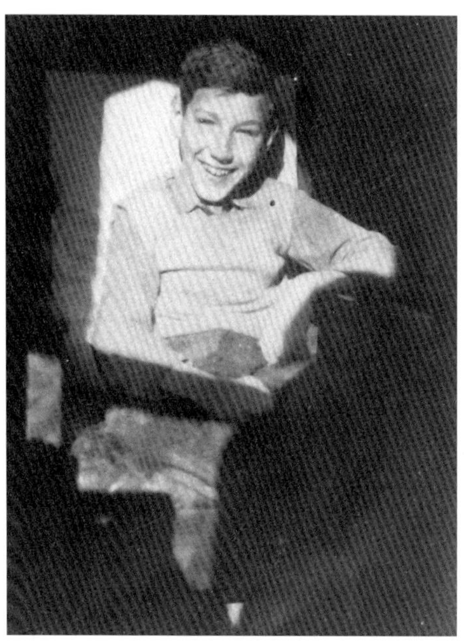

25 Robert Cornell smiling.

nature, his arcadian vision articulated. In a significant entry in his dossier he includes a quotation from Jean Renoir: 'I believe that during the past 50 yrs. man has been losing contact with his physical senses and is becoming too intellectualized. The artist's mission today, he noted elsewhere, is to recreate a direct contact between man and nature',[37] and Cornell goes on to discuss exact times and places where he experienced direct contact with nature. These moments he described as 'mystical dream episodes of bicycle rides through lonesome landscapes'.

The dossier itself shows how concerned Cornell was to develop a conception of himself as an artist with a certain kind of consciousness. Let us look first at the overall shape and aims of the dossier, and then at an individual episode, where Cornell catalogues the stages of the creative process ('The Floral Still-life'). I will then illustrate how Cornell sifted nostalgically through his own past by his strategy of parallel narrative, in this instance with a fictional character from Alain-Fournier's *Le Grand Meaulnes* (1913), first published in English in the USA as *The Wanderer* in the translation by Françoise Delisle (1928). The spiritual and mystical elements of the dossier, especially the connection with Christian Science, follows, after which I turn to Cornell's obsession with dreams. Finally, I present two boxes that are linked thematically with the 'GC 44' dossier: *Untitled: American Rabbit* (1945–6) and *Untitled: Paul and Virginia* (1946–8).

Donald Windham has described the basic physical characteristics of 'GC 44' as it appeared in the late 1960s (more than twenty years after it was begun): 'two grey cardboard boxes . . . hundreds of scraps of paper with things written on them and hundreds of mounted illustrations' (illus. 26).[38] If this dossier had begun, like others, in a loose-leaf folder, then by the end of the 1960s it needed box containers, for 'GC 44' was not only Cornell's most important dossier, it was also his largest, containing over one thousand pages. The references and diary notations pertaining to 'GC 44' extend even beyond this huge compilation: other dossiers and 'explorations' discuss it, and contain cross-references (Cornell comments on the 'rich

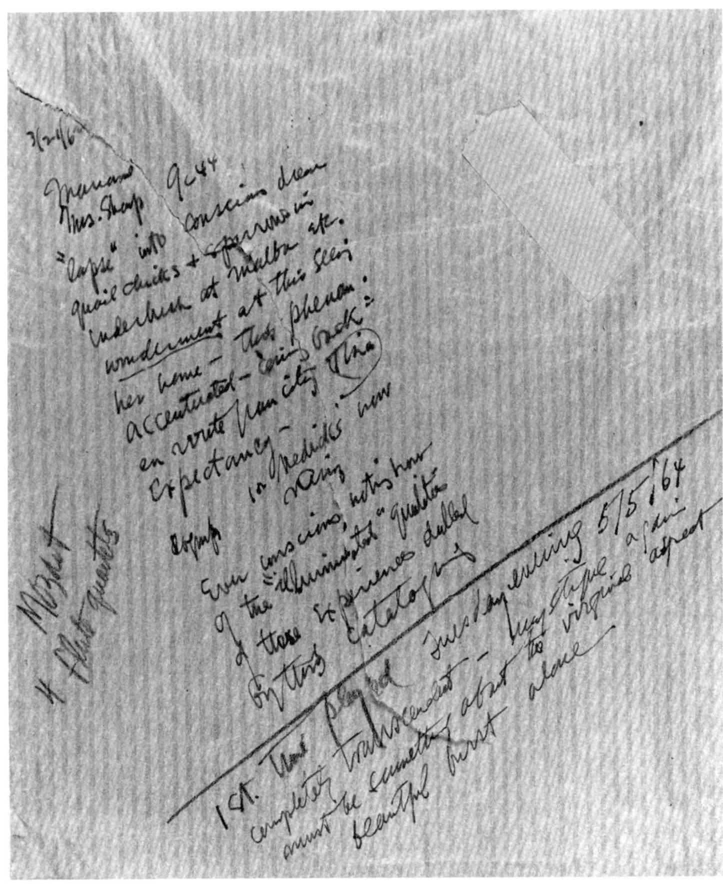

26 'GC 44' notations, 1962 and 1964.

cross-indexing' with this project). It is difficult to overstate the importance of this dossier to Cornell; as his sister Betty recalls, 'That was a big, big, experience in his life, "GC 44"!'.

'GC 44' is a 'bulging chaos' because of Cornell's compulsive habit of collecting.[39] David Hare was puzzled by Cornell's collecting habit; Susan Sontag thought it 'incredulous'; and even Cornell warned himself about it: 'A discipline will have to be acquired against the piling up of diverse material'.[40] Of further relevance to 'GC 44' was Cornell's notetaking. He was an inveterate notetaker. Whether on buses, in train stations, in the library, over his danish pastry in the automat, on the telephone, while enjoying the backyard sunshine, while sharing the company of visitors, Cornell was always to be seen with his yellow legal pad and a pencil, making notes.[41] He was as acutely fascinated by an anonymous face in the crowd as he might be by a poem he encountered or an Old Master painting he had just studied. He was constantly noting the ordinary, the everyday, as well as the eventful or the out-of-the-ordinary. The ordinary, of course, was promptly transfigured: a neighbourhood girl chasing her dog is a 'young Diana on the lawn with her hounds', for the local in Cornell's mind was transformed effortlessly into myth.[42]

While Cornell was watching outward passings-by he was also watching himself. He had a capacity to look at himself with a kind of objective interest, and in fact he had the same 'onlooker' attitude towards himself that he had towards life in general. He observed and described his dreams and his emotions, as well as cataloguing changes in his moods:

> Reaction rest of day after lingering by water. Naively poetic feeling evoked by Mother telling me to go out into the garden to say 'shoo' to the rabbit which would keep him away from the plants all night.[43]

He constantly qualified things, and endlessly expanded on his ideas. He was on occasion prolix, unfocused, but at times he displayed a determination to try and close in on a subject when he sought to be precise or needed to define a feeling or a mood.

We can see that as a 'museum without walls', 'GC 44' could have gone on forever. There is something about 'GC 44' and this period when Cornell was making notes for his art, something about his acute receptivity to things, that suggests he

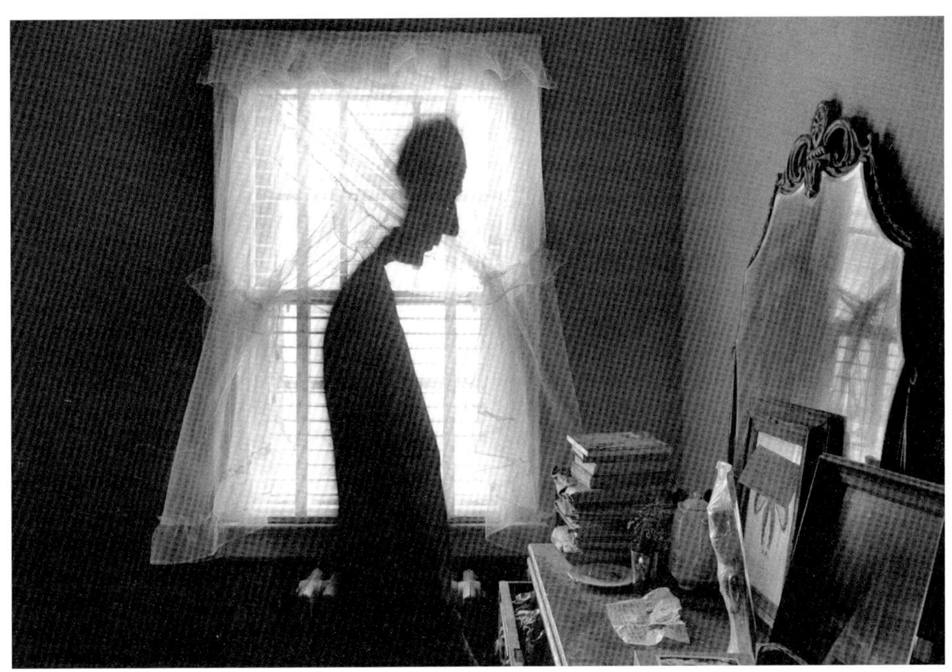

27 Duane Michals, *Joseph Cornell in a Bedroom at Utopia Parkway*, 1970, photograph.

was at the height of his artistic powers. He seemed to be in a constant visionary state. 'GC 44' has many references to his awareness of an overflow:

> rapid overflow of experience . . . overcrowding of incident and experience ever opening paths leading ever farther afield. Unbelievably rich cross-indexing (of experience) the ceaseless flow and interlacing of original experience.[44]

But Cornell, having decided to open up a 'museum without walls', had to find some clear-cut boundaries: 'undecipherable records desperately attempt to hold fast'.[45] Donald Windham has described what it was like when Cornell turned to him for help: 'It seemed to be that I, or somebody else, was to make the magical transition from this chaos to what was in his mind . . . I could never figure out what was in his mind'.[46] Cornell struggled to communicate his wishes. The difficulty lay in the very nature of what he wanted to speak about – visions, revelations, moments of inspiration, the 'rarified and spiritual', the 'sense' of things ('the sense of things set off in or against a field'), the metaphysical aspect ('the metaphysical aspect of this "expectancy", the "something"

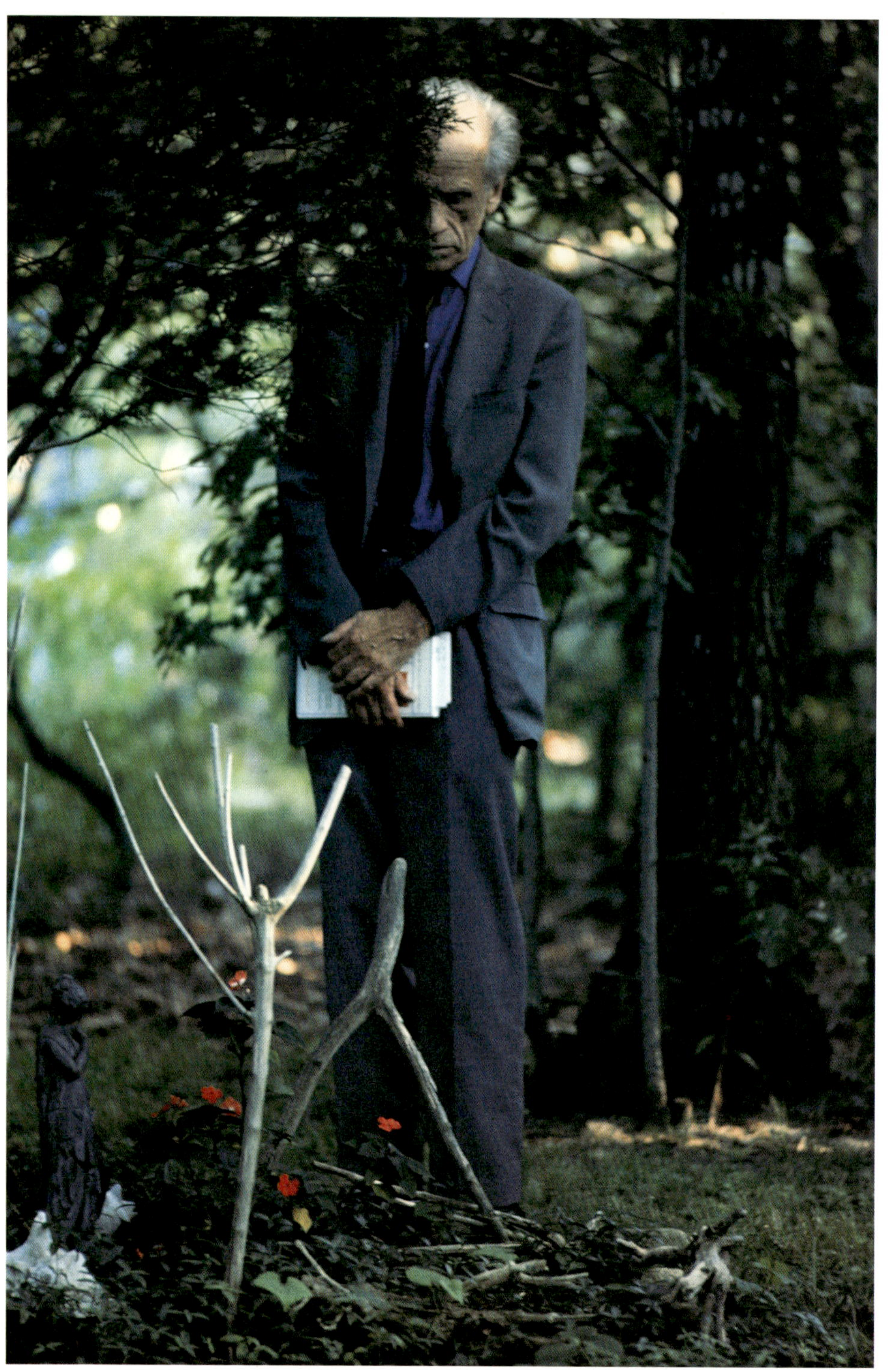

28 Hans Namuth, *Joseph Cornell by Woof's Burial Site at Betty Benton's in Westhampton*, 1971, photograph.

that might have happened').[47] As well as dealing with any number of complex associations, Cornell also sought to communicate what he called 'abstract associations'.[48] 'There are things in GC 44', Cornell wrote, 'which cannot be explained'.[49] And yet, throughout his life, he returned again and again to this dossier in his search for a way of explaining. In a diary entry for 9 September 1968, for example, he noted that 'GC 44 in the air today . . . 24 yrs now the Floral Still-Life section of GC 44 still unrealized'.[50] He experienced a religious awe in front of experiences, in the face of nature: 'the miracles of life and beauty . . . cannot be explained'. Later, he decided that some distancing from 'GC 44' was needed, having found himself too close, emotionally, to the material: 'some proper detachment may be felt but which nonetheless is indispensable to a proper evaluation of original experiences'.[51] His hopes for this dossier had been so high that his continuing failure to shape anything from it that satisfied him led to a sense of despair:

> an engulfing futility at the thought of formulation, a hopelessness of adequate expression . . . And so an emotion akin to that felt by the oriental poet which led him to burn all his works with the exception of a single haikai which is only an exclamation: (example)
> Ah, Ah
> Is all that one can say
> Before the flowers of Yoshino
> . . . a cry which has meaning only from the depths of the feeling out of which it rises, and only for the sensibility of the ear which hears it.[52]

Cornell felt that if only he could work through the 'GC 44' material satisfactorily then it would help him with all his work as an artist, with his whole corpus of working material: 'GC 44 realized successfully can become a "method" for crystallizing experience', he jotted down on one occasion.[53] Cornell had hoped to work out a way of moving from the mass of source-material to the artwork. He strove for a 'final distillation wherein the subject is almost lost sight of in a literal sense or glimpsed briefly in a doorway by de Chirico or a window by Apollinaire'.[54] 'GC 44' epitomizes his obsession with collecting, but also with his twin obsessions of trying to order his collections while somehow controlling the urge.

One way in which Cornell attempted to order his thoughts was by undertaking an odd kind of correspondence: he wrote letters ostensibly to others but that were ultimately intended to serve him. Their purpose was to help clarify to himself the moment of inspiration. 'GC 44' contains a letter to Mina Loy about an inspirational episode of 1944 that he refers to as 'The Floral Still-Life'.[55]

'THE FLORAL STILL-LIFE': LETTERS OF SELF-BELIEF

The clearest explanation Cornell gives of the moment of inspiration and the way the imagination works on experience is supplied in the journey/chapter labelled 'The Floral Still-Life' in the 'GC 44' dossier. The 'journey' is not separated out but is inserted chronologically among the dossier's other materials, yet certain distinct stages in Cornell's process are clear. There is the initial glimpse – the basis for a journey; a period of research and meditation on the subject; an initial articulation of the subject by letter; then finally an extension is made to the original inspiration. The following is a record of the dates and basic nature of each entry:

Summer 1944: original inspiration – 'Floral Still-Life' logo seen on goods wagon in fields near Flushing.
30 May 1946: associated image – snails seen near Lawrence Farm.
July 1946: 'extension' in church.
November 1946: moment of disillusionment when logo is seen divested of its visionary aspect.
21 November 1946: letter to Mina Loy articulating 'Floral Still-Life' episode.
5 May 1949: further 'extension' – image potentially associated with goods wagon logo found in a reproduction of van Eyck's *Ghent Altarpiece*.
27 February 1950: letter to Mina Loy revised – contents of the 1946 letter reworded and news of van Eyck reproduction 'extension' added.

Cornell was on his bicycle in the summer of 1944 riding in the direction of a house he refers to as 'Malba House'. He was cycling through fields beyond Flushing. Passing him on the road was a small goods truck with a logo or trademark on its side that advertised the meat and fish the company sold.

29 *L'Abeille*, 1966, collage.

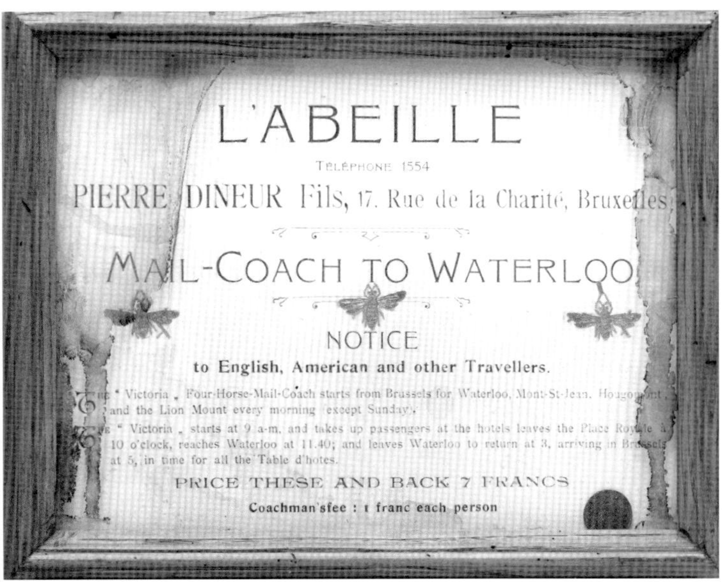

Because of the rural scene – fields, grasses, flowers – in which the meat and fish logo was glimpsed; because of the fact that Cornell was in the vicinity of 'Malba House'; and because he was riding his bicycle and therefore 'in motion', there was a 'metamorphosis of the sign into the more poetical'.[56] He saw a connection between the logo and still-life paintings by the Dutch masters that display 'flowers and edibles'.

All the various elements compounded to make the 'metamorphosis' into the 'poetical'. 'Malba House' was included because he could see in his mind's eye a still-life by one of the Dutch masters hanging there: 'a painting in the old house on the hill in an earlier day or dream'.[57] A number of his day-dreams and visions around 1944 had centred on this building, while Thomas De Quincey's essay 'The English Mail-Coach' (1849) served as a reference point highlighting the excitement of travelling.[58] Cornell noted 'wagons and vehicles in motion, vehicles of fantasy'.[59] The weather conditions were also significant, and became more so on Cornell's second sighting of the truck (the moment of disillusionment in November 1946). However, in the summer (or perhaps it was the autumn[60]) of 1944 he noted the 'dew on the side of the truck in cloudy weather etc, the sign thought of at a different time of day. Early morning going through fields and becoming part of the scene'.[61]

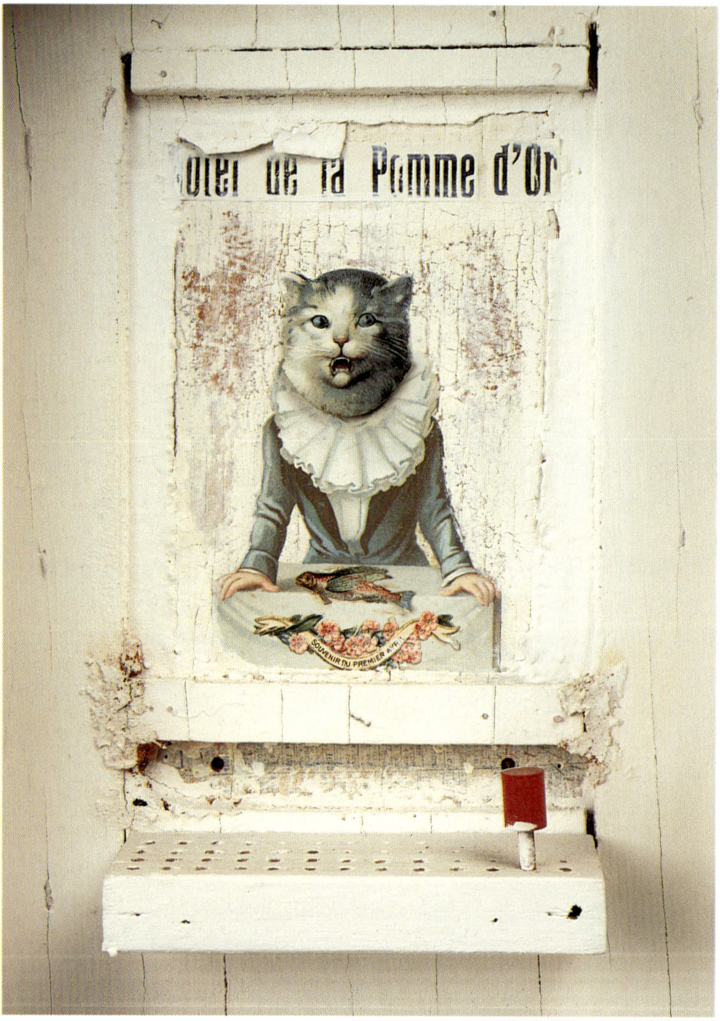

30 Detail of *Hôtel de la Pomme d'Or*, c. 1954–5, box construction.

The account of the moment of disillusionment is given in Cornell's letter to Mina Loy, which opens with a description of the weather:

> Autumn seems to be in such a quandary this year . . . And why am I writing to you about the weather? BECAUSE yesterday afternoon, hung about with mist, a really ambiguous afternoon for Fall; I came across a smoked-fish delivery truck parked on the shabby fringe of a shopping center near us. On the side of this small vehicle . . . painted an enseigne in the form of a still life of various stock, fat pieces of meat surmounted by whole fish in colors that

> make one think it might at one time have been a bright decalcomania, silvery whites and greys . . . Viewed close the background sky blue betrayed beneath black lettering of a former, less picturesque, version of a trade-mark. The effect as shabby and uninspired as the afternoon. What I am leading up to is the lesson in INSPIRATION that shabby little enseigne held for me. For I glimpsed that in MOTION exactly two years ago for the first time on a beautifully clear shining day on a ride on my bicycle to an unfamiliar section near the water wonderfully evocative of the American past in the unfolding panorama, rural, creative in its nostalgia and mellowness. That little still-life is still travelling in my 'chambers of imagery'; it has picked up many a gleaming and poetic bit since then. And so to see it stock still before one's eyes (the paint the worse for wear) no one in the least interested in passing before it as I did on my bike, well all this on such (I repeat) an ambiguous Fall afternoon, was all kind of a mocking challenge.[62]

The weather, the shopping centre (instead of a rural setting), and the fact that the truck was 'stock still' and therefore available for close scrutiny, brought about a totally different response. Cornell saw 'betrayed' beneath the sky blue, the black lettering of the former less picturesque logo. All this brought about a 'lesson in INSPIRATION' – the new vision of the sign became a challenge. Cornell was able through his continuing self-analytical dialectic to accept 'the reality' of the shabby logo as a challenge to his subjectivity. He had to develop a Transcendentalist subjectivity powerful enough to overcome all obstacles blocking its spiritual or visionary path. His letter continues:

> You see I have been discovering in the most unexpectedly delightful manner . . . that it is possible to see 'lightning strike in the same place'. . . . All of the above seems sometimes so evanescent and nebulous that I have never mentioned the trifle to anyone. But terms like 'evanescent' and 'nebulous' are defeatist, are they not, to those who like ourselves are tortured most of the time by their reality? I have generally paid a pretty high price for the above kind of experience, however silly this might sound to some. But way down deep these things can be unconscious, sturdy weapons against discouragement. And although my

> attempt at communication sometimes seems as shabby as the paint of the enseigne I can still rejoice that a glorious 'light' once illumined it for me in colors never to fade.

In the second part of his letter Cornell attempted to explain why he has chosen Mina Loy for his epistolary confession. Looking back to 1934 he noted that 'circumstances link in the most curious manner'.[63] He remembered 'the indelible impression' of the sky blue of Loy's paintings and how this mingled with his canvassing experiences when he worked as a salesman for a textiles company in 'strange out of the way parts' of Long Island and Brooklyn. He writes wonderingly of the way the 'essence' of 'commonplace experiences' remained with him. Also revealed here is the tone of religious affirmation to be found in Christian Science, where the mind is seen as the custodian of visions bravely withstanding the pressures of the external world.

The third major part in 'The Floral Still-Life' involves van Eyck's *Ghent Altarpiece* (illus. 31). 'Five years after the spring and summer of 1944 the events of the daily routine conspire to bring about an 'extension', 'renewal', a 'recreation' of one of the high tides of inspiration'.[64] An extension, Cornell explained, is a 'complement' to the original moment of inspiration.[65] This is how he described the extension:

> On Good Friday after taking Robert to the dentist's in the direction of the fields at Whitestone a copy of LIFE is noticed in a little store carrying copious color spreads of the van Eyck Altarpiece 'The Adoration of the Lamb' as a special article for Easter. A week or so later in the Bayside West section in a similar store and where the delivery wagon with painted enseigne (still-life) was observed at rest, again the van Eyck is noticed on one of those afternoons . . . Upon contemplation the van Eyck glows as beautifully realized, metamorphosed, sublimation of the original commercial enseigne with the feeling of the grasses, the fields, the flowers, the rarified and spiritual quality of the dream. The remembered incident of the little girl appearing along the top of the grasses of a field, turning out to be borne on her father's shoulders. The circumstances of finding the magazine in almost the same place yet removed by worlds. The manner in which all unsuspectingly the 'Floral Still-Life' comes to life naturally,

spontaneously, completely, an 'unfoldment' or 'extension' in which the Flemish master has obligingly allowed himself to be pressed into service for the concrete presentation of a vision.[66]

The girl travelling through the grasses connects in van Eyck's painting with the 'Virginal Procession through the Grasses'; the spires and towers in van Eyck have a 'parallel in seeing the spires and towers of Manhattan from these meadows on certain clear afternoons' (these are the meadows where the original sighting of the truck took place).[67] Here a moment of inspiration drawn from 'real life' connects with an extension found in what Cornell called the life of art – literally found in *Life* magazine.

Through his connection between 'The Floral Still-Life' and van Eyck, Cornell was able to make the altarpiece 'live' again within the realms of his own art. By the association of time and place regarding the truck and the magazine (bearers of imagery), Cornell made the altarpiece reverberate within the context of modern art. There is an extreme sacredness, a stillness captured by the formal, sharply defined, almost frozen elements within van Eyck's picture space, elements that are yet vibrant at the same time. It is the formal patterning of the arrangement that makes it come alive. van Eyck's altarpiece has what Cornell called a 'graphic' dream quality. Cornell

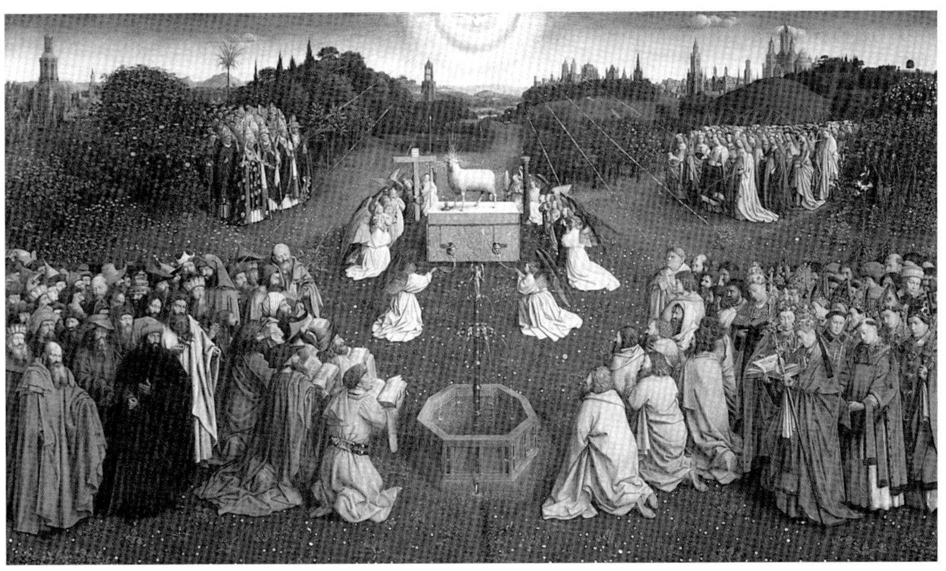

31 A detail (lower central panel) from Jan van Eyck's *Ghent Altarpiece*, completed 1432. Cathedral of St Bavo, Ghent, Belgium.

may have seen in van Eyck's work the possibility of portraying the feeling of magic, the atmosphere of spirituality, of sacredness, a dream mood from a highly realized, formal representation. In his letter to Loy, Cornell had mentioned that 'terms like "evanescent" and "nebulous" are defeatist, are they not, to those of us who are tortured most of the time by their reality?'[68] The clarity of van Eyck's image is an example of the 'concrete presentation of a vision'.[69] Geometric design is used to convey the spiritual atmosphere of nature.

This episode epitomizes Cornell's method of looking: he hoards his memories and works on retaining a state of readiness for when the associative faculty might strike. It is at the looking, notetaking, meditative stage that the important connections are made. His scrupulous documentation of detail in recording his own thought processes illustrates and embodies his attempt to hold onto the sought-after image. Most significant of all is the letter to Loy, for this is not a letter from one person to another but a letter of self-explanation or articulation: an attempt by the writer to explain to himself how the process of image-creation works and how it may be threatened. What he was required to do was to watch the self for its moments of weakness or doubt or disillusionment, and correct them so that the visionary reality of the original inspiration might be revealed in all its luminous clarity.

LE GRAND MEAULNES: CORNELL'S NOSTALGIC VOYAGE

In 'GC 44' there are frequent references to Alain-Fournier's novel of childhood, *Le Grand Meaulnes* (1913):

> a 'key' to the portfolio of plates and notes known as GC 44 . . . at the time of the experiences comprising this collection thought was strongly preoccupied with, impressed by, one of the supreme literary achievements of this century, namely Alain-Fournier's 'Le Grand Meaulnes', translated into English as 'The Wanderer'.[70]

Cornell identified with the 'seeker of visions', the young Augustin Meaulnes, who early in the novel 'wanders' and chances on a lost domain, an enchanted old house in a wood in which fancy-dress revellers are attending a magical night-time engagement party. Before dawn Meaulnes is led to the road that will carry him home, and since he both encounters and leaves the house in the dark, he is unable subsequently to locate either it or Yvonne, the girl he has met there.

The 'chance' element of Meaulnes's adventure appealed to Cornell. In 'GC 44' he noted how, on a bicycle, 'the manner in which riding blind, a succession of paths and by-paths would open up releasing unexpected and extravagant joy of discovery'.[71] Meaulnes, after all, 'without in the least meaning to', came off the road to Vierzon and was steering instead to the 'lost domain'.[72] Cornell's assessment of 'riding blind' echoes almost exactly Meaulnes's experience of stumbling across the lost domain, the fantastic, magical world of festivities, gaiety, grandeur, children, girls and love. In Manhattan, when Cornell had been employed as a travelling salesman, he had fruitfully extracted from the enforced necessity of trailing the streets; he had wandered purposefully, and in doing so found materials and inspiration. As Simic has observed, 'the city is a labyrinth of analogies, the Symbolist forest of correspondences'.[73] Even though Cornell's job as a salesman did come to an end, his habit of 'wandering' did not. Like Meaulnes, Cornell became a seeker of visions.

Cornell appears to have been fascinated by the organization of *Le Grand Meaulnes*: 'The titles comprising the sep. categor. of this compilation ['GC 44'] might be likened to the chapter headings of an adventure of a mystery novel but one in which the sensational element is entirely missing. ("Le Grand Meaulnes"of A.F.)'.[74] The first thing, then, that Cornell perceived in the novel was the significance of the narrative order or sequence. It led him to separate out some of the notes in 'GC 44' under headings that would suggest separate episodes or journeys – 'The Festival of Nature', 'The Little Dancer', 'The Floral Still-Life', 'The House on the Hill', 'The Old Farm'.

Specific landmarks in *Le Grand Meaulnes* parallel locations that were familiar to Cornell and which are reflected in his series boxes. There is the 'tumble-down pigeon-house' that connects with the 'dovecote on Willet Mansion' in 'GC 44' and the Dovecote series; the first sighting by Meaulnes of 'the mysterious domain' ('the spire of a turret above a large grove of fir trees') connects with visions depicted in 'The Floral Still-Life' episode: Manhattan as seen from Flushing meadows and van Eyck's altarpiece; and which also feature in the box *Owl for Ondine* (1952) and, earlier, in *A Swan Lake for Tamara Toumanova* (illus. 32); the 'some forsaken old manor'[75] that Meaulnes encounters connects with the Malba House of 'The House on the Hill', Willet Mansion, and Cornell's Pink Palace series; and Meaulnes's earlier pause at a lonely cottage that contained a sitting-room whose walls were 'covered like those of an inn with pictures from illustrated papers'[76] is picked up in Cornell's Hotel series and in the Juan Gris boxes, which carry the distinctive feature of walls of printed matter and newspaper or magazine-type illustrations.

Meaulnes's adventure was frequently punctuated by snatches of sleep, after which he woke to confront a 'transformed scene'. He dreams, day-dreams and recalls visions of his childhood. The girl, Yvonne de Galais, the symbol of youth, innocence and beauty, figures prominently in his reveries. She captivates Meaulnes, although he is only momentarily in physical contact with her: 'She was quivering at his side, like a swallow which had come to rest for an instant but was already trembling with the wish to resume its flight.'[77] This description of a trembling bird-like girl comes close to the way that Cornell himself often imagined the women who so preoccupied him at this time: he was besotted by ballerinas because of 'their release, their escape, their flight, their defiance of the physical world: their amiability; the subtler sense of light and air'.[78] Meaulnes's ill-fated passion, like Cornell's, is largely directed towards a creature of the imagination.

The imagery, mood, themes and spirit of *Le Grand Meaulnes* is reflected again and again in Cornell's writings and in the boxes he produced around 1944. Like Meaulnes, he allowed life to entangle itself with visions, dreams, memories and fictions; there is a constant process of to-ing and fro-ing that ultimately makes it difficult to discern what is and what is not real. *Le Grand Meaulnes* encompassed so much that Cornell identified with that he found himself using the expression 'Grand Meaulnes feeling' in his notes as a shorthand reference to a whole world of feeling and imagery.[79]

The distinctive mood of the first part of the novel is an acute nostalgia for an earlier, idealized era. Alain-Fournier's vision of the past – a pastoral, romantic, slightly decadent and theatrical nineteenth-century world – gives way in later chapters to the weight of moral obligation in the form of a

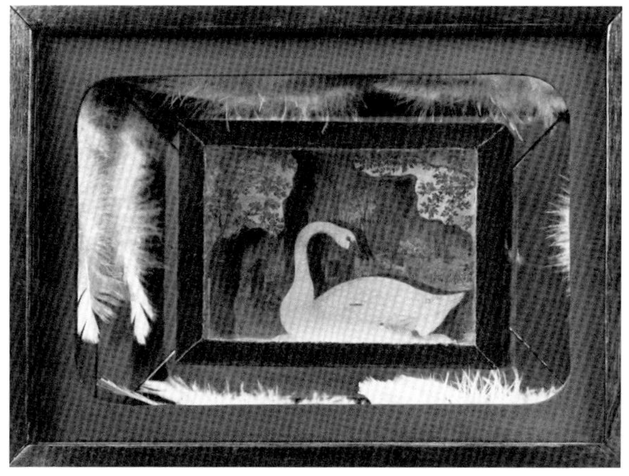

32 *A Swan Lake for Tamara Toumanova (Homage to the Romantic Ballet)*, 1946, box construction.

promise that must be fulfilled. This shift is part of the power the tale wields over its readers. Furthermore, it echoes history, and uses the young man (innocence), the girl (beauty) and the lost domain (vanishing world) as symbols of change. Cornell's own nostalgia was for a beautiful world redolent with an atmosphere of festivities, close family celebrations and magical sights, sounds and visions. They were among his most precious memories. His sister describes the change that came over Cornell when circumstances were dramatically transformed during their childhood:

> Before Daddy died – that was when he had a full sense of security. As soon as Daddy died then he felt that he should be the man of the house. And that's when all his dreams and terrible nightmares started. You know, in Andover he had a terrible time. He used to have these terrible nightmares and he'd yell for me. I would find myself running up the stairs, not even awake, saying 'I'm coming, I'm coming, I'm coming'. At one time he was cowering in the corner and he said 'it's a white antelope, it's a white antelope', and I didn't turn the light on, you know I had learnt not to startle him. So I said, 'It's alright Joe, it's just the sheet'. It was hard to convince him because he was in the grip of terror.[80]

His whole preoccupation in 'GC 44' with Malba House, Willet Mansion, Lawrence Farm – large homesteads with outbuildings set in the landscape – brought back a sense of the past, his own past, and nostalgia for a bygone era of imagined gentility. The disappearance of the houses was itself a mark of

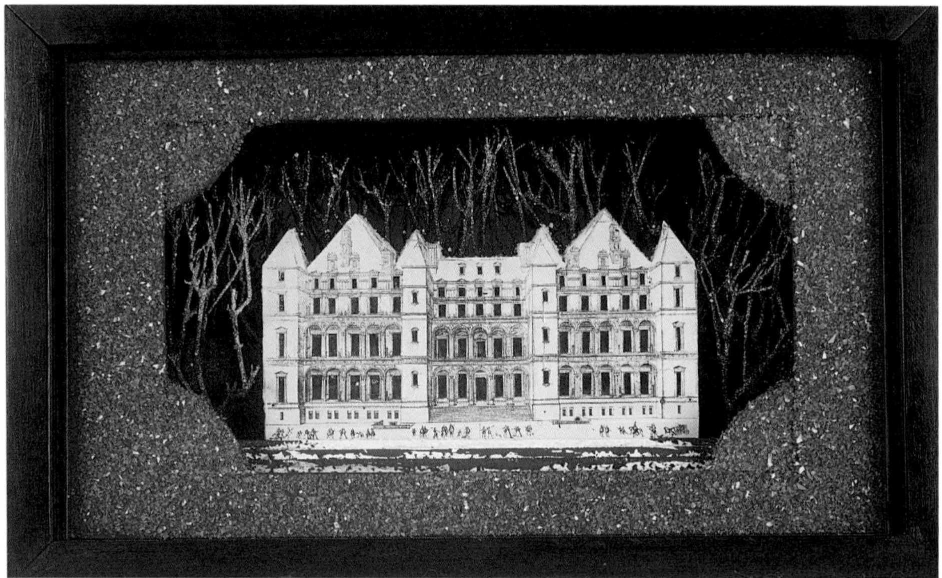

33 *Setting for a Fairy Tale*, c. 1942–6, box construction.

34 *Untitled (Dovecote)*, c. mid–1950s, box construction.

disintegration, but in addition the countryside was being ravaged by modern development. 'Unspoiled' is a word that frequently surfaces in Cornell's descriptions of his journeys into nature:

> beautiful country feeling through rural roads still unspoiled by developments . . .
> during the above period various countless contacts with nature – the meadows surrounding the Lawrence homestead, in the opposite direction towards the water, unspoiled stretches through Bayside via Bell Avenue, unspoiled stretches of Bayside West.[81]

Donald Windham, in the speech he gave at the memorial service for Cornell held on 15 January 1973, spoke of the 1944 period and of Cornell's awareness of Flushing's increasing urbanization: 'In the drawer of the *Cockatoo: Keepsake Parakeet* box which he gave me at about that time there is a small, pink, plastic Indian, with drawn bow and arrow, enclosed in a *Perugina torrone* box, a wild ostrich on the outside.'[82] In 'GC 44' Cornell shows that he felt personally responsible: 'Lawrence Farm, auction sign up . . . brought back wild asters and grasses a feeling of being a "custodian" of what is left of the original beauties of plant and grasses before complete oblivion'.[83]

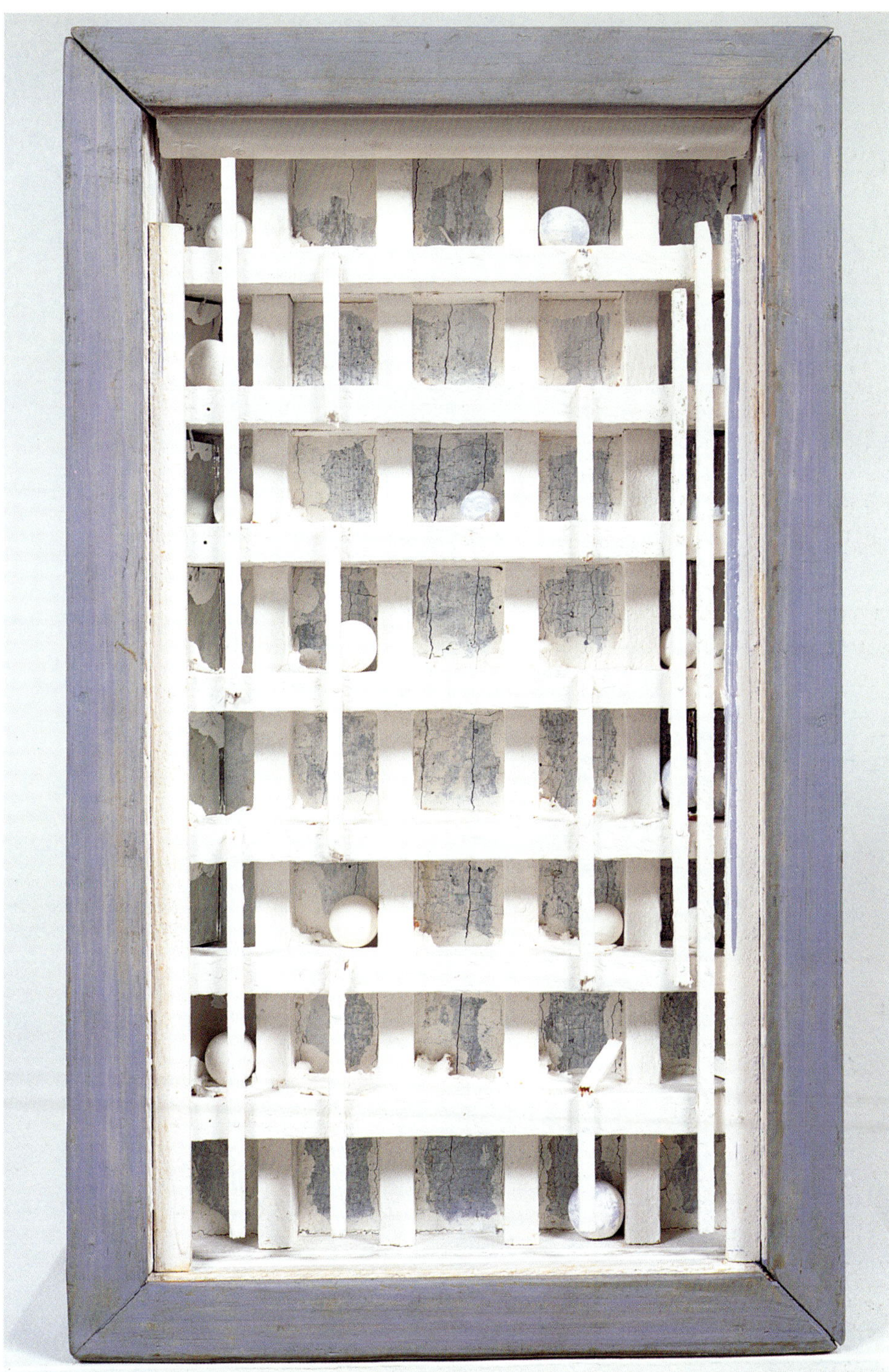

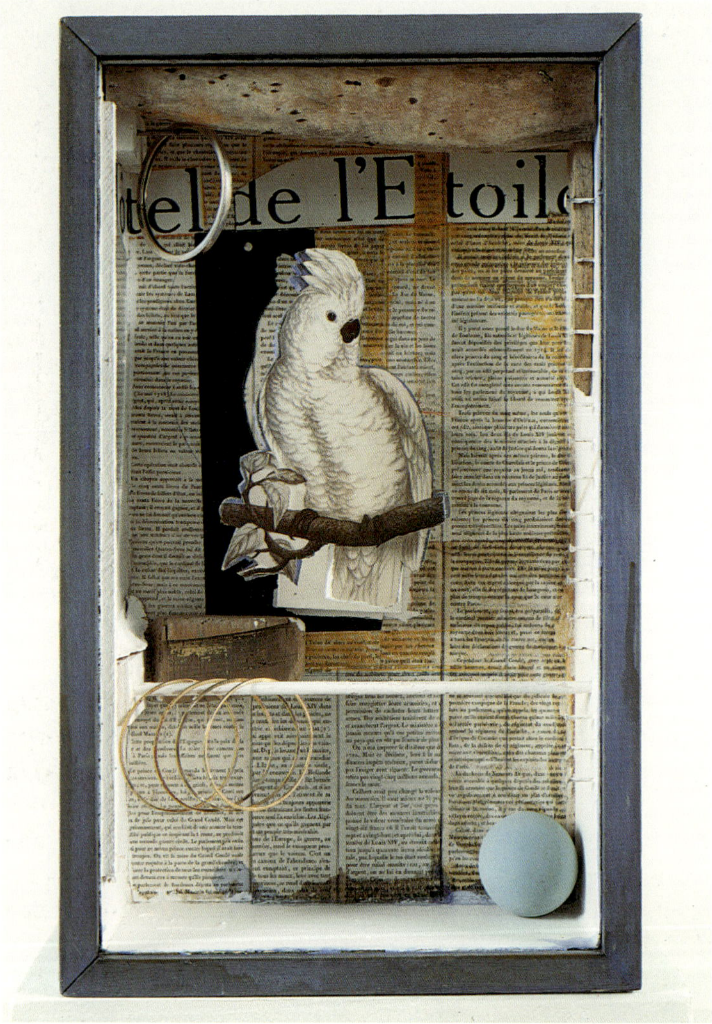

35 *Untitled* (*Juan Gris*), an undated box construction.

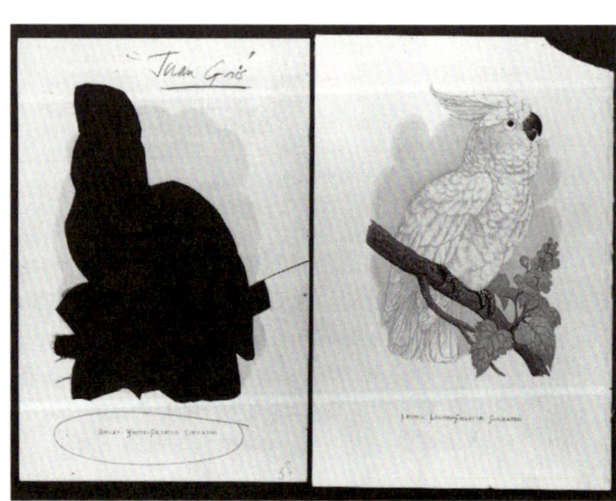

36 A pair of book illustrations of cockatoos – cut and inscribed by Cornell – from his files on Juan Gris, *c.* 1953 – early 1960s.

37 *Untitled (Bird and Corset)*, 1930s, collage.

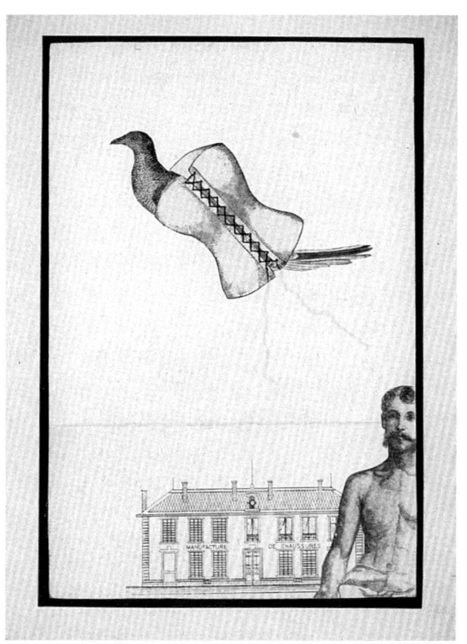

Listening to a radio broadcast of a panel discussing Proust's *Swann's Way*, Cornell noted a comment on it made by André Maurois: 'Perhaps the theme could be expressed in one sentence of Proust's himself: "Time as it flows, is so much time wasted and nothing can ever truly be possessed save under the aspect of eternity which is also the aspect of art . . . Yes, art because it gives the past a form, saves it from change and disintegration"'.[84]

Cornell incorporated the past literally as well as figuratively into his art by using up old nails found on the Lawrence Farm site, various grasses and bits of old bark, the wooden beading from Willet Mansion, as well as Audubon's nineteenth-century prints of birds.[85] This seems an extraordinary preoccupation if one considers the climate of art and literature that was current in mid-twentieth-century America. Nostalgia was anathema to most artists and writers; they were forging ahead to 'make it new'. Motherwell recalls the prevailing attitude among his contemporaries: 'we all felt that nostalgia was the enemy of Modernism, and his work is saturated with it'.[86]

Cornell was openly nostalgic when writing his dossier descriptions of Flushing's environs:

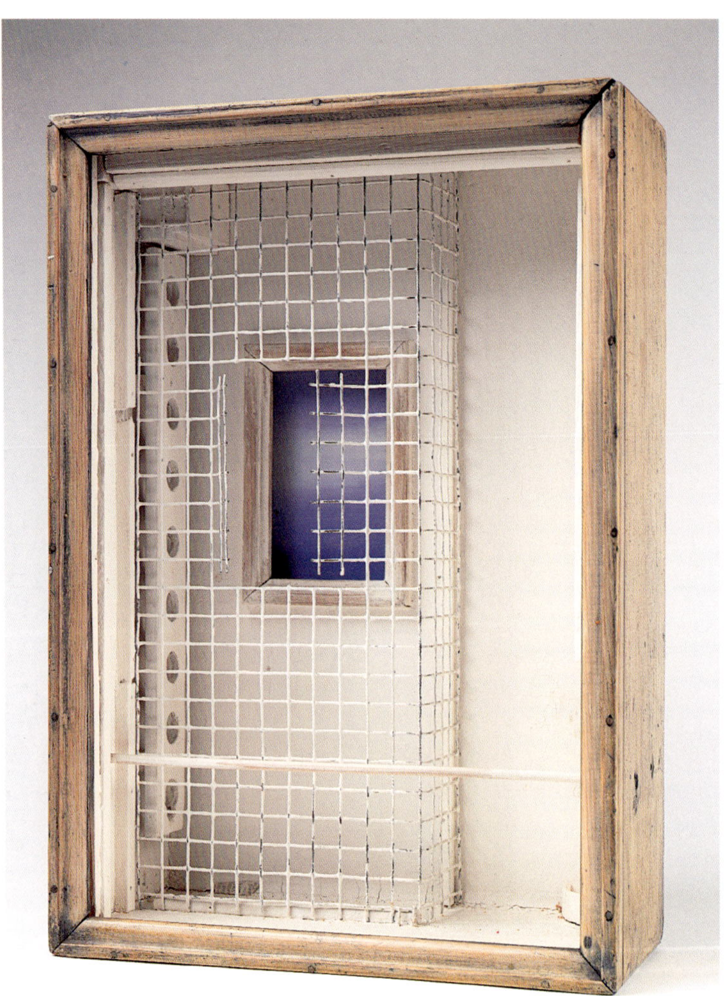

38 *Toward the Blue Peninsula (for Emily Dickinson)*, c. 1953, box construction.

Hundreds of white gulls beachcombing at very low tide – 3 men digging for clams – warmer than days before but an edge of sharp sun half hidden by grey clouds but with wonderful effect of subdued light on incoming waves – a shifting tapestry of silver before which the gulls disported themselves in their raucous droll manner, squeaking etc. a couple of terns among them – more rustling up in grass nearer road – a rare and beautiful mood in this late afternoon – a quiet mood but expansively picturesque and evoking the 'American Scene' also something of the past

39 *Untitled*, c. 1970, collage.

with a real awe and beauty. A rich and varied sunset, very dramatic. The house on the hill at Malba came to life authentically, naturally. The relationship of the water to the house, the association of flotsam and jetsam with the past, the Italian girl . . . An uncommon friendly feeling about the place. Riding brought back continued feelings of the appreciation of the familiar surroundings its former sense of strangeness and nostalgia etc. Feeling of being with Robert on late summer vacations going past homes adjacent to Francis Lewis Boulevard. Some fine pieces of jetsam

– one especially, a toy metal horse, beautifully corroded, lead with green and reddish coloring after the sea change. Preoccupation about the house of driftwood from different places and times . . . the renaissance by the country stream with its evocation of childhood, the American scene all its essence (see Audubon notes) and overwhelmingly transcendent serene state of mind – the vision (real) of the House in its immaculate setting of tree, shrub, lush grass, barns and smaller huts, well bushes in flower, serenely remote in its own dream in the early morning air of a new spring. All this remoteness accentuated by the yellow 'no

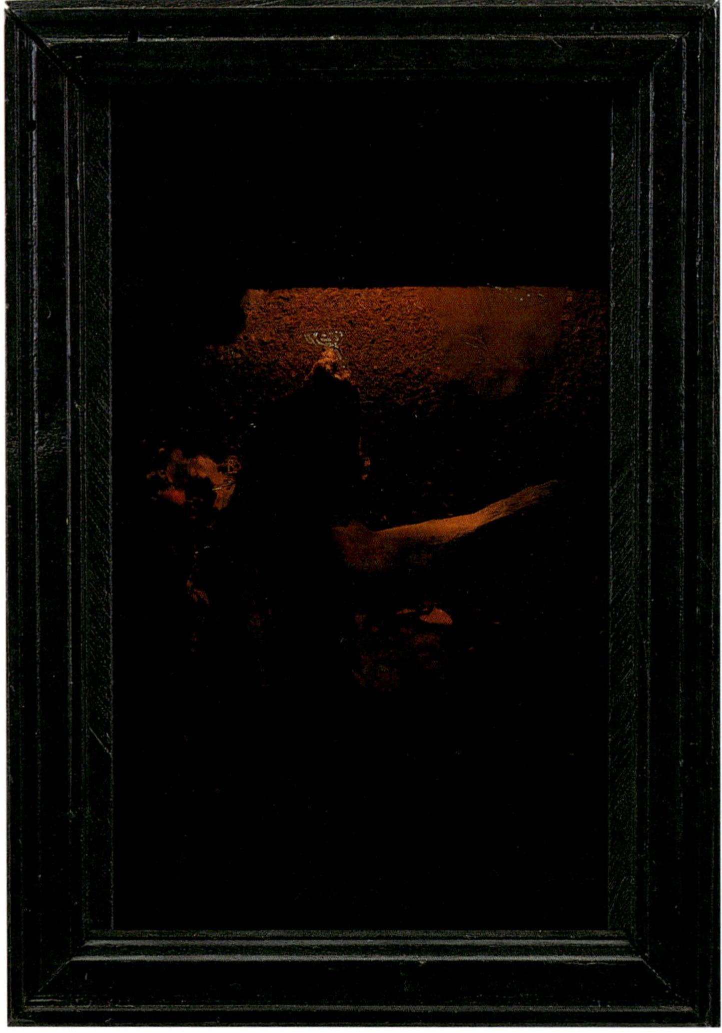

40 *Untitled*, an undated box construction.

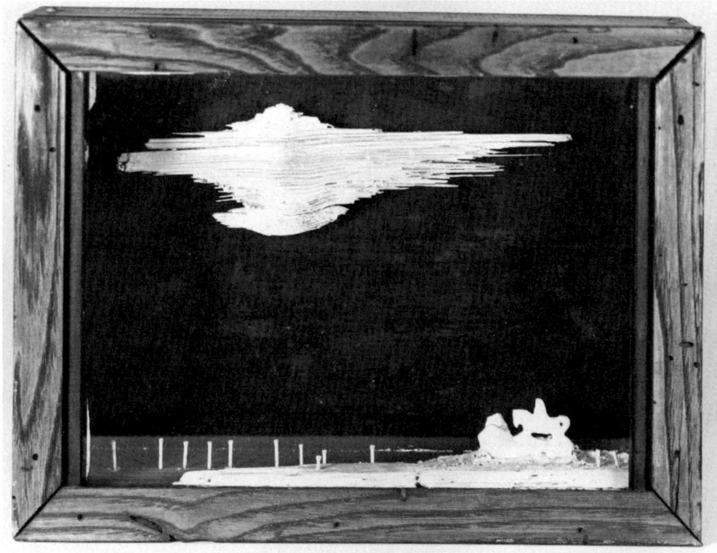

41 *Pleiades as seen with Unaides' Eye*, *c.* 1945, driftwood, nails and white china figure.

> trespassing' sign importing a kind of sovereignty making it seem all the more inviolate.[87]

In a passage in 'GC 44' entitled 'the past', Cornell attempted to come to terms with how the past was affecting him:

> A quickened sense of the drama of nature in diverse moods and the added sense of detail of commonplace experiences evoking something elusive (but real) of the past which made the present live with a significance more than sensuous enjoyment of spectacle (scenery, people, etc) a feeling that a particular moment of the past was transmuting the present with an unnamed but significant touch (a lyrical feeling although there was the ever lessening strain of morbid obsession with the past – a thing from childhood never outgrown).[88]

A young student, Steve Wood, on a visit to Cornell, recalls how in the midst of conversation the artist would allow a particular moment from the past to invade the present: 'He just kind of looked up at the sky, he raised his eyes up a bit and said "It's very quiet here today", talking to himself: "Thursdays are always mystical days. Mother was buried on a Thursday."'[89] This behaviour illustrated his determination to keep the past alive, but his active use of stored memories seems also to have been the counterpart to his obsession with the internal journey – the journey of the spirit.

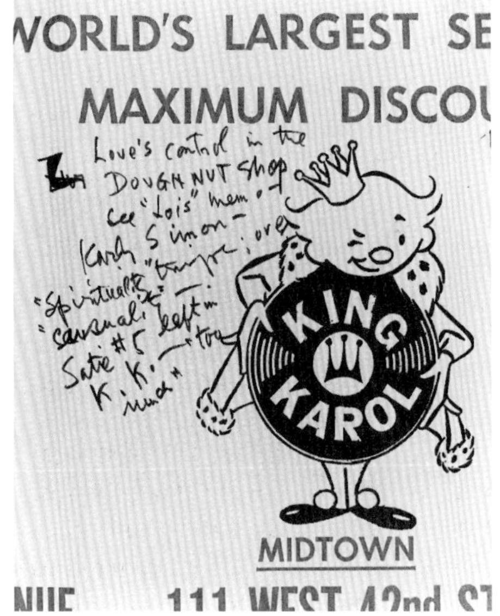

42 Cornell's notation on a paper bag from the King Karol music store.

DETACHMENT, INDIVIDUALISM AND SPIRIT

Cornell's other-worldly, preoccupied state was something that many of his contemporaries commented on. That his attitude to material things was unusual is easily learned from the remarks others made on his personal habits and social behaviour. Cornell did not conform to any 'normal' codes of behaviour: his sleeping, eating and working habits were dictated by his own system. He generally napped on a daybed and tended to work by night. He rarely joined social rituals, such as sharing a meal, or celebrations such as Thanksgiving. Even in the days when he was participating in functions organized by the Surrealists he would retire at eight o'clock. According to Dorothea Tanning, he was decidedly 'not a come-to-the-party boy'.[90] He was also awkward to work with, as the editor of *Dance Index* – who received contributions from Cornell in the 1940s – discovered. Kathryn Kuh, who edited a book of interviews with Surrealists, thought him 'too irrational. He didn't understand how to be interviewed . . . he wouldn't keep appointments'.[91]

Sometimes Cornell's unconventional behaviour brought him into conflict with the authorities. There were instances when he was hounded by the police because of his infatuation with young women and girls. He failed to understand how, for his subjects, his infatuations could become disturbing. He would follow them along the streets, or thrust parcels into their hands (boxes in homage to their images of innocence and waif-like beauty). Some young women were alarmed by phone-calls received at the dead of night; others by quirky cartoon drawings of the male organ distorted into the shape of a snail.[92]

Cornell seems to have adapted his life to detachment, to a kind of isolated living, yet a kind of isolation that allowed constant contact with people. He was a prolific letter-writer, and would spend several hours at a time on the telephone. But these methods of communication were at a safe distance; in face-to-face confrontations Cornell appeared awkward. The film-maker Rudy Burckhardt said of him: 'He never smiled just out of politeness. But if some thought occurred to him that pleased him he would smile slowly, from inside.'[93]

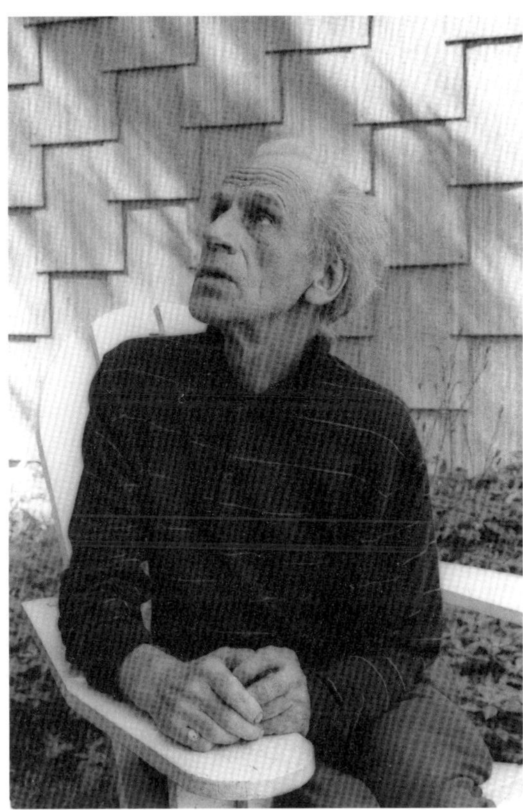

43 Hans Namuth, *Joseph Cornell*, 1970, photograph.

The art dealer Alan Stone even underwent a visit with the artist that took place with a wall between them, as Cornell on that occasion preferred to speak through the wall. If Cornell did share experiences with others – listening to music, walking or talking – his real enjoyment came later, in retrospection.

Cornell's attitude to food was extraordinary. He hardly ate. 'Joseph picked at food as though eating were a nuisance', John Bernard Myers noticed,[94] and has added that in the course of a whole day Cornell might share with a visitor a few pumpkin seeds, a few cookies and warm pineapple soda, or on another occasion a few sardines on a plate. He became infamous in art circles for his penchant for automatic diners, where he would consume Danish pastries and 'Jello'. Cornell also refused himself comforts. He often chose not to use the central-heating system in his home, for example, explaining to visitors sitting there in thick buttoned-up overcoats that if he felt the cold it was because of an error in thinking, because his 'mind set was not correct'.

Motherwell commented on the lack of physicality in Cornell; and in his art the lack of 'art brut':

> He neglects the fact that people sweat and snore, that a woman looks very different in hair curlers – he couldn't bear that idea, and there's not a trace of it in his work . . . I had a Welsh terrier, a very active one. The terrier jumped on his lap. Joseph gave a shriek of absolute horror. It was a terrific insight. It was the kind of shriek I would give if a rattlesnake jumped on my lap. It was so unexpected and for me a sudden revelation. His horror of anything physical: flesh, blood, appetite, realism.[95]

Motherwell also spoke about the way Cornell differed in style from so many of his contemporaries:

> Joseph would have played Captain Ahab in Moby Dick – the drive to find the white whale. The sentimental and the delicate misleads about the intensity of the obsession. I would imagine Lewis Carroll was not so different. Now Cornell's works are commodities, *objéts d'art*. He's neglected, underestimated. His fanaticism! I could imagine him killing over some scrap of film he found in some secondhand book stall. His artistic sensibility was rooted in Europe. As a man he ate junk food and dressed tastelessly. I've known lots of

poor artists, but usually artists have a way of wearing a scarf, you're very aware of a visual sensibility at work. For Cornell there was none of that at work. He was really *petit bourgeois*. I used to wonder, until the drugs scene, if alcohol was endemic among creative Americans. Joseph was always a teetotaller. I always wondered why, and suspected that at some time he'd had a drink and given something away, revealed something. He was secretive. Talking is one way of concealing what you think. In a curious way his art is almost a total compensation for what he's not – a world of grace, elegance, female beauty, mirrors, European culture – a gourmet art by a man who ate junk food.[96]

Motherwell was an admirer of Cornell's artistic achievement, but clearly this was an art very far from his own. Motherwell was quite open about the natural affinity he felt with certain artists: 'Physically what I liked was Matisse, Mondrian, Picasso and Léger – very masculine, broad, colourful, forceful, earthy, and for those days, abstract painters. Cornell was none of these things. On the other hand the Surrealists had a very strong feeling for poetry, and from that point of view I looked at Cornell as a poet.'[97] But there were others who met Cornell and felt closer to him psychologically and spiritually. Linda Scott was a young artist and a Christian Scientist:

He was an alchemist. Everything he touched, his nature, his relationship to reality as we know it, the material world, was that of an alchemist – to change in degrees, to change of a kind. He was transforming it. You even had the feeling that there was a witches brew on the stove, it was very powerful stuff. The house was filled with his fetish system. The attention that was given to everything – the attention that was used for transformation. I saw the degree that he was into himself. It's one thing to handle this other part that's going on when you think somebody's still eating three meals a day, I just saw that he didn't. He was a virgin, wasn't he?[98]

Cornell's eccentric behaviour may be at least partly attributable to his commitment to Christian Science. The denial of matter within the Christian Science doctrine and the absolute emphasis on mind control may help to explain Cornell's lack of interest in bodily needs, his refusal to allow his mind to be subservient to society's views, his overall detachment and preference for his own inner vision.

Eddy's *Science and Health* is the ultimate source of truth for the Christian Scientist, surpassing the Bible in its authority, for adherents may only interpret the Bible in the manner indicated in *Science and Health.* The essential doctrine of Christian Science contains four basic denials: matter, evil, disease and death. Apart from the overwhelming subjectivism that is advocated in these principles, it is certainly the case that the aspect of Eddy's teachings that has provoked most criticism is the denial of bodily disease. According to her, 'the cause of all so-called disease is mental, a mortal fear, the mistaken belief or conviction of the necessity and power of ill-health'. Further, 'the evidence of the senses is not to be accepted in the case of sickness, any more than it is in the case of sin'.[99] Perhaps the most significant point to underline here is that physical and mental health are guaranteed to Christian Scientists as long as they adhere strictly to the tenets of that faith: man's physical and mental well-being is the goal of the doctrine, and God is a means to that end. This is what most obviously and most radically separates Christian Science from other branches of Christianity.

As a philosophy, Christian Science approximates to subjective idealism, in that matter is declared to be unreal, while God or Mind are infinite. By affirming propositions such as these, Christian Scientists believe that they can raise the condition of the unreal material body to harmony with the real spiritual estate of man. For Sandra Starr, Christian Science is the key to understanding Cornell's work: 'around 1925, seven years before his first exhibition as an artist, Cornell became a Christian Scientist and so remained for the duration of his life. It was 'the single most important force not only in his life but in his work'. Cornell's philosophical position by this reading is fixed: he works, thinks, acts according to principle, and his artistic direction is seen to be determined and subordinated to his transcendental beliefs. Starr insists that Cornell was 'first and foremost a metaphysical scientist and religious philosopher who used art as a means rather than an aesthetic end';[100] moreover, that Cornell attempted to communicate the Christian Science doctrine 'that physical matter is a delusion of mortal perception and that true substance is reflected only in spirit and cannot be perceived in matter' through striving to 'eliminate art as material object and our perception of it as such', gradually replacing it with 'the substance of things hoped for, the evidence of things not seen'.[101] Starr's position, of course, leads her to undertake a highly convoluted reading of the boxes: 'It is in the shadows between the objects, and in the mirrored reflections that one finds the invisible Reality in Cornell's shadow boxes and his demonstration of the existence of Spirit'.[102]

Although Starr has too limited an explanation for the sources and goals of Cornell's art – 'It has been said that all roads in Cornell's earlier work lead to Marcel Duchamp. In fact, all roads in Cornell's art lead to eternity and a vision of the absolute'[103] – it cannot be denied that the tenets of Christian Science did have a strong influence. His writings abound with sympathetic statements about his religion:

> Aug. 17 1945 Decided to go out back alone and do some mental work to know the unreality of the claim of pressure at the back of head . . . went through the whole lesson on SOUL in Christian Science Quarterly and enjoyed it more than I can remember in a similar session in yard . . . Felt better after reading – lessening of belief, hatred, fear, all sensuality . . . yield to spirituality, and the superabundance of being is on the side of God, Good Health. In trying times I am citing this, which was read from the pulpit last week – and it has been helping me.[104]

Cornell also read about other branches of Protestant thought. Books he owned included *The Protestant Mystics: An Anthology of Spiritual Experience from Martin Luther to T. S. Eliot*. His diary tells us of his interest in the astronomer Kepler, a 'tortured mystic who stumbled onto his discoveries'.[105] Mystics everywhere agree on at least one thing: man must learn detachment from the self and from things of this world that tend to dominate him. However, in the state known as illumination, individual selfconsciousness remains and the consciousness of God may be mediated through the objects and forces of nature. This mediation was of vital significance to the artist. But there is another feature of Christian mysticism that would have attracted Cornell. With most other forms of mysticism the tendency is to regard the attainment of an inner state of consciousness (ecstasy or contemplation) as the goal of the inner life, whereas with Christian mystics the goal is action – a state of being wherein God acts in and through the soul. Christian Science also, we may remember, is a creed dedicated to action.

Another strand in Cornell's metaphysic was Chinese philosophy and art. In 'GC 44' he writes 'to the greatest *traveler*', and then notes down lines from Arthur Waley's *Three Ways of Thought in Ancient China*:

> Those who take infinite trouble about external travels, have no idea about how to set about the sight seeing that can be done within. The traveler abroad is dependent on outside things; he whose sight-seeing is inward can in himself find all he needs. Such is the highest form of travelling; while it is the poor sort of journey that is dependent on outside things.[106]

Cornell was a visionary whose involvement with his own mental states would, while offering him insights into reality, threaten his mental stability: 'states of mind bordering on the hysterical . . . all the emotionalism, persecution, fatigue, depression'.[107] Though he was clearly disturbed at times like these, he none the less nurtured the tendency to internalize, for its inestimable creative stimulus.

A letter to Susan Sontag of 17 February 1966 illustrates the way he would foster a state of being in which the mind would seem to be divorced from the body:

> It is the witching hour as I now pen . . . wide awake for the night and . . . of that Cartesian state wherein the prototype experienced visions in a state of extreme lassitude; and so minded reminded of poss, the most significant of all my explorations GC 44 – not completely cabalistic Garden Center 1944 where I took employment in a garden nursery 'center' which became the hub of an infinite no. of journeys.[108]

In 'GC 44' the oriental mind is applauded for its appreciation of spiritual development and for its approach to nature. One entry, labelled the 'Festival Of Nature' and subtitled 'Chinese Pictures Of Autumn', discusses the processing of grasses. Other examples of nature references that connect with oriental poetry and art include the following:

alone at home cutting grass after reading ALOYSIUS BERTRAND a realization of the nature of the extreme 'picturesqueness', the imagery of Bertrand's poetry – such as appreciated before in Oriental poetry, the 100 Views of Fuji of Hiroshige.

Observed tiny insect like miniature darning needle . . . but wings (transparent) more like a butterfly. Tiny ball shaped head red – undulating tail glossy black – only about an inch long – maybe Miss M. Moore will know its name – a feeling of calm similar to morning a week ago Sunday when this spot was alive with birds – went through the whole lesson on SOUL in Christian Science

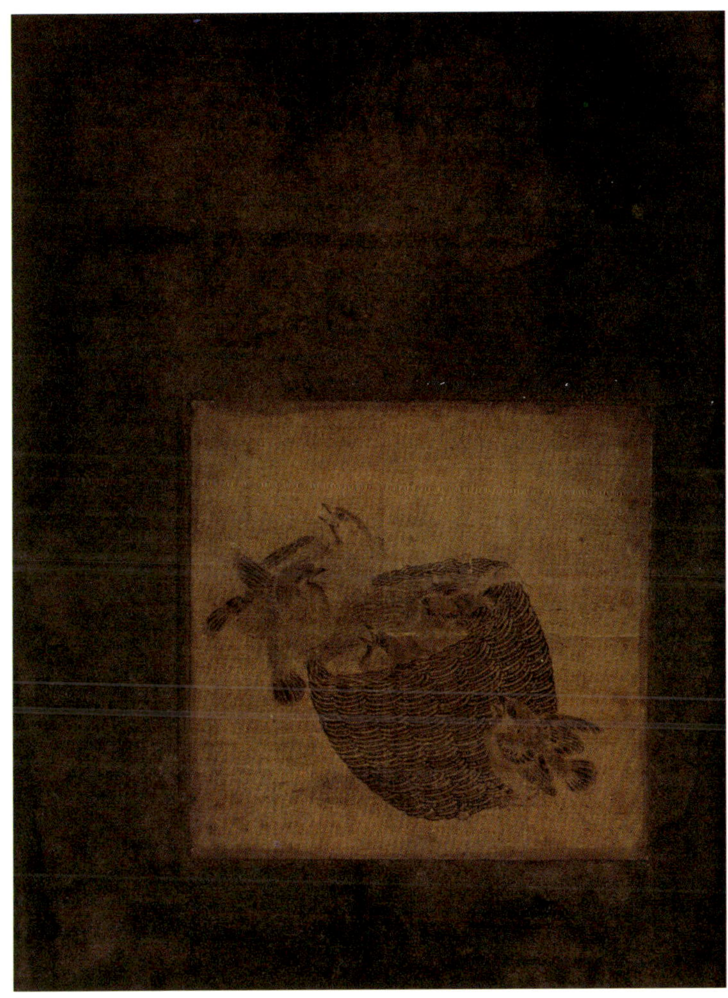

44 *Untitled (Young Sparrows in a Basket)*, 1967, collage.

> Quarterly and enjoyed it more than I can remember in a similar session in yard. Bird with brown back – greenish yellow breast flashed by two or three times chasing a different kind of bird. Speckled starlings strutting about and pecking at perforated cabbage plants in Backmann's plot in bright sun brought that wonderful feeling of the correspondences in nature treated so profoundly and beautifully by the Chinese painters of the SUNG period. The quince tree in bloom (what is left of the fruit that hasn't been despoiled by squirrels) also brings this feeling. Felt better after reading – lessening of belief . . . Feeling of peace too deep to get into words.[109]

Cornell's observation and recording of the activity in his backyard and the visual, tactile descriptions that are tied in to his thoughts on mortality and religion is in accord with Marianne Moore's poetry and led Cornell to the painters of the Sung period. His appreciation of oriental art is expressed not only in the dossiers but in the collages *Untitled (Young Sparrows in a Basket)* and *Quite Autumnal # 2* and in the box *Untitled (for Sheree North)* (1953–9).

According to Donald Windham, 'Joseph's mind worked by association and by passionate identification with specific things, and a very acute feeling of connections between specific things, but I don't think by intellectual theory. If he took something from astrology or mathematics I don't think it was Kantian, I don't think he was pouring over Aristotle's theories even if what he did fitted into them.'[110] Cornell's writings would seem to confirm this idea. He borrowed from various sources, and the items he lists in 'The Yale Student File' testify to the breadth of his influences. Cornell wrote down some of his sources in response to a request by a Yale student researching a paper: 'Odilon Redon, Hiroshige, Chinese Painters by Petrucchi, Adventures In The Arts – Marsden Hartley, Delacroix's Journals, Steeplejack – James Huneker, Monsieur Croche – Debussy, Christian Science Monitor – Home Forum Section'. As asides, he also mentioned 'De Chirico, Vermeer, Caravaggio, Van Gogh's letters, Goya's Child With Magpie, great joy of discovery in Jap. prints, Theater, Opera, Sense of the Past, Deep empathy for Currier and Ives prints, religion, sense of American past, Tina'. The bewildering diversity even in such a short list points to the way that Cornell's art developed through the multiplicity and fecundity of his associative imagination and not through rigorous extrapolation from doctrinal fixities.

Cornell certainly made strenuous attempts to constrain his tendencies towards proliferation. He wrote in 'The Yale Student File' of 'hueing to the line of true religious love as vs aestheticism . . . this reminder . . . is comforting and inspiring even. And fruitful in evaluating allegiances in the direction of French artists and writers.'[111] His discomfort at finding within himself sympathies that were difficult to align with his Christian Science beliefs is further indicated by his reflections on the French intellectual obsession with art and beauty, where he writes guiltily that 'upon reflection there has always been a quality of life about them'.[112] Later in the same passage he reinforced his determination to curtail the associative tendencies of his mind: 'the promise of so many countless things, people etc. in the light of C.S. [Christian Science] for philosophy and intellectualism per se cannot be reconciled; only emanated whatever enduring , beautiful or worthwhile surviving'. His difficulty was reconcilement. He was clearly involved in a constant struggle to bring all his divergencies into the mainstream of his religious beliefs without ever managing to 'reconcile' them. Though it is clear that Cornell was drawn towards a fixed position, his instinctive urge was to collect, and this is reflected as much in the divergent overflow of the 'thoughts' in his dossiers as it is in the 'things' shelved in his workshop cellar.

SURREALISM, DREAMS

Cornell's description of 'GC 44' shows the centrality of dreams and visions. He calls it variously, 'a dream-like accumulation', 'a world of authentic visions', 'a tower of visions' and 'a clearing house for dreams and visions'.[113] Recording his dreams and visions was the habit of a lifetime, and in this connection Dore Ashton has pointed out that 'although it was a Surrealist habit to try to capture the flow of dreams, one suspects that Cornell long before he ever heard of Surrealism, was busy excavating his nocturnal imagery. He often mentioned his long and sometimes terrifying dreams.'[114] Dawn Ades too has observed that 'Cornell was attracted, not to the purely painterly extension of automatic processes, but rather to that side of Surrealism which involves the exploration of dreams and visions and the annexing of real objects as material for the free exercise of the imagination'.[115]

It was not just the visionary state, the *dream state*, that pervaded 'GC 44', for Cornell drew on his actual dreams as well. One in particular centred on the ballerina Carlotta Grisi at Coney Island. This dream is at the heart of the journey entitled 'The Little Dancer' in 'GC 44'. Cornell wrote of the 'appreciation and gratitude for the workings of the mental processes that can transform a picture'.[116] He had found a picture of Grisi in *Theatre* magazine, and it was this image that had surfaced in the dream he had that became the basis for 'The Little Dancer'. He explained in another dossier that his inspiration often began with a key image, his poetic search following on from that.[117] The key image in Cornell's creative interior journeys is always something initially only glimpsed – a memory not clearly contextualized. In 'The Floral Still-Life' the original image of inspiration had been glimpsed when riding on a bicycle, the truck bearing the meat and fish logo flashing past him.

As a collector of dreams Cornell was obsessive. He collected not only his own but those of his sisters and brother also ('that dream of Robert's to follow . . . lurking treasure'[118]). 'It's awful the way I used to hound him to tell his dreams', Cornell confessed to his sister.[119] Betty's dreams would have been a useful source for uncovering elements of their childhood that may have failed to surface in their exchange of memories. Robert's dreams offered an even deeper penetration into a mind that was distanced from the world as a result of cerebral palsy. Cornell saw his brother as an untouched soul, pure and innocent, and he appreciated Robert's poetic and sensitive delivery when he summoned the strength to express himself. Robert did struggle, labouring for hours with twisted hands to record his dreams.

Cornell also recorded many of his own dreams in his diaries and dossiers because of the types of image, and the moods or atmospheres, he encountered ('the glow of the dream rapidly fades yet something is left delicate but real and comforting, as the imprint of Cinderella's glass slipper'), and for the confirmation of the worth of an image, such as the Grisi image from *Theatre* magazine.[120] In considering Cornell's use of dreams in relation to the Surrealists and their dream theories, which he

45 *Untitled*, 1959, box construction.

This box is an example of the unusual variety of objects Cornell could utilize for 'a genuine evocation' of dreams, daydreams and time passing.

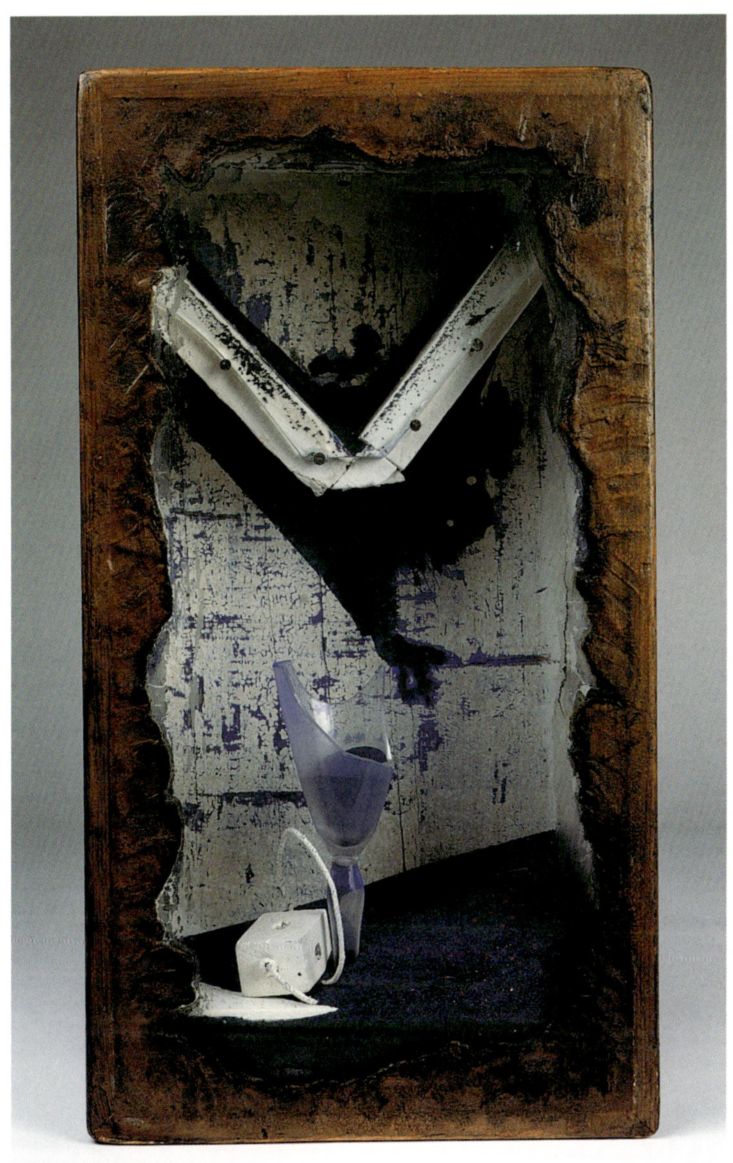

expressly dissociated himself from, it is illuminating to examine a dream episode recounted in the diaries.[121] This is a dream of the 'nightmare alley of Lower B'way':

> the re-creative force of the dream images and illuminated detail (although tenebruso and sinister) seems very important albeit very difficult to do much about in terms of

> communication. Strong sense of having witnessed these areas illuminated (also in waking hours just as much as dream) in the same way as Gérard de Nerval without his classical sense of form and genius of expression to help out. But this dominant and latent force must have some kind of present significance to evoke images of such splendid terror . . . going back to the 'Chien Andalou' days.[122]

Cornell's affinities with the French poet and short story writer Gérard de Nerval have frequently been acknowledged. He was drawn towards Nerval's insistence on dreams and the 'double aspect' of existence, particularly in the poetic and hallucinatory collection *Aurélia, ou la rêve et la vie* (1855): 'Our dreams are a second life. I have never been able to penetrate without a shudder those ivory or horned gates which separate us from the invisible world. Here began what I shall call the overflowing of the dream into real life. From that moment on, everything took on at times a double aspect.'[123] Cornell describes dreams as, 'a dominant and latent force', but they need a 'classical sense of form and genius of expression'. He did not believe that, unhindered, the dream could be tapped and an uncontrolled passage opened up from the dream to the creation of a work of art, as the Surrealists attempted in their automatic writings and drawings. Dawn Ades reminds us in *Dada and Surrealism* that Arp was the 'most naturally unconscious artist and yet he didn't like the Surrealists' theories of automatism because he says "I am no longer doing the forming"'.[124]

According to Dorothea Tanning, 'When I first met [Cornell] he was so obviously possessed, a *person habité* as they say in French, *habité par ses rêves et les phantasms*'.[125] She felt that their association continued because what she was doing was parallel to what he was doing. When she met Cornell she 'was living in a bit of a dream world and my pictures had some sort of . . . definite undercurrents of rather violent dreams.' Her relationship with Cornell was largely maintained by correspondence, because in 1943 she and her husband, Max Ernst, moved from New York to Arizona. Prior to this she had met with Cornell at the Levy Gallery and at Gypsy Rose Lee's house, 'a very pretty house in East 64th'. Gypsy Rose Lee 'was fascinated by what he did. He used to put together these old movies so we had a couple of seances at her place where he showed the movies'. Once, Tanning had been out to Utopia Parkway with Max Ernst, Jeanne Reynal and a couple of others: 'At one point Joseph offered to take us out to the garage where he kept all these things, it was quite impressive I must say, but he said "the ladies only", and Max was rather miffed'.

Expressions of feeling between Tanning and Cornell are well documented in their letters: 'Dearest Dorothea, I have a dossier on you Tante Dorothea from which I send you a precious feuilleton or even better, copy some material so that others may know in what esteem I hold you.' She would respond in the same tone: 'Sometimes I think the only true and satisfactory means of contact with those we love is by writing rather than talking. So it seems to me that our letters are far more the barometer of our feelings than when we speak for a few over-charged moments in New York.'[126] They exchanged drawings (Tanning) and collages (Cornell) by mail and gave accounts of their feelings and dreams. Advice about galleries would be offered by Tanning (she was a connection for Cornell with the Copley Gallery in California, and later with a gallery in Paris that was also showing Ernst's and Duchamp's work). (Dickran Tashjian, in his *Joseph Cornell: Gifts Of Desire*, has much of interest to say on this connection between Cornell and Tanning.) On a different level of indebtedness, Cornell was occasionally a provider of imagery for Tanning; she would use him, as others did, as a sort of image library. She said 'it was a mutual, charming little exchange of ideas, of letters'.[127]

One exhibition of Tanning's – held at the Levy Gallery in April 1944 – was especially important to Cornell. He mentions it in 'GC 44', saying that it was a part of the initial circumstances of the 'GC 44' experiences, and that it was influential in terms of his state of mind at the time. Cornell mentioned on several occasions the painting of 'the boy with the flowered leg'.[128] He treasured Ernst's words about the show printed on the slim handout that accompanied it: 'I like the work of Dorothea Tanning because the domain of the marvellous is her native country'.[129] These words would have struck a chord with Cornell then, for almost daily he felt he was discovering anew the wonders of his own country. However, he would also have connected with Tanning's expression of the 'tumults of the child's soul' and with her 'courage in taking a precise and difficult position amid the general confusion of ideas which characterizes the artistic situation of our time'. Ernst summarized this by talking about the 'too-comfortable monasteries of the abstract, with its easy and vague nebulae' on the one hand and yet the 'exigencies of an orthodox surrealism' on the other, which needs a vow of obedience. 'Precision is her mystery', says Ernst, 'thus she acquired the faculty of leading us with the surety of the somnambulist through the real world as well as throughout the imagined world'. 'My dreams, my illusory impressions and my waking life are all so mixed and con-

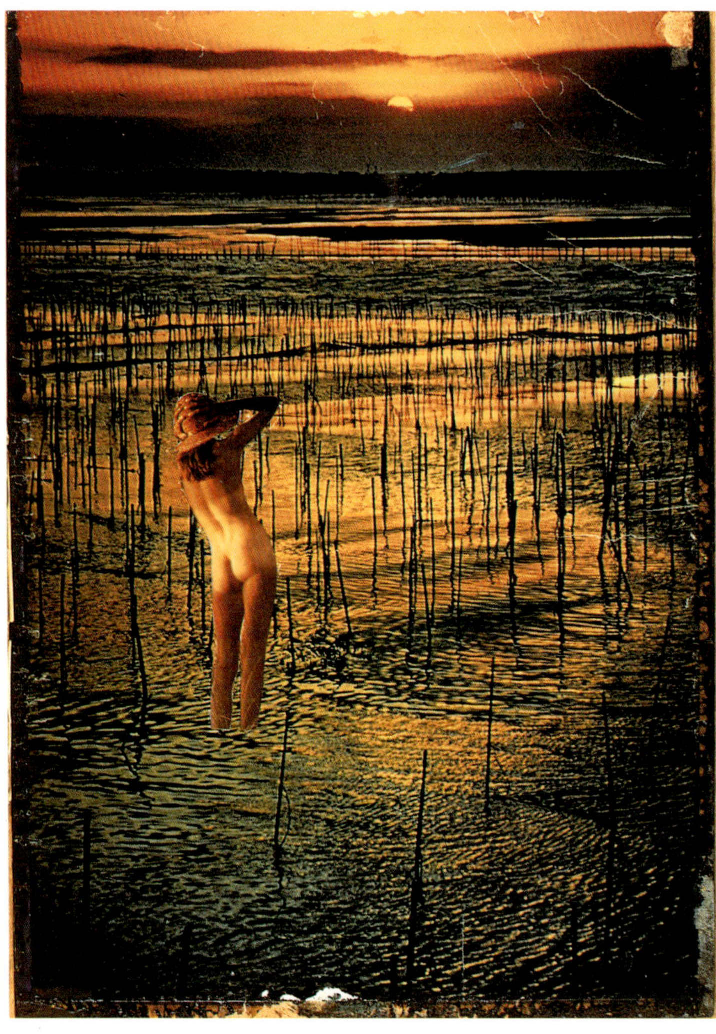

46 *Untitled*, c. 1960s, collage.

fusing that I sometimes wonder if there is any reality at all', Tanning told Cornell.[130]

The two artists had much in common, including an ambivalent attitude towards Surrealism. They both felt great respect for the movement, but chose to remain independent from it partly because they wished to retain an American aspect in their work. They both struggled to define the creative mind; they both aimed to establish precision and deny vagueness; they both sought for authenticity in their work. Besides this they were also sympathetic to similar sorts of images: the little prince of Tanning's dream in his 'doublet with long silk stockings' and the little prince of Cornell's Medici Machines are closely linked; and they were both drawn to the world of children, particularly favouring images of young girls in dream-like atmospheres. They both wanted to 'let the poetry in and keep the revulsion out':

> That is something that you, of all the people I know have somehow managed to do. How did you do that Joseph? I wish I were not so aware of what the rest of the world is doing. Maybe that is your secret, maybe that is what you keep out.[131]

TWO BOX STUDIES

Sitting in the backyard for most of Cornell's adult life were some plastercast rabbits from the Garden Center, which were therefore a part of that momentous experience in 1944 – and subsequently a daily reminder of it (illus. 49, 50). According to Betty (to whose yard the rabbits were removed following Cornell's death):

> Some people have said that the rabbits were banal, but those people don't know what a rabbit meant to Joe because Robert drew rabbits and we had a Bunny society in our family. We made it up. Robert and I made up a Bunny society because of my grandmother's sister Aunt Wina . . . we used to say 'she's like a bunny'. She had these dearest little pink round cheeks and a little nose, and when she smiled it kind of wrinkled. She was the most precious thing. So Robert and I used to say 'she's a bunny' or 'he's a bunny' – that was the highest praise we could give people. And so Joe played along with us. And so rabbits had a special place in our family. It was personal.[132]

Robert's drawings of rabbits were incorporated into collages by Cornell after Robert's death in 1965. One of their favourite rabbit drawings was 'Prince Pince', which features in a number of Cornell's collages. He would treat the photostat reproduction of Robert's drawing within the collage context in the same way that he might attend to a reproduction of a Magritte painting or Man Ray's rayograph of Breton's head, or Dürer's drawn self-portrait. That is, Cornell would paste on the reproduction and then impose on top a small constellation or some stamps, a bit of glitter, some ink staining, mathematical shapes or pencilled markings. *The Heart on the Sleeve* (1972), *Untitled (Prince Pince)* (1967) or *Satie and Ravel* (illus. 47) became 'the Cornell brothers doing a balancing act'.[133] However, Robert's drawings were different in that they were treated similarly within the collage space, but within the public sphere they were elevated. Cornell organized an exhibition solely of these works:

> I was with him when he had the show for his brother, his brother's drawings and his own constructions at Schoelkopf

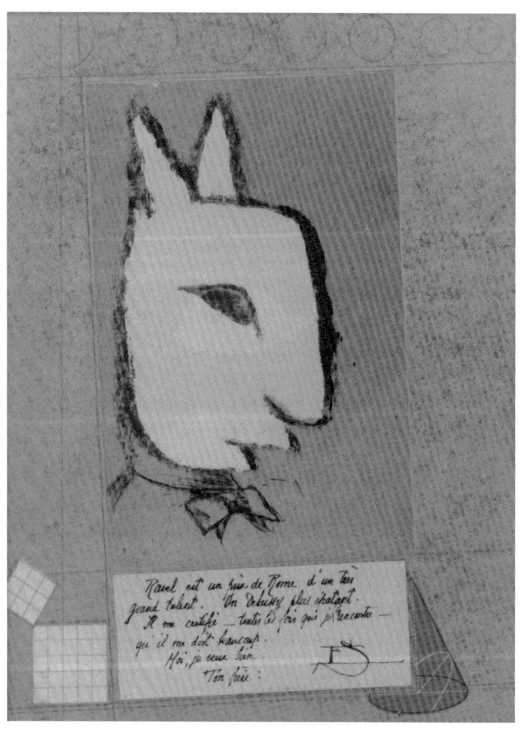

47 *Satie and Ravel*, *c.* 1960, collage composed of cut and pasted commercially printed papers, with graphite on untempered masonite (including Robert Cornell's rabbit drawing).

48 *Untitled (American Rabbit)*, 1945–6, box construction.

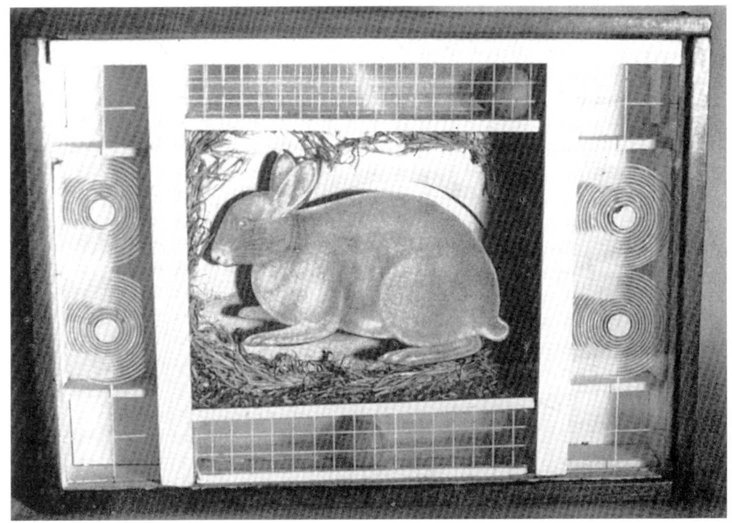

> – and how concerned he was that this was the right person to show Robert's work. He was so emotionally involved it was difficult for him . . . In some way I felt there was a non-resolution with the brother's death. Joseph immortalized him in many of his works, particularly the collages of the rabbit.[134]

In the cellar workshop Cornell had enlarged photographs propped up on shelves. Among those on the top shelf was a blown-up photo of Robert taken when he was a child, in among the 'prince' images (by Goya and others). On the second shelf was propped a picture of a rabbit peeping out from foliage. The significance of rabbits, then, began in childhood and the image of the rabbit became a symbol for Robert.

Rabbits were manufactured at the Garden Center, and they feature in the 'GC 44' notations in more general diary-type records. More specifically we can see how a box like *Untitled (American Rabbit)* (illus. 48) could emerge from inspirational passages contained in 'The Floral Still Life' episode, for example:

> the sense of the moving vehicle with the painted enseigne against fields, grasses, the lushness, the sense of imagery, the sense of things set off against or in fields, the sense of the 'expectancy' of animals lurking, shrubbery etc the metaphysical aspect of this 'expectancy' the 'something' that might have happened with a little more patience in

> not scaring up something whose presence was realized too late. The 'renaissance' by the country stream with its evocation of childhood, the American scene, all its essence . . . an overwhelmingly transcendent serene state of mind.'
>
> A quiet mood, but expansively picturesque and evoking the 'American Scene' also something of the past with a real awe and beauty.[135]

The formal element of the box construction is arresting: there is a symmetry and balance in the top and bottom and two sides and four corner compartments that border the central image. The grid-like patterning and the target impressions add to the formal impact. This basic formula for a box – a large central area with slender bordering compartments, grids and spheres making up the echoing resounding shapes in the side chambers – is also the formula found in the 'Medici Slot Machine' and 'Caravaggio Boy' series and in the *Penny Arcade Portrait of Lauren Bacall* (1945–6). These boxes, however, all stand vertically, whereas *Untitled (American Rabbit)* lies horizontally. *Untitled (American Rabbit)* has a white background – white struts of wood separate out the compartments, and a natural wood case holds the whole construction together. It is not a hutch that has been built for the rabbit, for the grid/cage markings look more like something one expects to encounter in a science laboratory. Perhaps it is the predominance of white paint that makes the box appear clinical. It has a limited colour range. The red solid circle (ink staining) is like something caught in orbit; there are four red circles, and each one is shifted slightly, moved into a different position but yet still within its own determinate orbit, just like the red balls in their narrow confining chutes/channels at the top and bottom of the box, or like the rabbit in its cage. The red may be connecting with the pink of a rabbit's eye; the grasses are the warm reddish/orange/brown hues of autumn grass.

The rabbit has been cut from a leaf of paper in a book or from a print and it has been brought forward in the box construction and tilted over just a few degrees. The rabbit looks poised, about to pounce. By leaving the burrow-shaped hole in the background and by tilting the image of the rabbit in the foreground a quivering energy is conveyed – the side coils or

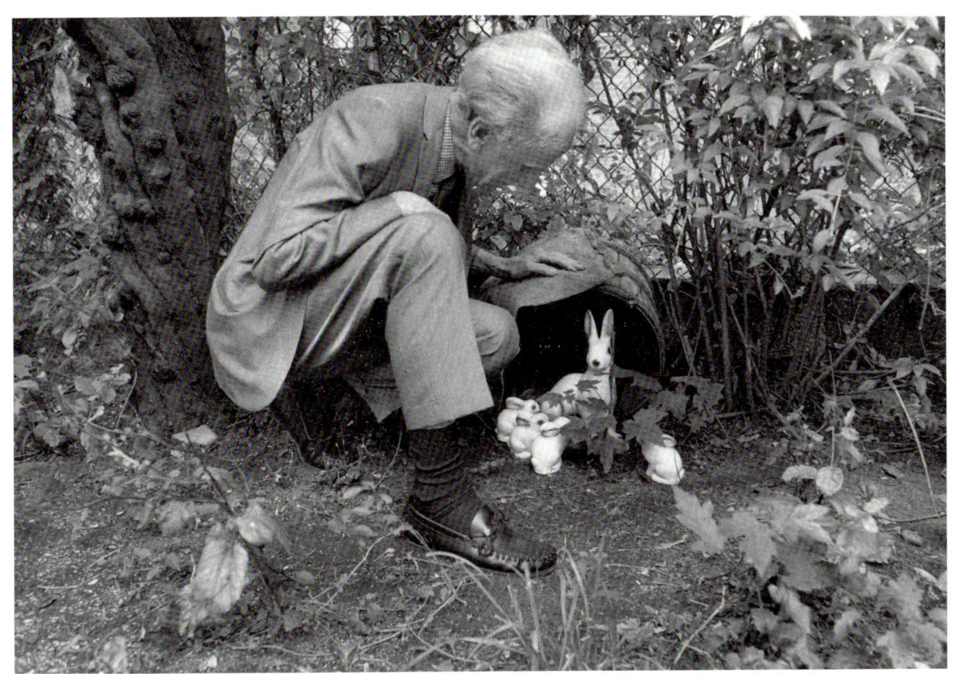

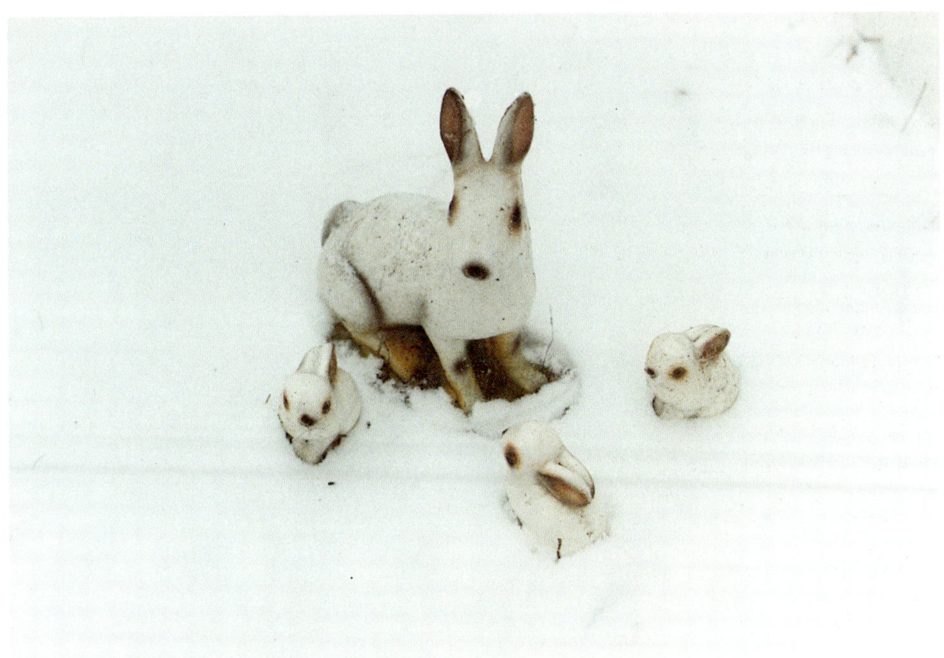

49 Duane Michals, *Cornell in his Garden, c.* 1970, a photograph taken at Cornell's request.
50 Harry Roseman, *Rabbits in Snow: Joseph Cornell's Backyard*, 1970, photograph.

springs reverberate to continue this dynamic. The atmosphere is one of expectancy: 'the sense of things set off against or in fields, the sense of expectancy of animals lurking'. There is a soft focus about the definition of the rabbit, naturalism about its depiction and, of course, it is squatting among real grasses. Cornell is not removing the rabbit from the context of the illustration from which it was lifted: peeping from behind the real grass in Cornell's construction is a pictured image of grass. The naturalism of the central compartment is engineered. A conscious contrast is built between it and the outside compartments with their clinical elements and arrangement. The rabbit is a warm image. The concentric circles and red ink staining and red balls rolling along grid-marked chutes act as optical illusions, giving the impression of flickering movement. Animals encased in their natural habitat are another link with Cornell's childhood: Cornell's father was a sportsman who enjoyed hunting and fishing. Betty remembers particularly trout that were caught and encased,[136] although her father once returned home with a deer's head. Cornell often visited the Natural History Museum

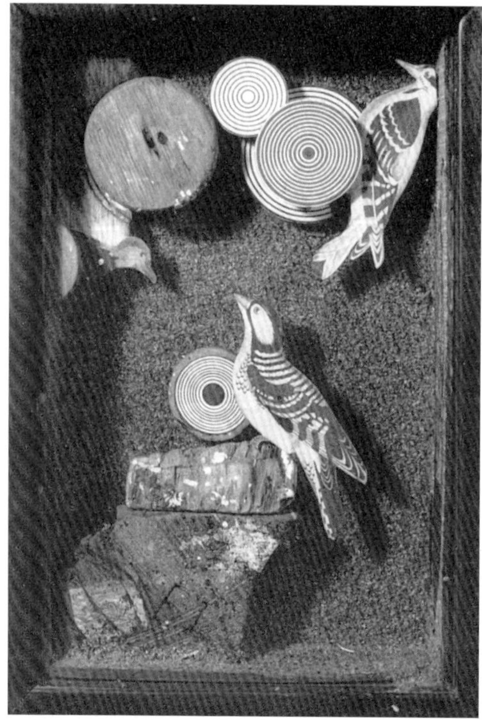

51 *Untitled (Woodpecker Habitat)*, 1946, box construction.

in order to see birds and animals staged in their look-alike natural habitats.

Untitled (Woodpecker Habitat) (illus. 51) is an interesting box to examine briefly as a point of comparison to *Untitled (American Rabbit)*. *Woodpecker Habitat* has the concentric circles of the other box; however, here the connection is very obviously with targets and shooting ranges – the birds are still and stilted and look the clay pigeon type. There is a fairground atmosphere. The symmetry and balance is missing from this box construction: there is an arbitrary arrangement of the birds and of colouring. Comparing the two images points up the range that Cornell could reach through the sophisticated grasp of formal elements to evoke different atmospheres and suggest different facets of nature.

American Rabbit (illus. 48) defines an attitude to nature through form: repetition, arrangement, demarcations, compartmentalization, colour coding, associations, the use of synecdoche and so on. If we think of Cornell's treatment of nature, of his stuck-on birds, the lifeless representations he selects, images that would seem to be contrary to the sense of 'living nature', then we notice that it is through the combination of the elements that the dynamic is created rather than through the representations themselves. By wrenching things from their naturalistic form and forging them together with anomalous surroundings, by stripping away conventional associations and a conventional perspective on things Cornell made nature come to life and instilled in it a new energy. In borrowing things from apparently dissimilar worlds a charge is created, the meeting of opposites becomes a source for a new chemistry. Cornell subjugated natural elements to his own code of classification.

The second box study, *Untitled (Paul and Virginia)* (illus. 53), is derived from the romantic tale *Paul et Virginie* (1788) by Jacques-Henri de Bernardin de Saint-Pierre. Bernadin's young lovers come to terrible grief – indeed, from the outset it is a love affair that seems to be ill-fated. The romance is set in an ideal world of beauty. Paul and Virginie have grown up together on a tropical island (a French colony) in the Indian Ocean. They are raised there in relative isolation (though their mothers are with them), and nature, the lush nature of that island, is both their playground and their means of education. Virginie is then sent to France, and is distraught to be parted from Paul. She later returns, aboard the *Saint-Géran*, but, within sight of the main island and close to the tiny Isle d'Ambre, the ship is overwhelmed by a sudden hurricane. Virginie is drowned, and as a result Paul dies of grief. The pining for love in an ideal world is the subject of the tale, and the mood of Cornell's box is one of nostalgia. Cornell remembers seeing hanging on the wall in his grandfather's parlour a print of Paul and Virginie.[137] He and his brother Robert had also once come very close to being drowned themselves, in the hurricane flood that hit America's Eastern seaboard in 1938. As Betty recalls:

> They were in the only house left with stairs . . . Joe had broken his ankle the night before. He and Robert were both in bed. And mother was coming out on the train. I had been down to wipe up the floors, have the place look nice. I had left to get the eggs ready to take to the train and in the meanwhile the hurricane came . . . We started to take our eggs to the train, this was when the hurricane was over on Montauk Highway on the way down to Speonk and we saw a brook going down the road . . . and we saw all the trees down . . . and then we saw down by the mill the top of a car and all the rest was water . . . And then it hit us . . . I almost went mad. [*Betty and her husband, Jack, attempted to reach the two boys in the house near Westhampton Beach, next door to Halix Farm, which they knew was already under water*] We tried to go down Jaegger Lane but it was choked, you couldn't get anywhere near . . . Jack went ahead of me, we slipped on eels, on worms, it was slimy from all kinds of things from the bottom of the bay. There were boats in this lane . . . there were rooftops . . . I kept going and kept calling 'Snickey, I'm coming, I'm coming Snickey', yelling at the top of my lungs . . . When it began to blow, Joe got out of bed; he went to look out the windows. It was a big lawn, a huge lawn before you got to the bay and there was a gazebo on it. He stood there and he said it was the queerest sensation: he looked but he couldn't see any bay. He said to Robert 'I can't see any water.' The hurricane had siphoned the water out of the bay. Then he went and looked again; he saw the water and he saw the gazebo slowly knocked over and then he saw the water coming up the lawn . . . He collected *Science and Health*, the Bible – the

52 *Untitled (Young Lady in Blue, Paul and Virginia)*, *c.* 1960, collage.

53 *Untitled (Paul and Virginia)*, *c.* 1946–8, box construction with hinged door.

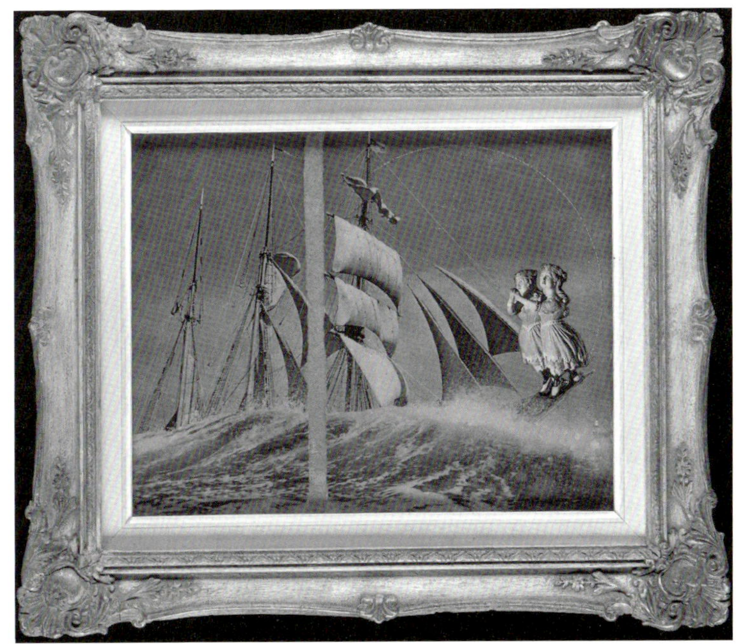

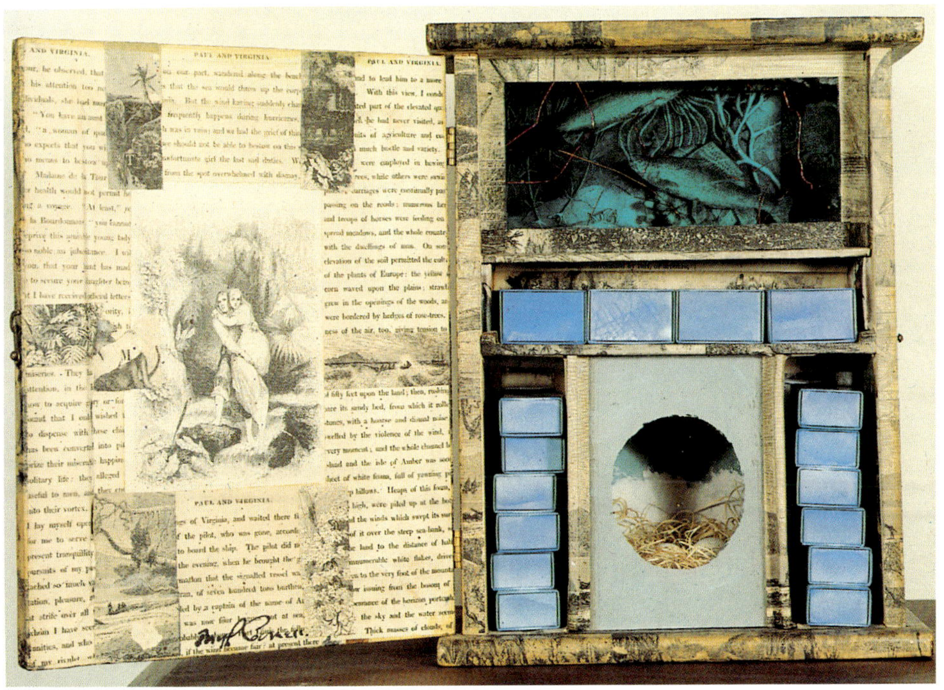

> day before he'd been to Ringport with a friend and bought an old-time film – he grabbed that and Robert. They didn't know where they were going . . . Uncle Fred was there and he carried Robert. If you could see the distance that he carried Robert with water up to his knees and coming! They sat in the kitchen (in the main house) until the water started to lift the linoleum. They went upstairs, the waves were dashing up onto the windows. There was a window with a tree very close to the house and Joe said to Robert 'with that strong left arm of yours' – cos Robert's arm was very developed, the left arm, 'I'm going to put you out of the window and you grab onto one of those branches with your good arm and I'll be holding on to you and I'll come out . . .' They had it all set and Uncle Fred walked in. He said 'It won't come any further, it's all over now, it'll start going down.' Then it started to go down and down. They had heard this car horn and they thought it was somebody signalling to them that they were coming to get them, but it was a car in a garage that had shorted from the water and the horn just kept blowing. Robert said it was a good feeling to hear that.[138]

This frightening experience had a lasting effect, for neither Cornell nor his brother chose to return to Westhampton for quite some years. No wonder that the appalling hurricane described in *Paul et Virginie* became of particular interest to Cornell. The extract from it that he selected as a decoration for the door of the box tells of a 'hoarse and dismal noise . . . swelled by the violence of the wind . . . the isle of Amber was soon a sheet of white foam . . . the winds which swept . . . unfortunate girl . . . overwhelmed with dismay'. And, as if to further illustrate his own interest in the tale, Cornell included an illustration of the winds lashing the sea into fury.

Balance, symmetry and order characterize the space of *Paul and Virginia*. Cornell gives us different depictions of nature: the young couple (extracted from Bernardin's novel) and pictures of elements from their private island radiating outwards – the couple at the core – like a star between the lines of text that tell their tragic story. On the inside of the box, within the main space of the box, looking through a peephole, there are two eggs (real ones) lying in a nest, and a blue cloudy sky provides the backdrop. Two fishes (engraved images) swim among the sea's vegetation. A dark aquamarine ink staining covers the illustration, and because of the elongated shape of the image it looks like an aquarium, while the fish look like specimens. There are a number of sky-blue boxes stacked either side of the eggs and lined up across the top. The boxes are matchbox size. Cornell draws attention to the blueness of the sky by his unexpected choice of form. It is almost like the effect that is achieved in jewellery, the way in which an intense energy may be retained within a miniature representation. There is a condensation of immensities within Cornell's stack of coloured boxes.

A cloudy sky is a well-worked symbol for the imagination, so for Cornell to risk using the image meant that he would first have to retrieve the image from its familiar setting in order to bring it back to life. The naturalness of the eggs in their nest is contrasted with the extreme geometry that depicts the doorway into the world (the real world). We open the door of the box and confront a second threshold: the door or window through which we can peer into 'life' (as symbolized by the eggs and as suggested by the fact that these are 'real' elements, the only real elements within a box containing representations of reality). The sky-blue boxes are like little building bricks – and here is another of the shocks of presentation – the idea of making sky out of bricks. Bricks are solids, not gases. Here it becomes a metaphysical issue: if it is possible to distort the elements – sky as the essence of spirit being made into bricks – then Cornell is breaking down what is traditionally an absolute barrier between spirit and matter. Matter as an extension of spirit becomes central to Cornell's art process. If he is able to make body or matter resonate like spirit, to imbue objects with spirit or magic, then he is succeeding on his own terms.

Cornell's intention was to create 'white magic' in his boxes. He tried to imbue that which is concrete with magical properties. There is an extreme realization, in physical terms of objects, and then by association he made his objects resonate with a spiritual electricity. The process involved drawing from physical things their energy, turning an idea (mental energy) into a physical thing (an object) and then trying to make that object 'live' again so that it would transmit its energy in its relation to other objects.

2 Origins of Selfhood

CHILDHOOD AND CHILDREN

Childhood was for Cornell the subject and the source that generated all other subjects. The inspirational counter-world of childhood conceived of symbolically as a place of confinement seemed to offer him a sort of security that ensured his vision was not corrupted by the world. The elevation of the child's vision by the artist had been established by the Romantics more than a century before: 'Wordsworth and Jean Jacques Rousseau, Blake and Nerval reasserted the virtue and happiness of childhood as something inevitably stifled by education and society . . . Artists became increasingly willing to accept the child's wonder and spontaneity and destructiveness as not inferior to adulthood.'[139] Cornell's attitude to childhood was, however, not one that was totally derived from the Romantic blueprint as it was one that shared with the Surrealists a consciousness of Freudian elements: the fascination with dreams, ambiguities and the absurd, and at times an undeniable sexual charge. Unlike the Surrealists, though, Cornell's vision was unashamedly nostalgic.

The first place to explore Cornell's attitude to childhood is his own childhood. It was there that Cornell sought most tirelessly for glimpses of the self. We have seen how he reached for those things in his daily life that might offer him an element of surprise, and it is within the context of childhood memory – the apparently known – that the unknown afforded him most pleasure.

Even so, the aura that surrounded childhood was not something that Cornell monopolized within the family. The affection, the tone of voice, the delight in remembered details, is present also in his sister's reminiscences:

> My grandmother and grandpa had three cherry trees. One of them was supposed to belong to each of us. They had little boys come and they had long ladders. These boys would go up the ladder and pick the cherries and bring them down in these bright, shiny tin things. Well, that's a

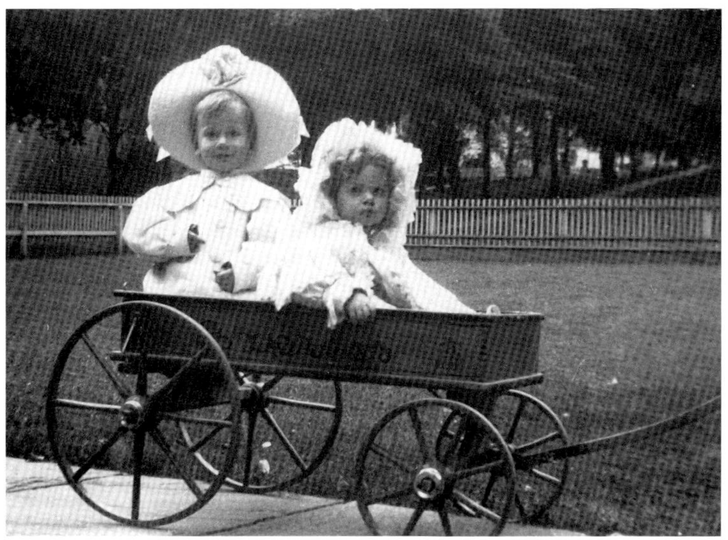

54 Cornell and his sister Betty in a box pram at Nyack, *c.* 1905.

big, big item in our memories. Joe used to *love* to remember about those boys going up those trees with the shiny tin pails. Everybody's grandfather didn't have cherry trees in their backyard. And a grandmother that made jellies. For Christmas they would fill the top of the piano. It used to be an upright piano. And, that was Nana's place every Christmas to put her preserves for us: her spiced grapes, her peaches from their own tree, grapes from their arbour.

Another thing Joe would love to remember: grandpa going out and he would get a gross of little white paper bags. He would tie the bags around every good cluster of grapes to keep the birds out. And Nana would make spiced grapes. You've never tasted anything like it: grape jelly, white grapes, black grapes, red grapes. He never had to spray the peach trees, and the peaches, the juice would drip down.

Her kitchen was downstairs. When Joe and I went up to Nyack this time, I guess it must have been to this funeral, we went to Nana's house. It was like we were going to the holiest place that you can imagine. Almost as if we were going to the Mother Church in Boston. We, both of us, we couldn't talk. It had quite steep steps up, with a porch. Then you had a thing that you turned to ring a bell. Then to the right there would be steps and what they called an airy way and then you opened the door and there was the

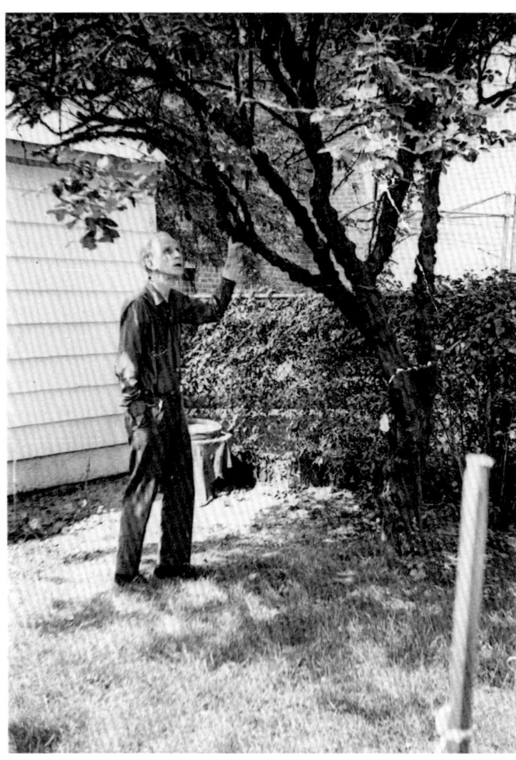

55 Cornell and the quince tree, 1964.

The quince tree was planted by Cornell's mother, and in time this umbrageous corner became a significant spot for reflection, reading, and thinking on religion, poetry and nature.

> kitchen downstairs. And it had a coal stove and it had brackets for kerosene even though we had gas in our house. Nana, at that time, still had kerosene and she had a fire cooker. She made soap in these big things. She'd slice it down, she'd mix wood ashes and lye to make the soap. This was not the way of the people round about, Nyack was a commuter's town as much as it was anything else. It was not rural. But Nana had these old-fashioned ways. . .
>
> It was such an innocent time. I never remember anything nasty. None of mummy and daddy's friends were ever cross with us. They were so kind.[140]

Cornell's attitude to childhood certainly differed little from that of his sister. First it was a storehouse for visual memories – just as Betty focuses on the pails, so Cornell himself used his grandmother's sewing-machine, the ice wagon, the scientific instruments, the books, the neighbour's parrot, as images in his boxes. It could even be inferred from Betty's description of the compartments of the house that they would find an echo in the compartments of the boxes – Cornell of course always looked back with great nostalgia to the large houses in Nyack. Then, in Betty's account there is the accent on the home industry in the grandmother's house: the making of soap and the commentary on rural ways in an urban location. This is something of a tradition that Cornell continued with pride in the preparation of his boxes:

> the many trips made by bicycle gathering dried grasses of different kinds the fantastic aspect of arriving home almost hidden on the vehicle by the loads piled high, the transcendent experience of threshing in the cellar stripping the stalks onto newspapers, the sifting of the dried seeds, then the pulverizing by hand and storing in boxes. These final siftings were used for habitat (imaginative) boxes of birds, principally owls. The boxes were given a coating of glue on the insides then the grass dust thrown in and shaken around. All the sides had an even coating to give them the aspect of a tree trunk or nest interior. Although used in the construction of objects, the nights when the cellar was filled with the aroma of these acrid scents with all the good richness stored in them by afternoon moistures . . . working like a herbalist or apothecary of old with those sweet scents in my own fashion this discovery of making boxes so like a bird's own nest was inexpressibly satisfying in such a warm and redolent atmosphere.[141]

Finally, we recognize in Betty's account the evocation of a spirit of refinement echoed in all Cornell's own memories of childhood. This is no celebration of primitive instinct. Quite the opposite, it is where the world of childhood is characterized by order. It is the memory of a cultured, civilized upbringing in which there was an insistence on custom and ritual, family ties, innocent behaviour ('I never remember anything nasty') and an attention to the sensuous surface of things. Leila Hadley has spoken of this element in Cornell:

> It was sort of the refinement of things, the very perfect dance, the very beautiful and very pure, and very spiritual and very mystical. He wasn't interested in primitive cultures, in James Frazer and *The Golden Bough* and things like that. He didn't like anything like African Art, or the South Pacific, or Oceanic Art. This was ugly. He loved things like all the fairy tales of Hans Christian Andersen, or

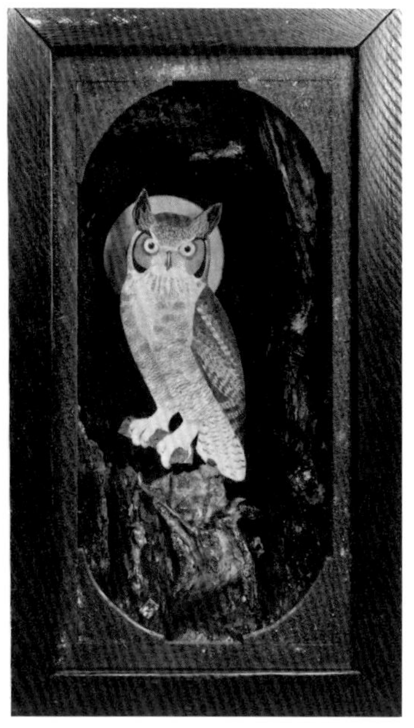

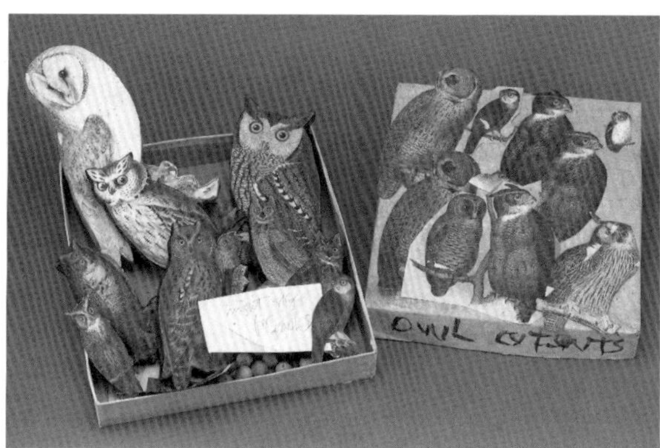

56 *Untitled (Great Horned Owl with Full Moon)*, c. 1942, box construction.

57 Carton of cutouts from hand-coloured lithographs, etchings, engravings and aquatints from John James Audubon's *Birds of America* (1840–44).

a mermaid . . . much more than the Grimm brothers. He wanted everything to be sort of perfect and beautiful.[142]

Almost all critics have commented on the toy-like aspect of Cornell's work. It has been placed half in the category of toys and half in assemblage since he first started out in 1932. Julien Levy included Cornell's work in a 'Jouets Surrealistes' exhibition in that year, and he spread the word that Cornell had actually started to make boxes to serve as toys that would entertain his younger brother.[143] Howard Hussey discusses Cornell's 'toys for adults' and John Ashbery refers to the 'sanctity of childhood which informs all of his art'.[144] In an article by the artist Robert Morris, Cornell is given a prestigious position as one of the four major cornerstones of American art, and still his art is described as toy-like.[145] Some critics recognized serious intentions behind Cornell's 'toy-world', notably Parker Tyler, in a handbill for an exhibition held in 1939:

I can remember when, as a child, I thought the dimension of the Universe was a shoebox because I peopled it with images, objects and drama, which it appeared to contain. Its boundaries were visible, neat and portable. It is easy to think of the world as a toy when you are a child, impossible to do so when you are grown up. However, Joseph

58 Cornell's toy Ferris-wheel.

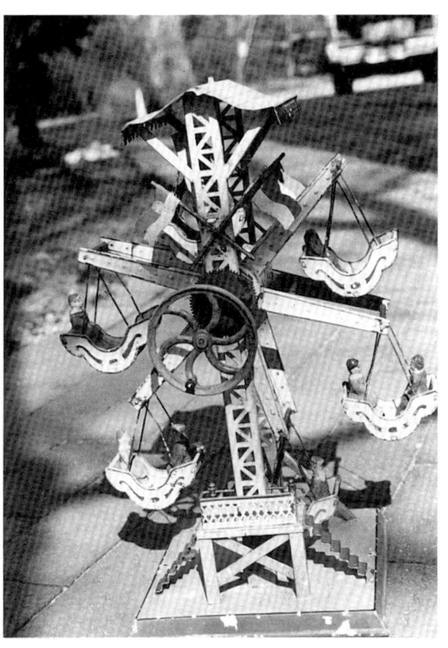

> Cornell shows that toys can be created and presented to the adult world as legitimate objects. These are creative toys, these princely and poetical contrived objects of Joseph Cornell. Their envelopes are all boxes but sturdy ones, closer in significance to a jewel-box than a shoebox, but with all the power of Pandora's chest in their mysterious, but beautiful and untrivial machinery.
>
> The instinct of the child to reduce the world to conform to his imagined, tender and scowling Godhead, reappears in Joseph Cornell as a ritual and a projection of the adult imagination...
>
> The poor, children and old people collect strings, useless articles, fetishes beyond price. Joseph Cornell transforms this practice and raises it to an art. We would transform our world into a more liveable one, a kinder and more solidly glamorous one. Joseph Cornell, master of the world as a bilboquet, transforms the tired brooding on messy things into the crystal perception of form and color; he cathedralizes thought too silly to mention and returns lost articles of the imagination.

Tyler focuses on the structural element: Cornell 'transforms the tired brooding on messy things into the crystal perception of form and color', and on the consolation element: 'We would transform our world into a more liveable one, a kinder and more solidly glamorous one'. Behind the manifest poetry-magic that is the surface attraction of Cornell's child-world art there are two underlying convictions that add structure and purpose to all his undertakings: logic and design (form), and a transformation, substitution theory (content).

Cornell immersed himself in the world of childhood. He mixed with, and observed intently, the local children of his neighbourhood in Flushing: he would invite them for afternoon tea and then afterwards exchange letters with them. (They trusted him to keep their secrets safe from adult ears, often addressing their correspondence 'Dear Mr Werewolf'.[146]) He read children's books and incorporated the stories and imagery he found there into his art.[147] He organized exhibitions especially for children: the first, in 1950, was in the Children's Room of the New York Public Library, it had the theme of Hans Christian Andersen's tales; the second, in 1972, an exhibition solely for children, was placed on low pedestals (head-height for the little ones), and cookies and soda pop were served for refreshment.

The respect that Cornell had for children is clear. He often felt adults to be insensitive – he thought they made 'stock' responses to life. Donald Windham illustrates this point:

> One of [Cornell's] statements was: 'some people see more than others not because they have sharper vision but because they want to see as much as possible and make the effort'. It amazed him, he added, that many people never noticed the tops of buildings.
>
> In the afternoon Joseph would arrive bringing me finds for the issue [of *Dance Index*] we were working on, and amaze me, not with how much he noticed, but with the almost Jack-in-the-box delight with which he shared his discoveries.[148]

Charged with inviting children for afternoon tea, Howard Hussey, one of Cornell's assistants, describes the grandeur of the occasion, the ritual and preparation that went into it: special cream cakes were ordered in advance, the table was set, and Cornell himself – freshly shaved and dressed in a suit and tie – appeared to receive his guests.[149]

Cornell was interested in children and in childhood, but it would be a mistake to describe his work as childlike, naïve or unsophisticated. He was not interested in mimicking the artistic efforts of children in the form that we know them (drawings and assemblages). Certainly, he wanted to see as a child, but then to advance and ally this vision to the sensibility of the artist and the skills of the craftsman. He admired above all else the wonder and spontaneity of the child's apprehension of the world. 'The only sure voyage of discovery would not be to visit strange lands but to possess other eyes, to behold the Universe through the eyes of another'.[150] It was this Proustian journey that concerned him, and the eyes he desired were the eyes of the child.

Some delightful stories told by friends and family illustrate how Cornell constantly regenerated 'wonder' in his own personal life, how he set up situations that could prompt spontaneity. This sounds like a contradiction in terms, but perhaps the stories themselves explain more clearly, for example this one by May Tabak, the wife of the New York art critic and writer Harold Rosenberg:

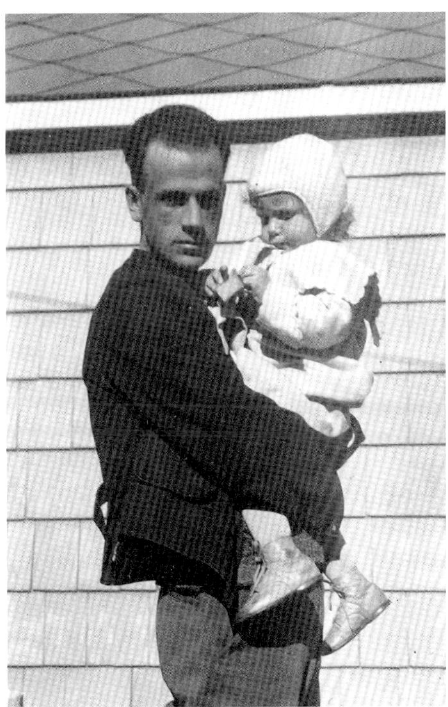

59 Cornell and his niece, Helen Jagger Batcheller, in the early 1930s.

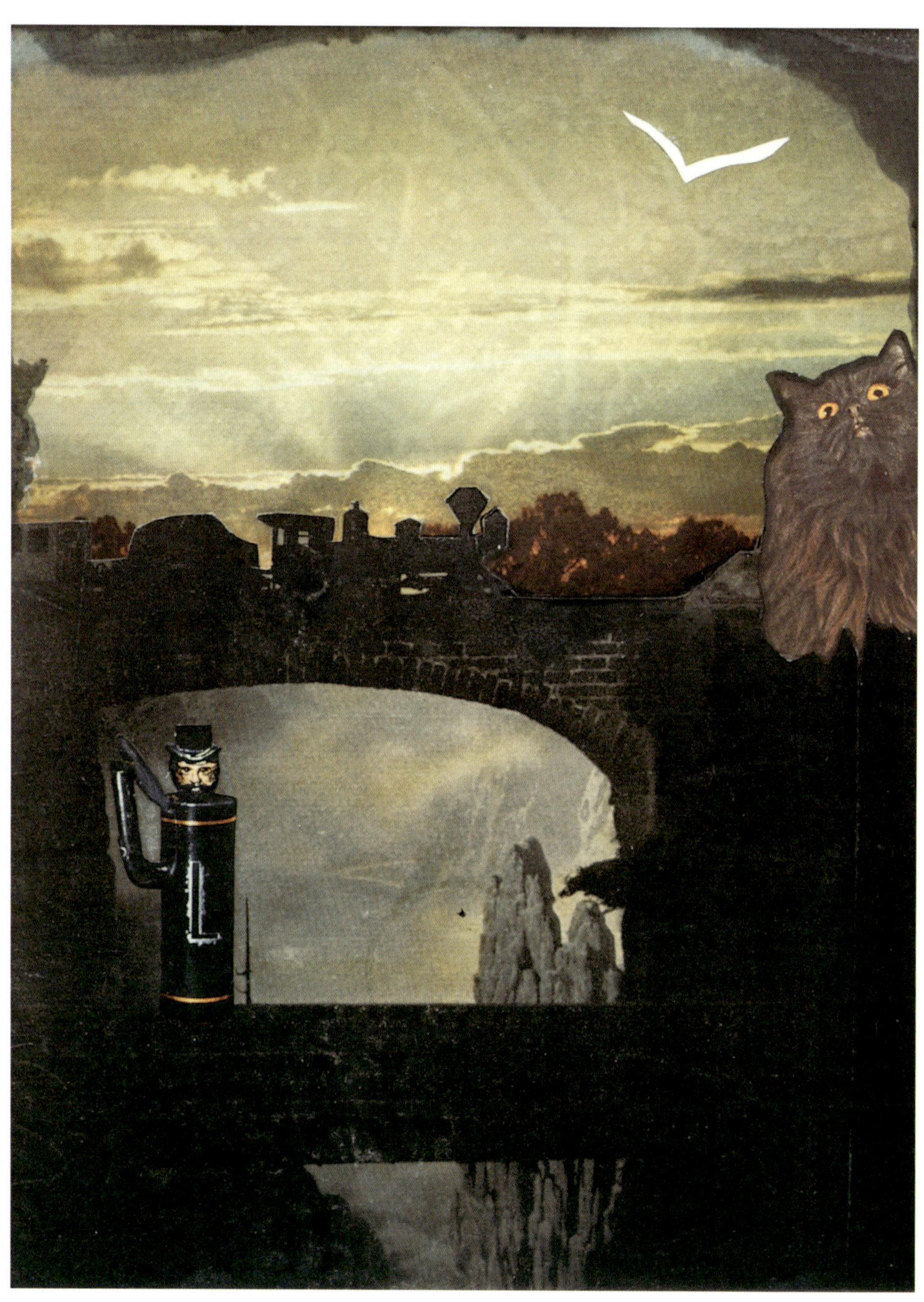

60 *Untitled*, c. mid-1960s, collage.
The imagery and syntax Cornell adopted in the mid-1960s for his collages shows how he sought to re-enter the world of the child: the way he manipulated relative sizes, for example, in this work dramatizes the wonders of growing up.

One day he called – it was a terrible day, it was raining and miserable. He said could he come and see me and so I said 'sure' . . . When he came he had a large packet, he didn't want to take his coat off, he just said could he leave the package with me . . . He said, 'just put it any place in your closet and I'd appreciate it, just keep it safe'. I'm dying of curiosity – why he had come from wherever he came to leave that package with me in this neighbourhood instead of other neighbourhoods that he passed and he didn't give any explanation . . .

So, then again he suddenly calls me up and asks to come over, very shy. I said 'sure'. I thought he wanted to come for his package. Instead of that he arrives with another package, exactly the same sort of package. And he talked about a lot of things and I see all of those things that we are talking about are simply politenesses, you see. So I wait. Then again he asks if he can leave the second package. He looked at the other package – I hadn't even moved it . . . He said he would like to go into the closet himself, so he went in, and then he came out . . . I must say I got about 4 of these packages which arrived at odd times. . .

Actually, what happened was, it went on for about a year and a half. I didn't know what to say, it would be like prying to say 'What are you doing? What's it for?' Then, maybe it was two and a half years, suddenly he came and he took a package. Just one. He came with a package as usual to leave, but then he said that he would like to take a package. I said 'It's all yours, take whatever you want to'. It was really very peculiar to have this growing collection of packages, all looking the same and not knowing what was in them. From that time on he would bring some and leave some. Sometimes he would bring two wrapped separately. They were wrapped in brown paper, they looked very professional but there was no way of knowing what they were . . . He said that he wanted to give himself a treat but he wanted it to be a surprise, so he began buying these records. But it wouldn't mean anything if he just took the records home because the surprise would be just going out to find them. This way when he finally began to commit himself to taking them away, he didn't know what it would be. But then he didn't take it home and open it and

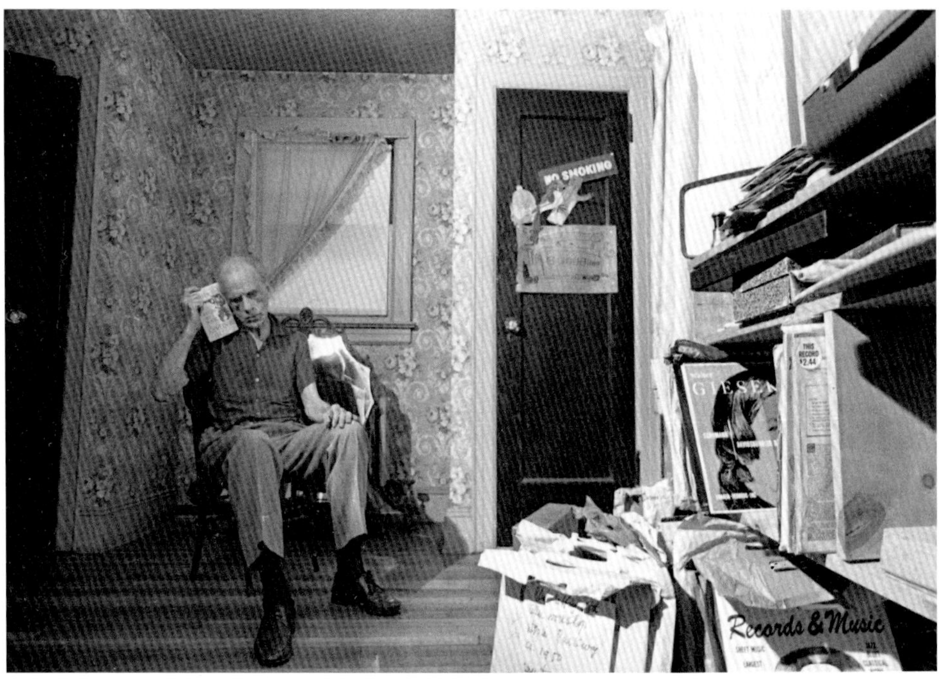

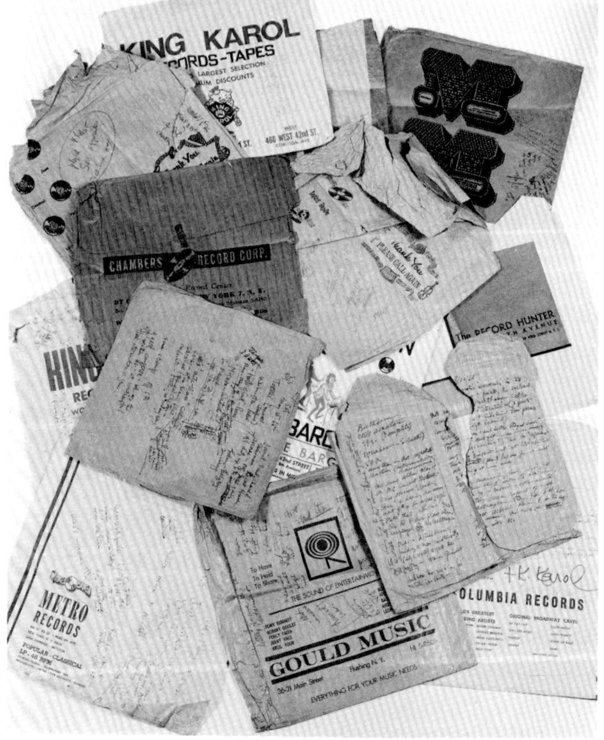

61 Hans Namuth, *Joseph Cornell, with his record collection, 'listening' to a book*, c.1970, photograph.

62 Assemblage of brown paper bags from music stores with Cornell's handwitten notations on them.

> play it, he took it home and he put it down and it was like something 'if you were a really good boy' . . . He finally managed to open the first and he called me up to tell me that he'd played it and what it was. I'd partook of the secret you see, but neither of us knew what he'd hear first so he called and we were dancing up and down with delight . . . They were very good, high fidelity records of very great music of different kinds . . . But that was so marvellous that he could have invented this thing. I didn't feel like telling my friends because it seemed like a confidence.[151]

The picture of Joseph Cornell that emerges from these accounts can be expanded by the character of his diary writings:

> real miracle of beauty under the canopies of Stern and Woolworth – 'people' – faces – movement of the crowd – the red umbrellas . . .
> recently ORIENTAL tin of Huntley and Palmer opened . . . sudden surprise of pink centre (shortcake) and extravagant joy.[152]

What is remarkable about the above passages is the way in which Cornell received impressions from the outside. He seems to have been like a child whose senses are opening out to their very first exposure to a wider world. He displayed a rapture and delight in the multiplicity of things. The very incompleteness of a child's knowledge makes the child open, whereas an adult may well be pre-emptive and closed off. Cornell's generous mind seems naturally like that of a child. Intuitively he sheds the adult's code of responses, the *a priori* rules. Instead, his eye expands eagerly.

TWO CHILDHOOD PROJECTS

> Cousin Ethel inherited this wonderful old Hudson river-type house – it's a museum of antiques. Joe was very welcome and he loved it there. And one day – he must have been in the cellar or the attic – he saw this doll, and when he left the doll left too. He wrote that he had kidnapped this doll from Cousin Ethel. And that was the Bébé Marie. Cousin Ethel didn't know that he'd taken it because he

> never would have got it out of the house. Cousin Ethel was very possessive of her things, especially her childhood things. The doll was never played with. She was an only child like mother, but she was a different type: their people were much more worldly, she had beautiful clothes and she was more sophisticated. Joe admitted that he used the doll in Bonwitter's window and then for different illustrations in magazines and then he encased it.[153]

Betty's story of the theft of the doll that eventually became the celebrated *Bébé Marie* (illus. 63) is a striking one, especially in the light of Motherwell's critical remark to Cornell that it was as though he was attempting to fashion his art from the stuff from his grandmother's attic. Motherwell expected a verbal tirade from Cornell in response, and was surprised when the artist smiled and on several subsequent occasions asked him to repeat it. Motherwell was directing his criticism at the nostalgic element in Cornell's work (something that was anathema to Motherwell), but it was exactly this sort of mood that Cornell strove to create. Bébé Marie is a female form enmeshed in a space. She appears behind a screen of vertically arranged wood splinters, and her narrow box compartment contains her form. However, the image is not threatening. Bébé Marie is a Victorian porcelain doll with a dress of silk or taffeta; her screen implies a forest of glittering twigs and her boxed encasement is speckled like a quail's egg or a schoolroom jotter. The atmosphere is a quiet nineteenth-century one with more than just a hint of sentimentality and traditional charm. Before her encasement, and indeed after, right up until Cornell's death, the Idol held a special place in the artist's own personal environment. He used her, as the photographer Duane Michals explained, as a prop for portrait photographs. Cornell did not enjoy being photographed; he was not an easy subject. Not a person to 'snapshoot', Michals has said.[154] In one of his portrait photographs of Cornell, Michals used elements from the central composition of Cornell and the doll in the box, and found echoes in Cornell's habitat, in his bedroom at Utopia Parkway. The wooden struts of the bed's headboard, the twigs within the *Bébé Marie* box, and the stick-like legs of the grasshopper can be read like the visual puns so beloved by Surrealist photographers; the shapes made by Cornell's fingers in his mouth echo

63 *Untitled (Bébé Marie)*, early 1940s, construction (papered and painted wooden box, with painted corrugated cardboard floor, containing doll in cloth dress and straw hat with cloth flowers, dried flowers, and twigs, flecked with paint).

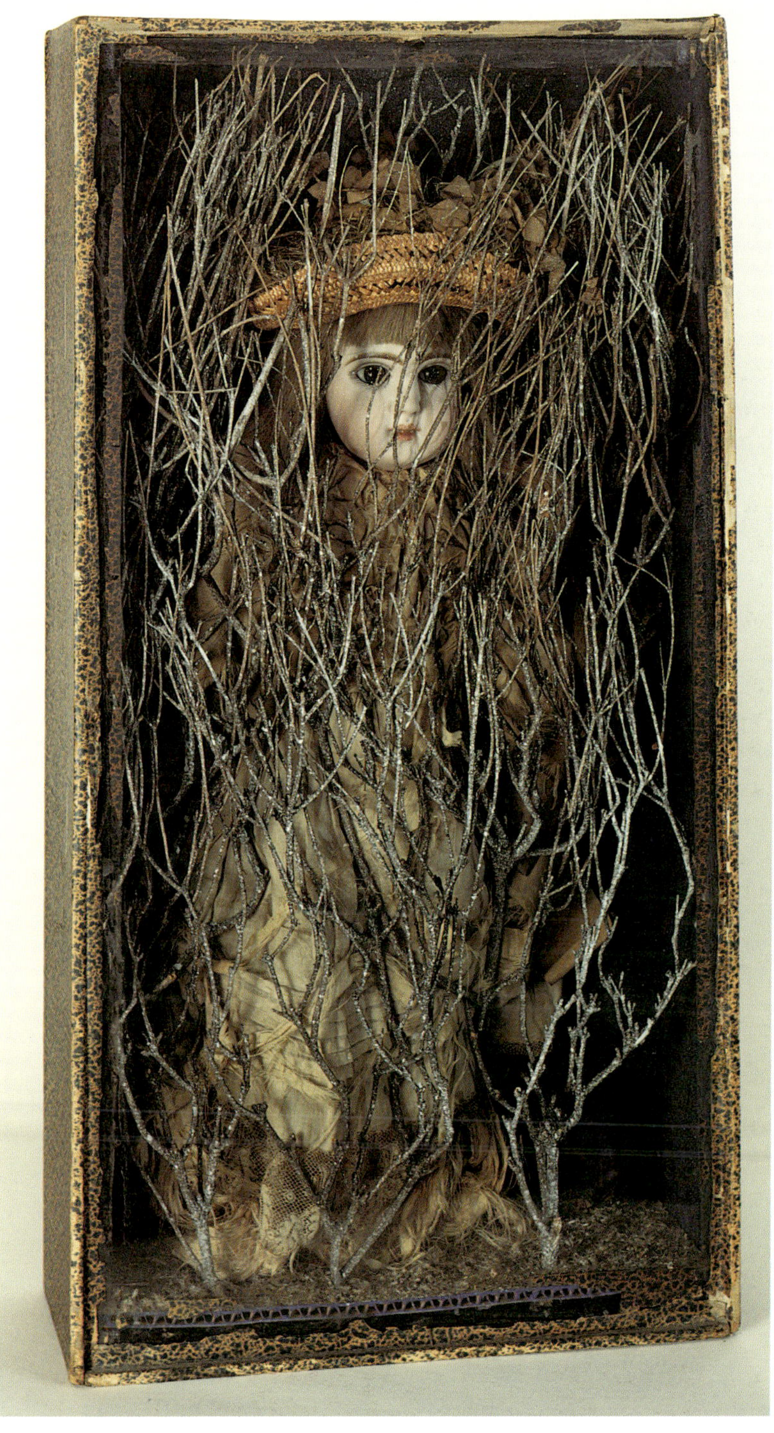

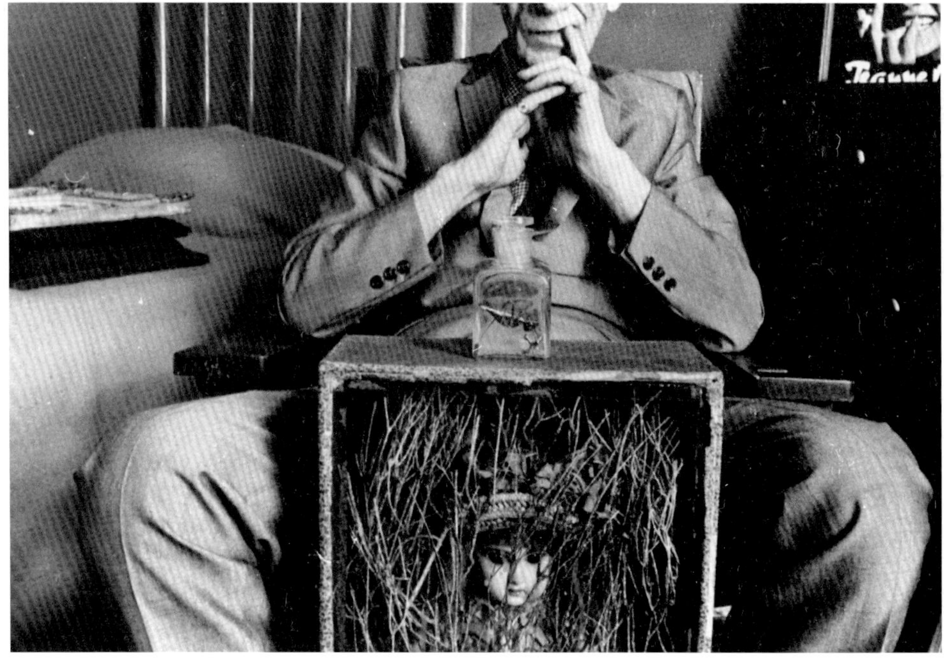

64 Duane Michals, *Joseph Cornell with Bébé Marie*, c. 1970, photograph.

the fingers of Jeanne Moreau in the photograph on the dresser behind. The grasshopper is contained in the small bottle, Bébé Marie in her box, and Jeanne Moreau in her cropped poster, but Cornell is also constrained by the photo: his head is savagely cut, and his legs likewise. When we examine his pose we cannot ignore its architectural formality: the pyramid shape made by his head, body and legs is echoed in the pediment of his arms over the truncated portico of the *Bébé Marie* box. This is a highly contrived photograph in which Cornell explicitly presented himself as created. Cornell also shared with his female 'subjects' a mood of inwardness or preoccupation. Bébé Marie is definitely a solipsistic doll who forever inhabits a realm of dreams. Michals explained that the grasshopper was included in the photograph because Jacqueline Bisset was appearing in a film entitled *The Grasshopper* at that time. We are conscious here of the constructed images of women as movie stars, as creatures or as dolls; but are they, Cornell asks us, any more constructed than the artist himself. Michals's own introduction to Cornell was through the *Life* magazine spread by David Bourdon that included a photo of Cornell holding up a

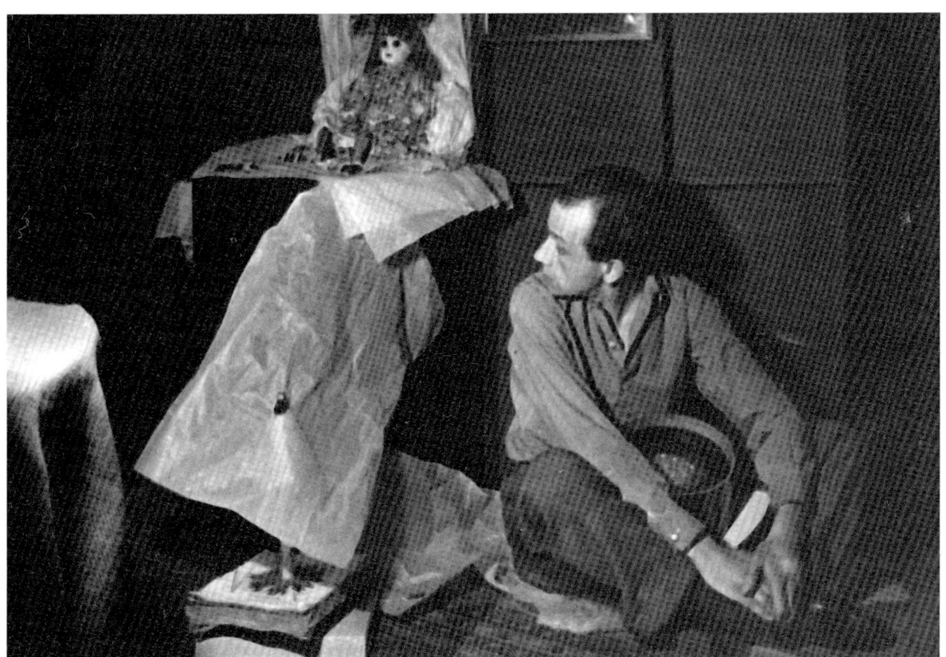

65 Cornell with Bébé Marie before she was encased, 1930s.

huge rock in Central Park to save a Victorian doll from being crushed.[155]

The Bébé Marie doll as she appears in *View* in 1943 lies flat, covered with autumnal leaves, as if abandoned. She is like the tin soldier lying in the gutter, or – forgotten in the attic – the once cuddly bear covered with dust and mildew. *Mélisande* (doll in box, *c*. 1948-50) continues this theme – she also has been lost to share her fate with the elements, but luckily for her, Cornell was on hand to effect a rescue.

Bébé Marie, the doll, must remain half-hidden. It is essential to her aura that she be not wholly revealed, for her perfection is such that she cannot be exposed to the air or to the gaze of the viewer. The box is here at its most fetishistic, it contains the unspeakable, the tantalizing glimpse into the spectre of desire, and yet what can be more innocent than the doll wrapped safely in its box?

A group of linked images shared by Cornell and the Surrealists are dolls, mannequins and automatons. The mannequin is of course synonymous with the origins of Surrealism (in the works of De Chirico), and represents a literally constructed female (androgynous) form. Some direct

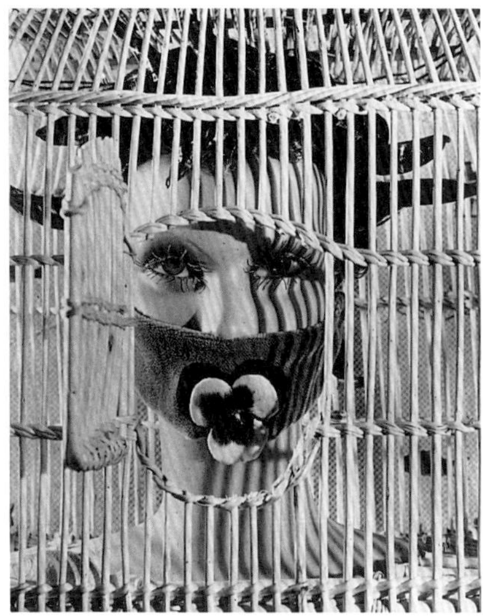

66 Raoul Ubac, *Mannequin*, 1937, photograph.

comparisons point up the distance (and at times the link) between Cornell and the Surrealists in their approach to the female and/or the love object.

Cornell selected the following quotation for the 'Romantic Museum' pamphlet (1946) on the subject of dolls:

> Playfulness is their life and they are earnest about it . . . Their movements are shy and angular, afraid of being taken seriously, of being seized strongly. In smiling evasiveness they keep life in due distance and clasp its fragrance in the tinkling of puerile colours . . . It is needless to say that they live in freedom, for their moral discipline is beyond reproach . . . calamities are borne without complaint, for in spite of their frailty, they are immortal.

On the subject of Bébé Marie alone, he wrote that it was 'not like the dolls of the present day, which are imitations of the faces and forms of human babies, but like the dolls of the old days which strove, parallel with humanity, towards an abstract ideal of feminine beauty'. This comment illustrates Cornell's attitude and his reason for using dolls in his work: he saw them as an ideal of feminine beauty. They keep life in 'due distance', and 'some cozy corner' has been reserved for them in 'the nursery of the imagination'.

Cornell's box has almost the opposite mood to the modern, chilling, nightmarish *Mannequin* (illus. 66), a Surrealist piece by Raoul Ubac. Ubac's photo is of the mannequin constructed by André Masson, in which the caged head of the female 'has her prey in her mouth' and 'thus evokes the mantis', says Rosalind Krauss in her essay in *L'Amour Fou* (1985).[156] She adds that 'this mantis which possesses is simultaneously possessed by the mesh of space'. This theme is, however, one repeatedly shared by Cornell and the Surrealists: Man Ray's triptych of Lee Miller is viewed from behind the cross-hatching of a net curtain, and in Boiffard's *Untitled* (1937) the female face is caught in a spider's web. There is no doubt that a sinister element is present in some of Cornell's doll boxes (illus. 67). It is impossible to exclude the element of desire from the combination of doll, cage and bondage. In this sense his dolls are not so far removed as perhaps might at first be assumed from the dolls of the Surrealists. It is more a difference in mood rather than a difference in content or sexual orientation. Hans Bellmer's dolls plunge the spectator into a

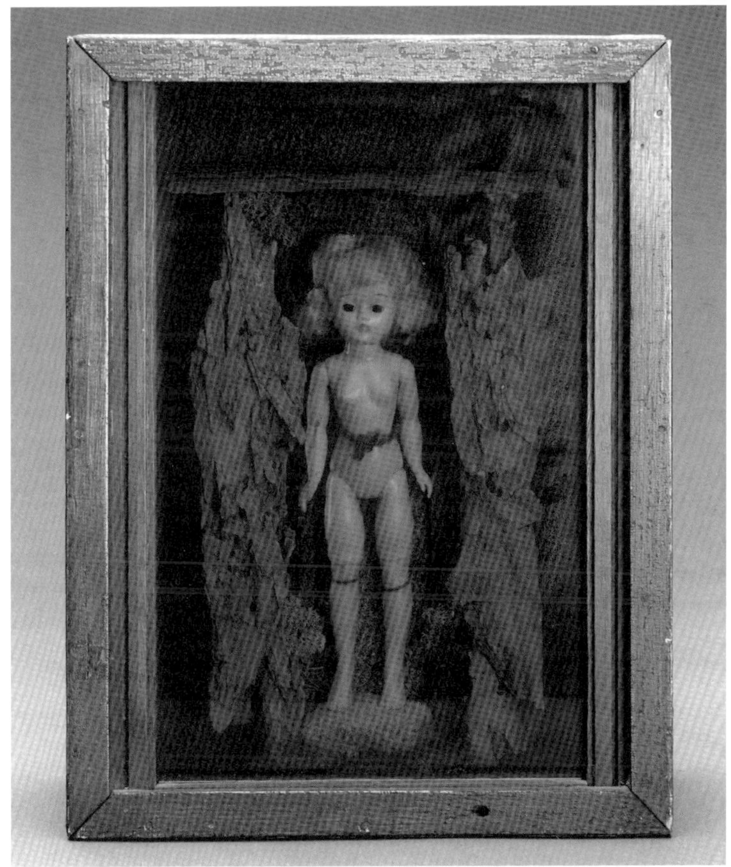

67 *Untitled (called 'Sequestered Bower')*, 1948 (painted, paper-covered, glazed wooden box for an assemblage of amber glass, wood, bark, plastic doll, twine, wire, dried plants, mirrors, and sawdust-like substance).

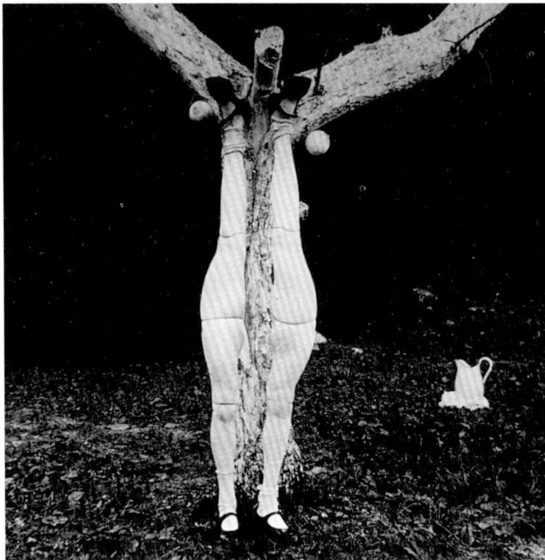

68 Hans Bellmer, *Doll (La Poupée)*, 1936/1949.

world of fantasy, nightmare and sexual displacement – a world removed in atmosphere from Cornell and his dolls. Bellmer's dolls frequent banal surroundings: kitchen, garden, stairwell, parlour, bedroom. They are not held captive but are instead presented in a state of reconstruction or dismemberment, the obsessional re-invention of an always-the-same creature recontrived, repositioned in ever more grotesque postures and alignments in other 'ordinary' environments. The doll is clearly phallic, often deprived of arms; pairs of legs are doubled up; and she/he possesses limitless swellings and bulges while undergoing transformations (illus. 68). Like the other machines or machine parts that the Surrealists incorporated into their works, the dolls are no longer little marvels of perfection but are instead transformed into disturbing, threatening, irrational objects.

For all the difference in the kinds of dolls selected, there may yet be something in the second part of the Surrealist aesthetic of the *explosante-fixe* that is suggestive of latent meaning in Cornell's use of dolls: the frequent sense of eeriness of waxwork figures, artificial dolls and automata can be attributed to the way these objects trigger 'doubts whether an apparently animate being is really alive; or conversely, whether a lifeless object might not in fact be animate'.[157]

This is one of Freud's examples (via Jentsch) of The Uncanny, the confusion between the animate and the inanimate.

Freud analyses this propensity to see meaning or life in nature or in things as a sign of regression to an animate stage of Primitive man, where the world was peopled with the spirits of human beings by the narcissistic overestimation of subjective mental processes. A fascination with dolls and a tendency to attach significance to coincidence and to personal mental states is a clear example of one drawn to The Uncanny. 'The uncanniness that seems to surround certain repetitions of names, or numbers, or concentrations of objects within one's everyday life forces upon us', Freud acknowledges, 'the idea of something fateful and inescapable where otherwise we should have spoken only of "chance"'.[158]

Our second childhood project, *Cherubino* (1959), does not focus on a glamorous figure, for example Lauren Bacall, Marilyn Munroe, Raquel Meller or Fanny Cerrito, all of whom were treated in other Cornell projects, nor was it centred on Manhattan. *Cherubino* was an obsession about an ordinary young girl, a local girl who worked in a store on Flushing's Main Street. Cornell did, however, mythologize her, and lifted her far beyond the bounds of an unnoticed life. Initially he managed this by giving her the name of the page in Mozart's *Le Nozze di Figaro*, then by the sacred associations he bestowed on her (he saw her as an angel or saint), and finally by personal association as he gradually connected the obsession with his own childhood and with his brother Robert.

The source material for *Cherubino* is contained in three wooden boxes. Handwritten notations, duplicates of a photo, printed books and booklets (religious) and a large stash of cheap plastic objects comprise the project. This is the only material for which Cornell made a remarkable request, writing on the lid 'Not to be opened for ten years after my death'. There is at least one collage that is directly extracted from the source material: *Fountain of Youth* (illus. 70). The collage title is only part of the full title of the project, which Cornell inscribes inside source box # 2, 'Cherubino, Fountain of Youth (relating to our childhood)'. It is also worth mentioning here his film *Nymphlight* (1957), a short (and plotless) film focusing simply on a girl (Gwen Thomas) aged about twelve, running round a fountain in her mother's flimsy white dress (illus. 72). As in much of Cornell's work there is the intense spirituality in the elision of bird and female subject as

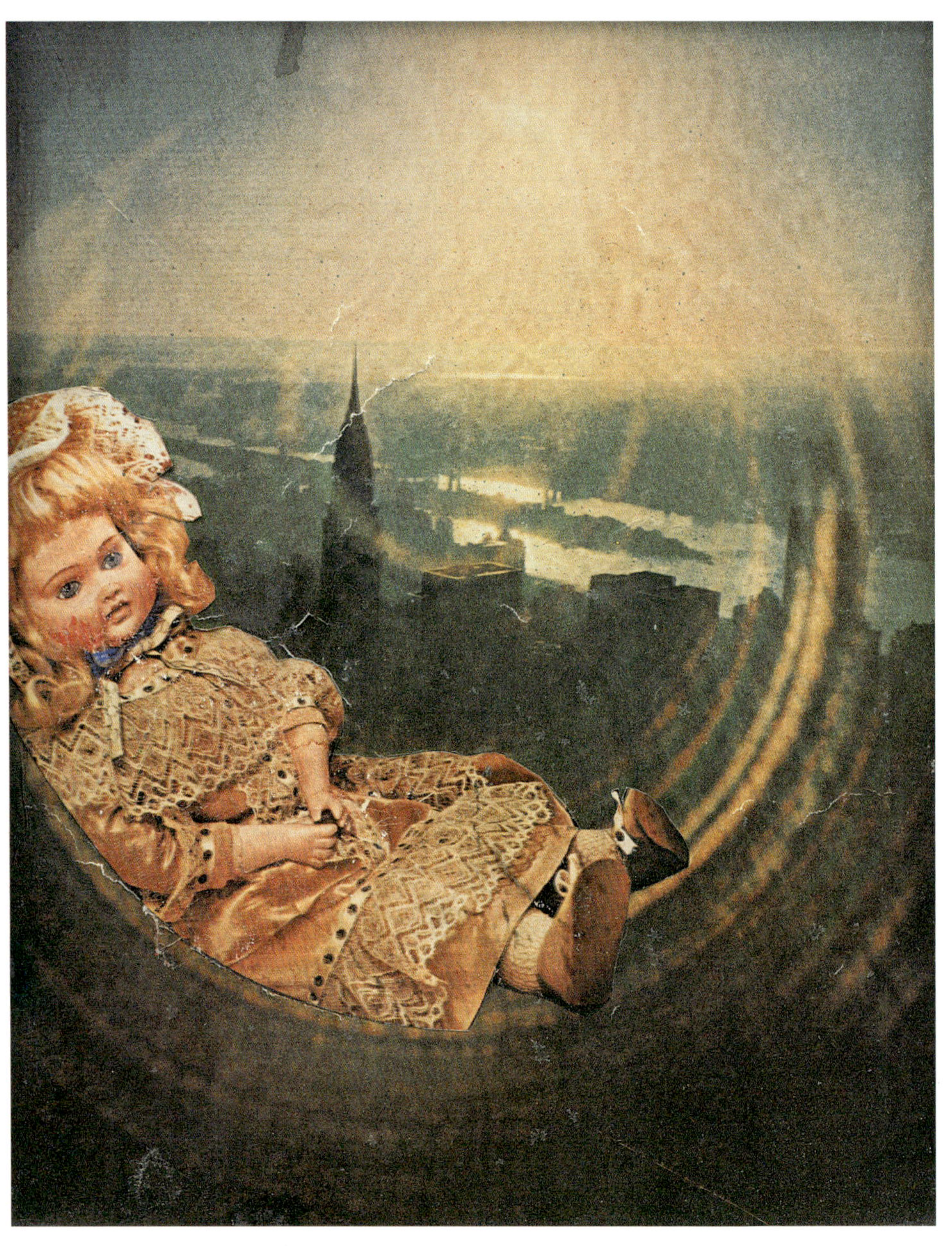

69 *Untitled*, *c*. 1960s, collage.

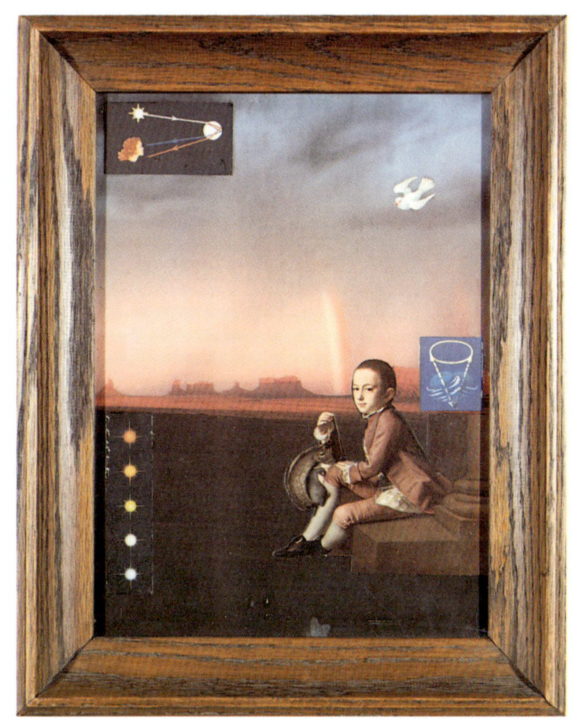

70 *Fountain of Youth*, 1959, collage.

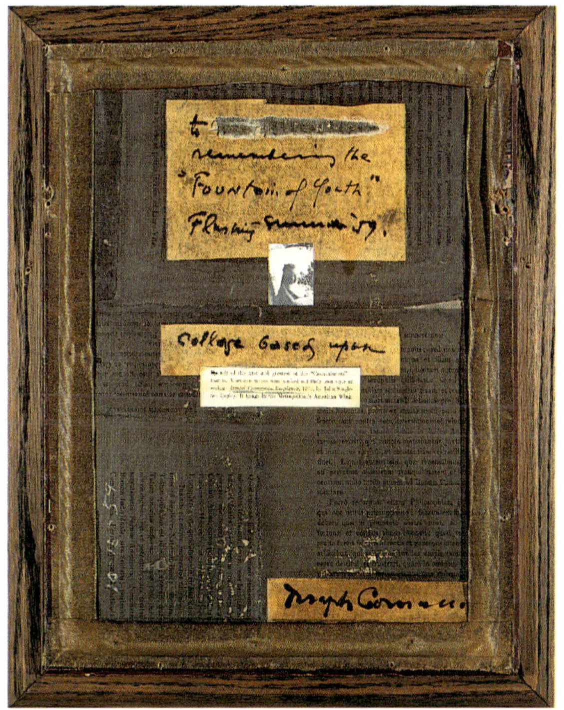

71 *Untitled*, 1959, verso of illus 70.

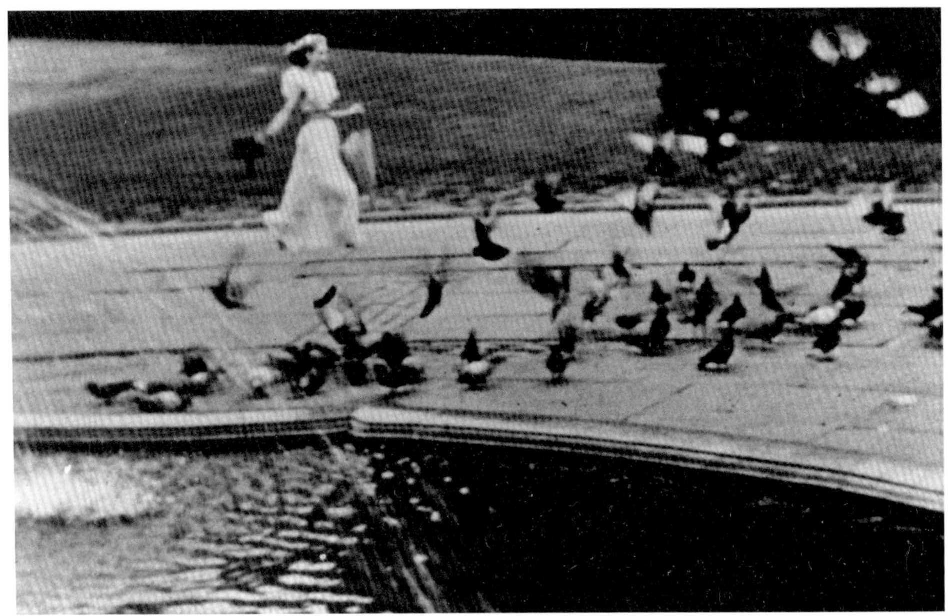

72 *Nymphlight*, 1957, a still of Gwen Thomas in Bryant Park.

well as the wistful, romantic mood and poetic structure, and yet there is in the images the lingering, unextinguished element of desire.

In the *Cherubino* project sacred associations came about because Cornell discovered a book in Flushing Library that coincided with a sighting of Cherubino, and because of Cornell's vision of her as encapsulating eternal youth: 'sense of clear youthful freshness so beautifully beheld in the person of Cherubino'.[159] The book was *The Ancient Secret* by Flavia Anderson, published in 1953 by Gollancz in London. One fragment of text that Cornell highlighted refers to the representation of St Barbara in art. She is described as the patron saint of warriors and often depicted carrying a miniature tower. The name 'Miss Barbara' was to become interchangeable with 'Cherubino' in Cornell's writings. This brings us again to Cornell's favoured working method: association through synchronicity. For example, he writes in his notes: '5 talismans found in the same shop as day of finding this little volume in the aftermath of Cherubino (Miss Barbara) – 2 bracelets with charms bought and 2 crystals (ice block and pick) and globule with portrait – (jewellery shop opp. library).'[160] Already we are beginning to enter into the complicated web of Cornell associations. Five becomes significant because he happened, by chance, to pick up five talismans ('5 tokens bought unwittingly'[161]) on the same day that he discovered *The Ancient Secret* in the 'aftermath' of Cherubino, and five is from the motto on the title-page: 'Five things were missing in the second temple: the ark, the mercy-seat, the cherubim, the heavenly fire'. Cornell copied this down and then added 'Cherubino cherubim'. Thus he rhymed and chimed, and noted 'carry this 5'.[162] He did, for we can see in the *Fountain of Youth* collage of 1959 (illus. 70) a block of five stars in the lower-left corner.

As the obsession grew, Cherubino became in the scheme of things not only associated with St Barbara, but also with an angel – 'wanted by the angel Cherubino'.[163] He wished for her special powers: 'thinking of Cherubino at F.B. soft drink counter – in thought telling her not to grow any older – meaning to keep her adorably generous manner and keep young all those with whom she comes into contact.'[164] A girl graduate from Flushing High School then employed at *Fisher Beer, Discount Variety Stores* had smiled at Cornell. And this smile had touched him deeply.[165] This had been the beginning of the obsessional pull.

On 26 August 1959 Cornell received some photographic work he had requested from a local store, *Morse and Victor,*

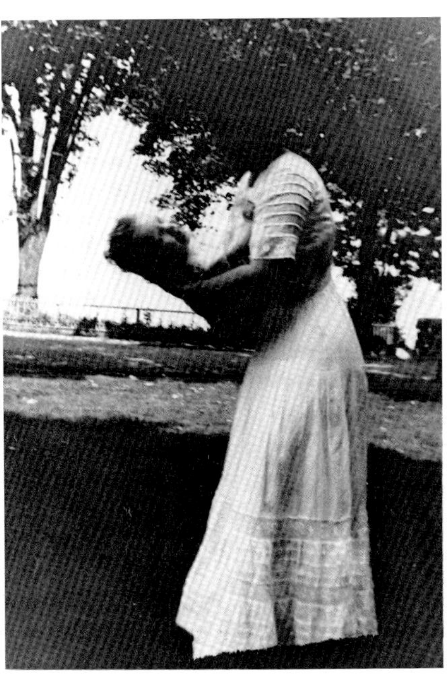

73 Robert being swung in his mother's arms ('Cherubino'), *c.* 1911.

Flushing Camera. The package contained a large photograph of Cornell's mother with Robert, when a baby, being swung in her arms (illus. 73). The face of Mrs Cornell was curiously absent, sort of erased. A note inside explained: 'One of CORNELL children. ca. 1907 Nyack, NY. 1910 or 1911 Robert.'[166] Two pictures of Robert had been extracted from the large image and five small copies made of both the mother and Robert, again with Mrs Cornell's face blacked out, as if in shadow. Wearing a white dress, she is barely an outline against a tree, a ghostly image. The package was labelled 'FOUNTAIN OF YOUTH (Cherubino) relating to our childhood'.[167]

Two days later, on the Friday, Cornell noted:

> F. of Youth aftermath': day fol. the inspiration not continued enough for one of those sublime occasional 'carry-overs' –
>
> still – the image of the youthful outstretched arm – and of the baby arm enfolded some -'wisps' (bringing bk Cherubino) . . .
>
> 'The Fountain of Youth' and the co-incidence of picking up childhood image of Robert framed to reveal a beautiful coup – love sideways encompassed by arm of mother.[168]

Robert held a very special position in the family because he was like an eternal child: he needed constantly to be nurtured and cared for. His cerebral palsy, his permanent affliction, meant that physically he couldn't advance. Although he was aged 40 when he died in 1965, his milieu in the family sitting-room had always been made comfortable for him by means of his well-loved 'toys' – his magic lantern and train-set.

For Cornell the whole concept of Robert's particular state had an unusual twist. Cornell believed that if you had a severe physical disability then you possessed other (God-given) gifts, such as an unusual degree of purity and a direct access to innocence. (Of course, a non-active sexuality was an important part of this sanctified state.) Cornell once asked Leila Hadley if any of her four children were disabled. The answer was no. 'What a pity', he said.[169]

If we look at the portrait image central to the *Fountain of Youth* collage, connections with Robert begin to emerge. The image is of a boy-child sitting posed and curiously motionless. We see The Uncanny element here: is it an image of a living person, or is it a doll? We know it derives from a painting by Copley because inscribed on the verso is:

> collage based upon one of the first and greatest of the 'Coonskinners' – that is American artists who worked out their own style of seeing – *Daniel Crommelin Verplank*, 1771, by John Singleton Copley. It hangs in the Metropolitan's American Wing.

And he added: 'remembering the 'Fountain of Youth' – Flushing – summer '59. 10-15-59'.

The Fountain of Youth is cut into two: the bottom half comprises the Copley reproduction; the top half is a panoramic skyscape extracted from a Luminist painting. There is no attempt to blend these two represented worlds: the dark shadowy, architectural world containing man and the brilliantly lit expansive world of nature stand apart, except for the boy's head, which is cut and pasted to overlap. Another late collage in which the significance of this same contrast is made more explicit is the undated *Untitled (Cherub With Kitten)* (illus. 74). Here too the collage is divided, but this time vertically. On the one side is a dark formal interior and on the other a snow-covered outdoor scene visible through the grid patterning of the window. In both collages, images of childhood are presented indoors within abstract, architectural elements of permanence. In *Cherub with Kitten* the 'fountain'

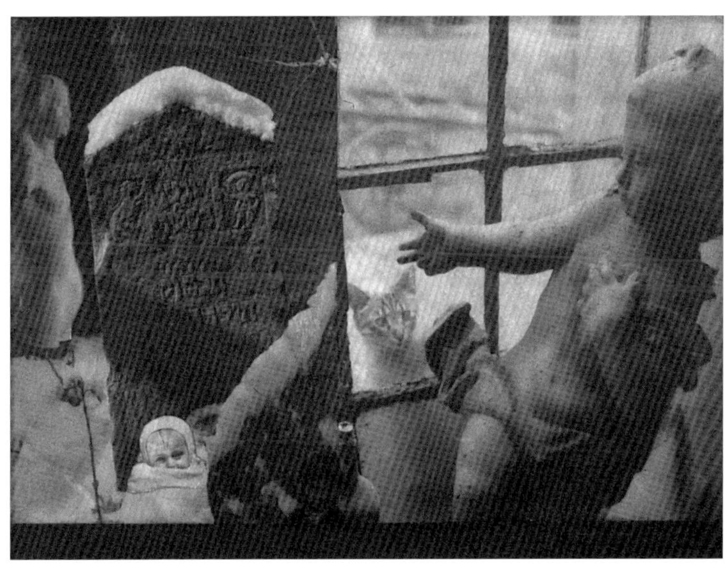

74 *Untitled* (*Cherub with Kitten*), an undated collage.

of youth is represented in the putti, the plastic doll, the statue and the Dark Age Pictish carvings. In 'art there is the possibility of eternity', wrote Cornell, remembering the quotation from Proust in a radio broadcast.[170]

The child in shadowy light, like a Caravaggio painting, is one image Cornell would have kept from his own childhood as this was the standard form of the posed studio photograph. For such pictures the family was gathered together – formally dressed and utterly still – and the light, flooding in from one side, would then illuminate an ovoid edge to the faces, but still leave a dark shadowy backdrop to the figures.

Fountain of Youth has, in addition to the formality of the environment that the child inhabits, a formal blocking in of the various elements over the image as a whole. We have already mentioned the horizontal division: the light and dark, the exterior and interior. In the lower-left there is a strip of five stars, the five tokens for Cherubino; top left is the angel Cherubino demonstrating her 'vision'; on the right a dove may be a symbol of innocence or purity, or it may represent 'maleness' (Leila Hadley used to joke with Cornell about the Spanish slang for dove, 'La Paloma', which was also slang for the male organ.)[171] On the right a diagram of a top spinning vigorously works to accentuate the motionlessness of the picture. The top is also the synecdoche for childhood toys. What is the ambience and mood of this collage? It is summed up in a few lines lifted from the Cherubino writings:

> continued bewilderment at being pulled back into unneeded heavy sleep vs the sublime joy of early morning – . . . dream-like? aspect of these notings . . . the quiet consolations, sudden joys, touches of beauty in people nature – in performance of the day's round . . . serenity felt drift direct from C. without stiffness.[172]

The Cornellian child is not the child of nature, but one whose activities become blocked into the shapes of fulfilment. The child's sense of fulfilment is achieved by a journey through constructed passages. The shapes, spaces, containers, geometries, constructions of Cornell's created worlds are satisfying because they mirror the processes of the mind. Also, and this is perhaps the main point, it is only in a constructed world that ephemera can have significance.

In *Cherubino* the ephemera are overtly fetishistic. Things

become animated with spirits; they become sacred objects because they can be connected with a thought or a sighting of Cherubino. Consider the following:

> returning 'the Ancient Secret' to library and Cherubino . . . going in with sweet girl grads from Flushing High – spoke to the one – in Bicks – with party . . .
>
> house – heavy o' cast shard of glass falling out of cracked pane . . . a grey let down and the smile remembered Bick's girl grad.[173]

The shard of glass is kept and stored within the Cherubino box. Then, '3.15 PM. 8/26/59 only a partial root beer from the hands of Cherubino'.[174] The beer-bottle cap is kept, and a toy alligator that was 'taking part' the day after the 'title unfolded'. Cornell remembers 'Monday June 6.60 reminder of how the trouvés humbler tokens also partake of something miraculous talismanlike – to be treasured and shared in such a spirit'.

Rosalind Krauss has argued that the scandal of Surrealist photography was its 'fetishization of reality', and worth considering here is the shared fetishism of Cornell and the Surrealists. The fetish is the third principle in Breton's aesthetic detailed in *L'Amour Fou*, in which a found object or a found verbal fragment signify to the recipient a desire of which he was previously unaware.[175] Breton discovered a slipper spoon in the flea market and realized that this was the fulfilment of his desire to find a Cinderella ashtray. Freud, of course, reckoned that the fetish is a substitute, a substitution of the unnatural for the natural. Its origin lies in the refusal to accept sexual difference. The fetish is the substitute for the once-believed-in phallus of the mother. The Surrealists were clearly drawn to Freud's interpretation. Levy went on to define fetishism as the 'Doctrine of spirit embodied in or attached to, or conveying influence through certain material objects. In the terminology of psychoanalysis, the transference of the libido from the whole object of affection to a part, a symbol, an article of clothing.'[176] This fetishistic element is undeniably found in much of Cornell's work. He was forever collecting items of clothing from young ballerinas, attaching massive significance to objects associated with his young female subjects, exchanging gifts with his female associates. The suggestion that this activity was free from sexual longing is untenable. When we look at Cornell's boxes – especially the ballet boxes or those that contain dolls and young female subjects – it is impossible, for all their emphasis on the innocence of childhood, to ignore the lingering presence of the strong desire that originally caused the boxes to be made. One commentator has referred to the fact that certain boxes are 'fraught with plangent erotic content', and it must be admitted that something of the intense impact felt on seeing these boxes derives from the onlooker's own sense of guilt at being implicated in the artist's voyeurism.[177]

'THE CRYSTAL CAGE'

'The Crystal Cage' (illus. 77) is unique in two ways: this is a dossier with no box constructions that relate to it, and it appeared as a verbal/visual 'exploration' in *View* magazine in January 1943.[178] After 1943 Cornell encased the documents, photos, prints and other memorabilia that comprised 'The Crystal Cage' and made a 'boxed edition in facsimile' that looked like a travelling suitcase containing loosely piled papers – images and writings. What we see in 'The Crystal Cage' exploration in *View* is a series of sightings, descriptions

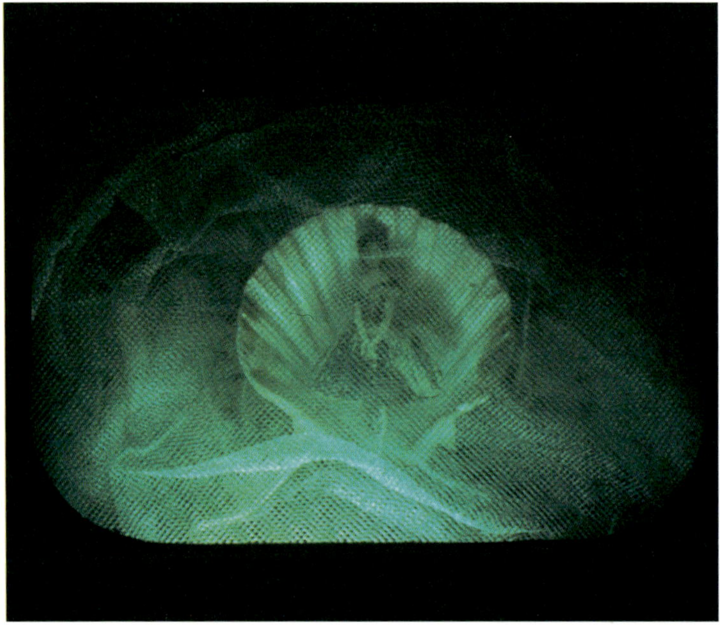

75 *Untitled (Ondine)*, c. 1944–6, box construction with electric light.

76 *Untitled*, c. mid–1950s, box construction.

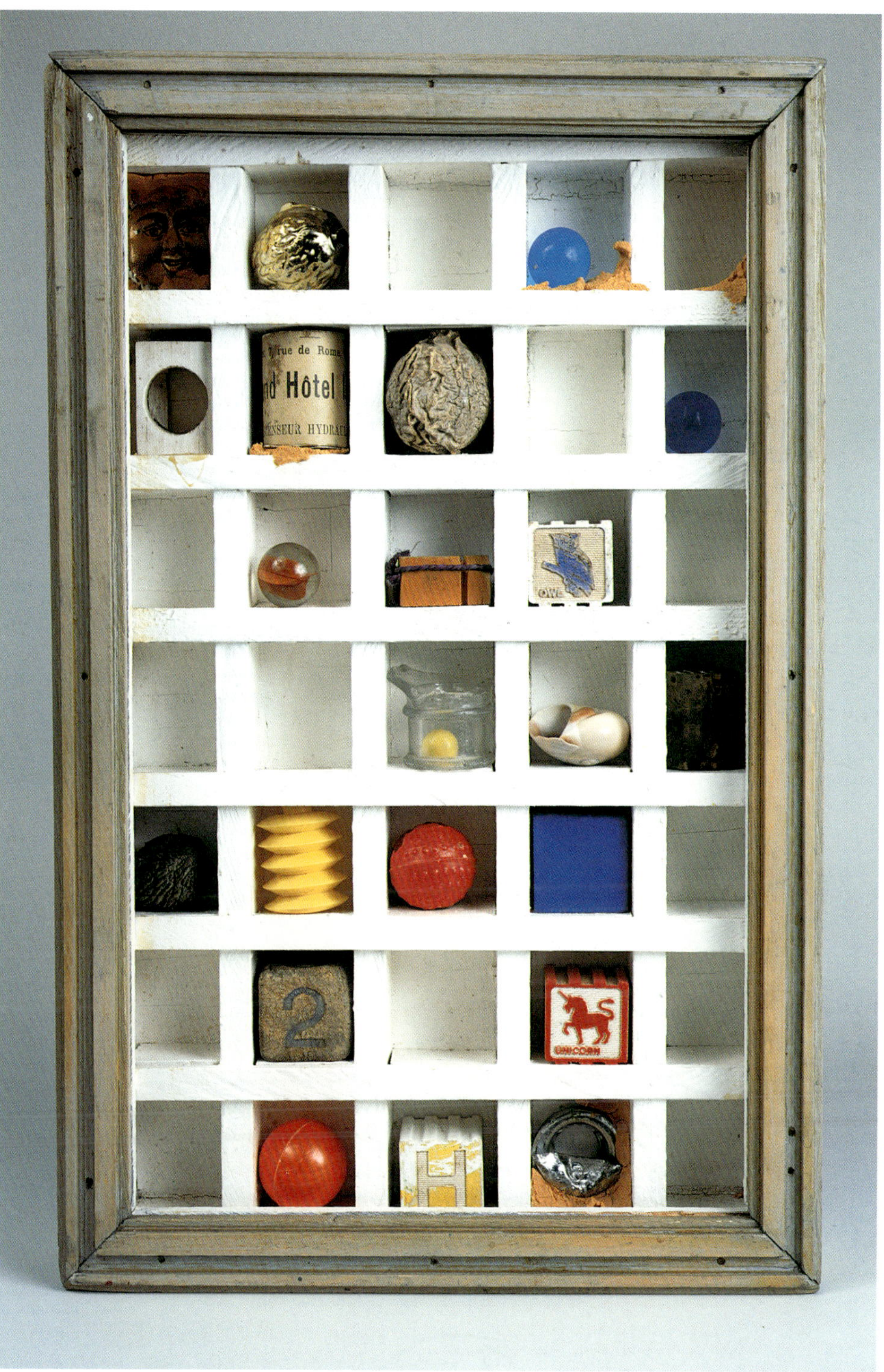
rue de Rome
Hôtel
2
UNICORN
H

and representations of a phenomenon that may have existed.[179] The 'series' as Cornell's favoured method of working – we normally recognize through the repetition of a formal motif or layout; here there is a thematic connection: Cornell gives us a series of perspectives. With regard to the 'language' of Cornell's art we should notice that this investigation of credulity, documentation and vision shows his fascination with form: each page is selected to be set against another in the sequence of the essay/exploration according to formal considerations – the general shape of an image/mass of words, the abundance of images or words on a page, and so on. Cornell stretched the role of the artist, becoming a journalist, editor, correspondent, graphic designer and archivist.

Turning the pages of 'The Crystal Cage' is like unpacking a trunk or recovering precious items collected in a childhood scrapbook. Like many of Cornell's other creative projects, 'The Crystal Cage' is two-dimensional paper material; it is in black and white and has been inserted within the pages of an avant-garde arts magazine. The project has the character of a picture pullout pamphlet, but it contains words too: in addition to photos, montages, collages and prints it holds word constructions, poetic associations and snippets of what appear to be documentary information. It has a formal title-page and a subtitle: 'Portrait of Bérénice'.

In a substantial and scholarly publication devoted to 'The Crystal Cage', Sandra Leonard Starr offers many insights. She sees it as Cornell's homage to his own childhood and takes Bérénice to be 'the universal spirit of childhood and renewal, not subject to age, illness, death or decay'. Less convincingly, perhaps, she also interprets Bérénice as 'a metaphysical astronaut' – the embodiment of Cornell's faith in Christian Science. Here I restrict myself to explaining the opposition of influences in 'The Crystal Cage' so as to show the importance of the child's counter-world for Cornell, and, most importantly, to show the way that the tower – in its imprisonment/creativity dichotomy – exactly parallels Cornell's own attitude towards the boxed-art format.

Cornell's essay allows us to piece together the story of Bérénice and her pagoda. Bérénice, a young American girl, discovers a Chinoiserie pagoda while in Europe and asks her parents if this extraordinary edifice could be transported back to her home in New England. This pagoda, as it happens, really exists. Cornell discovered that a 'Pagode de Chanteloup' had been built for the Duc du Choiseul, one of Louis XV's leading ministers, in the late 1770s as a folly in the Duc's landscaped park in the Loire Valley.

In 'The Crystal Cage' version, however, Bérénice succeeds in having the pagoda shipped to America, whereupon she throws herself into simple scientific experiments. From the pagoda she makes a study of the skies, of distant panoramas, of hot-air balloons and the stars in their constellations. She lives in a wholly rarefied world, a kind of American version of Lewis Carroll's *Alice* stories. However, the difference between Alice and Bérénice shows that the fantasy world of the child has changed from an earthborn fable with fairytale characters (Carroll) to an airborne circus. Thus Bérénice encounters – instead of the sleepy dormouse and the mad hatter – cupids, angels, flying ballerinas and high-wire artists.

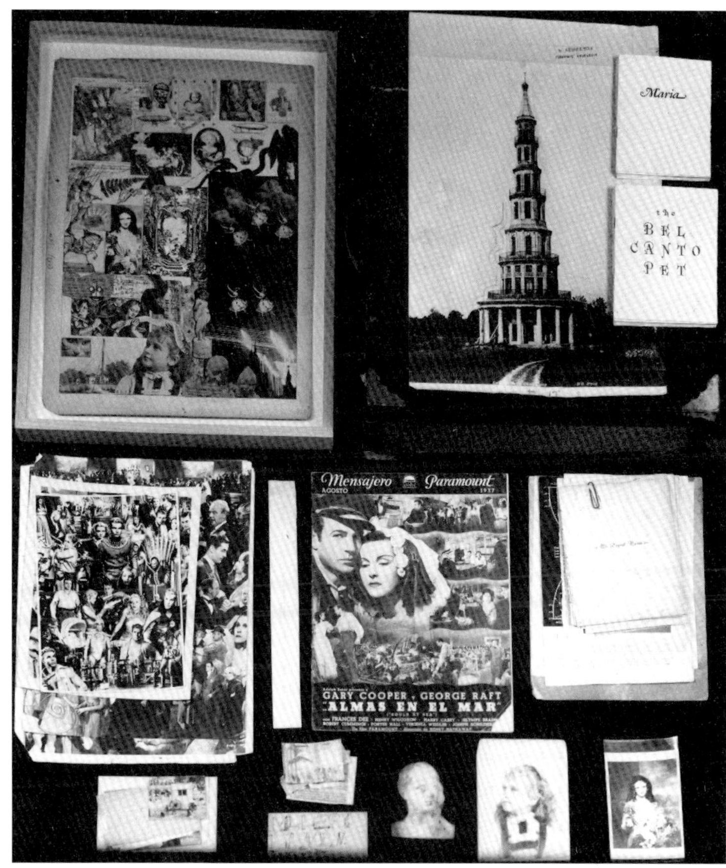

77 'The Crystal Cage: Portrait of Bérénice', *c.* 1943, valise containing documents.

Bérénice's story is contained in three paragraphs written by Cornell on page three of the essay. The remainder comprises a title-page, a pagoda of words (including a minute illustration of Bérénice at its base: illus. 78), two letter excerpts describing children's activities (on the same page as Cornell's tale of Bérénice), a full-page picture of a pagoda (looking a little faded and ramshackle in its grandeur), a full-page photomontage of Blondin (the celebrated tightrope artiste, a child prodigy), a collage of small images with an accompanying key on the final page (illus. 79), and a final small image of Bérénice peering into the windows of her pagoda (illus. 80).[180]

The word-pagoda is a construction with the outline of a pagoda but with the inside filled with words: lines of words or beginnings or ends of words thicken and thin out according to the contours of the pagoda, as shown opposite. It is possible to pick out phrases or groups of words that suggest significant content clusters. For example, Cornell mentions – from the hundreds and hundreds of words – the Great Wall of China, Fingal's Cave, the Blue Grotto of Capri, the Tower of Pisa, the Black Forest, suggesting that he is listing the wonders of the world. Or is it possible he is making a list of prima ballerinas (Lucile Grahn, Cerrito, Taglioni) and the great artists (Leonardo da Vinci, Giorgione) and musicians (Erik Satie, Liszt), and so on? The pagoda brims over with images, ideas, associations, all vaguely to do with the child's vision of the world and all apparently randomly assembled. Much of 'The Crystal Cage' is like a game that invites you try to puzzle out and then link the various elements. Perhaps the collage page at the back of the essay appears, initially, like a jumbled pile of paste-ups from a child's scrapbook. All higgledy-piggledy, a mass of images are crammed onto the page. Mozart appears with Carlota Grisi, some lifeboat survivors, a baby duck, a woman who looks like Mona Lisa, a child with an umbrella, a hot-air balloon, a Zeppelin, Cupid, some shooting-stars, and the blown-up features of a cat. The connection between all these things is, however, obscure. Again the feeling of release, of a spilling over of a generous embrace of things, is what is communicated rather than a tight hold, a restriction on planned, placed imagery. It is the same essential feeling we have with the word-pagoda, only here it is with images. The imagery on this page, however, as with the pagoda, does have selection, planning and

78 Calligram of the Pagode de Chanteloup in 'The Crystal Cage', 1943.

lamps Mozart
ird son
malibran
fireworks
rainbows
high nc
un dials
ightropes
ersian whe
e sunbursts
Berlioz rabb
himney swoops
a Belle Cordie
kylights Baedeko
iero di Cosimo od
parachutes emeralds
pageants Aerial atolls
strolling montgolfiers
camouflage colonnade
Madame Saqui Diana
Italian villas camel
fanfares La Fée Dra
peony bushes Archimedes
ns Christian Andersen N
soirées de Vienne violo
covered Switzerland celo
Rosiphèle snow bowls ph
ndigo Brigliadoro green
daguerreotypes balloon
Edgar Allen Poe marvels
hooting stars Israfel a
winding staircases pan
World's Fair of 1940 as
Francesca Corrito golde
Hotel de l' Ange lightning
soap bubbles solariums Kub
flower covered vallies fa
Harold in Italy snow crys
rambler roses Kirscher ra
glint Mignon Gulliver
minstrels canaries mirage
e Citoyen Hauy moles Carpaccio
hases of the moon now coins ex
ss in Boots Taglioni ice cubes
digo orange star-lit fields phen
palaces of light Cendrillon ascer
ighthouses constellation of Feu
tropical plumage Bouguereau si
Liszt barometers owls siphons
Queen Mab ascensions high noon
agic lanterns Karl Maria von W
eber panoramas twilight bees f
usical instruments of glass e
Columbus aviaries illuminatior
fountains of the moon Kepler d
St. Elmo's fire skyscrapers hisl.
adame Blanchard silk cord Milky Way
aerial flights of Carlotta Grisi homage
automatons Benjamin Franklin Vermeer y
iracles of perspective Cygnus Gemini
Lac des Cygnes calliopes ladders ga
eather vanes roosters Caravaggio ufi
dioramas butterflies mines ropes han
leaning Tower of Pisa microscopic g
ountains rope dancers flutter wheels
La Dormeuse de Naples ceilings hydrograp
sanctuaries waterfalls Erik Satie kaleidosc
eflections Colossus of Rhodes bear market f
Couperin ropes of stars Rimbaud candel stre
white marble statues Neopolitan fisher boys
Persian wheels cupolas string quartets opti
recious stones birds of the Black Forest em
lue tints les nuages de Claude Achille wind
oral islands Mer de Glace lanterns Alice in
Fresnel's system camera obscura Leonardo da
Trevi Chinese gardens flights Seurat Napoli
planetariums diadem of Marie Felicité steel
engravings zootropes Chatterton castles cinematography
diamant au coeur cycloramas treasures Great Wall of China
stoor dust spires festivals marvels of motion swimming bir
dramas of light Raquel Meller Giorgione dawns wind bells r
compasses snow Paganini look-outs windows Gilles the golden city
Seraphim Albeniz aquariums Auriga trumpets crowns pet crows sextants
Johann Strauss Montgolfier Mignon dovecotes toy merchants of Pekin hail k
eclipses transparencies Blue Grotto of Capri chrysalises botanical gard
searchlights Ingres Sunday afternoons flowers calliopes Giant's Causew
spectrums edelweiss Galna Ursa Major sunken cathedral of Ys chart
ose of the Winds birds' nests keys rivers hummingbirds Artesian wel
skylights chains of glass distant hills Sleeping Gypsy of Rousseau
songs in the night hurdy-gurdies Penthesilea fauna strolling mounteba
Miranda buoys Fingal's Cave Paul and Virginia rain snails verdant uh
Perdita radiance salamanders coral atolls Cockaigne Tyll Eulenspieg
mill red yellow subterranean brooks J.J.Grandeville storks' nests er
Pierrot mocking bird of Giulia Grisi circuses Lucille Grahn Mimi opti
habitat groups under glass voyages celestas Watteau irese velvet uge
velvet Phrigian caps Virgi tho Magi of Gozzoli entran
ope luminosities Euryanthe a Ondine serenades branche
ose tyrien tailor-birds re ponsions stalagmites dosit
iope Parizade cirro cumulu Blondin Novella d ' Andrea
Speltarina pomegranites Ki cond of Bavaria snow sleig
Corot distant music mermai ests Coppelia Niagara Fall
ists mirrors celestas Aure gs Atlantis voyages circus
The Snow Image iridescent shells Linnaeus Andromed
Wallendas sirens Neptunes i animals ephemera Floring
ets Courier of St. Petersb shafts of light Rastelli
Lilian Leitzel Trixie Grim Bois Dormant Fratellinis
Fanny Elssler noctuelles D irs chansonniers valses le
kests Zecca La Fontaine Th -go-rounds Hanlon efflores
leo de Merode shells la Périchole rocaille equestrians scenic railwa
Sontag Cordusan la fille au cheveux de lin Algeciras Garcia Offenbach
landas Baudelaire explorations crickets Baroque zoos galleons ladybu
pangolins La Belle au Bois Dormant 1900 Thérèsa Bird Millman ascensc

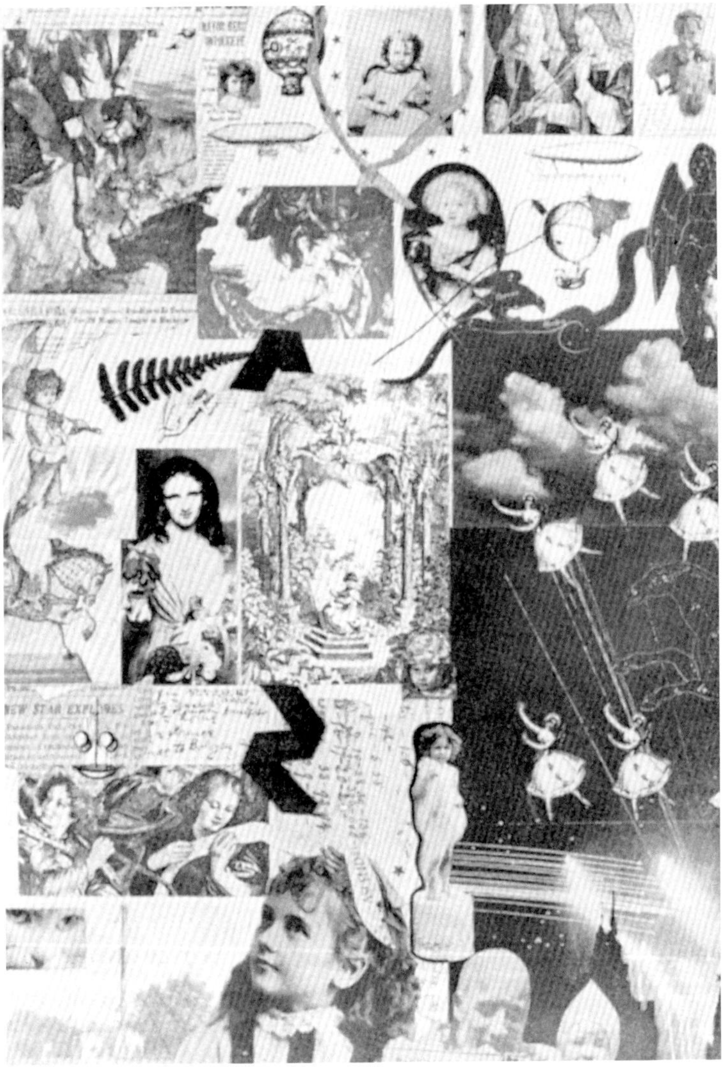

79 Collage from 'The Crystal Cage', 1943.

arrangement behind it. Thematic consistency holds the collage together: children and their concerns.

But as is so often the case in Cornell's work, it is the abstract/structural properties of the piece that makes visual sense of the diverse components. Formally we can see how Bérénice is placed bottom centre with her eyes turned upwards and a ribbon through her hair. The ribbon spells out 'ASCENDET' and we ascend up via the dark zig-zag, the silhouetted fern leaf, the tail of the 'Hydra' and the stem of a flower through to the image of a younger Bérénice sitting in all her glory surrounded by stars and ribbons at the top of the page. Some delicate handling of the photomontage makes the fingers holding the ribbon in Bérénice's hair echo the curling fronds of hair that frame her face: the ribbon links Bérénice to the angels placed next to her. She is all of the images. She seems to be lots of different little girls, all of whom have roughly the same appearance, a Victorian look – curly hair, a gaze that is serious and penetrating. And she also looks rather like a cherub.[181]

'The Crystal Cage' itself is illustrated on page four of the essay/exploration. This is the grand and beautiful structure through which the small child views the world. On page three of the pamphlet Cornell explores the fabric of this construction:

> In the glistening sphere the little proprietress reared in a severe atmosphere of scientific research, came to love the rarified realms of constellation, balloons, and distant panoramas bathed in light, and drew upon her background to perform her own experiments, miracles of ingenuity and poetry.

The kind of atmosphere that Cornell was striving for is contained in a newspaper article, 'The Private Worlds of Youth' by Alan Pryce-Jones, one of the items in the travelling suitcase:

> I hope Mrs Molesworth is still read. A few years ago *Herr Baby* was out of print; but a good many nurseries still seem to be faithful to *The Cuckoo Clock*. Like all good children's books, hers give an intense pleasure to grown-ups; but they offer children what I take to be the harvest of surrealism: the distillation of an object into an atmosphere. For queer events in themselves leave a child perfectly cold; exciting events also. Without what can be called a high dream power, they only amuse grown-ups.
>
> *The Cuckoo Clock* has that power. It creates a secret untransmittable picture: the turn of an ancient staircase in the evening, a dark labyrinth of wainscotted corridors. I cannot remember any of the events which were less important than their overtones; and I believe all imaginative children only use books as a lever to set their private world at work.

> The books can be quite worthless but they must have that power of distillation. There was a book by Louisa M. Alcott, *Eight Cousins*, which had that to a high degree. An uncle had returned with a trunkful of curious presents – the presents revealed to me, all the excitement of far places, all the life and room of the unfamiliar. They were from China and the Indies, as far as I can remember: a tea service, embroideries, ivory, sandalwood; and the whole book because of that chapter, was bathed in brilliant sunshine. It gave me a mystical feeling for trunks. Yet I do not suppose it had much merit as a book any more than *The Secret Garden* or *Anne of Green Gables*, both of which opened exactly such avenues in my ten-year-old mind as I should look for now in the poets.
>
> In the end the dangerous pleasures of the private world is, for those who can afford it, the only panacaea. No wonder we remember affectionately the budding of that world, the peaceful beginning when it could absorb with confidence as much of the real world as it chose, and reject the rest. Even when the real world was one in which the skylights in a big house had to be painted over, so that Zeppelins could not find a mark by night, a child was only pleasantly affected by it. For the Zeppelin was less real than the Cuckoo Clock, and one's mother playing with the violin, and the fun of using saccharin instead of sugar.[182]

Certain phrases employed by Pryce-Jones – 'the harvest of surrealism', 'the distillation of an object into an atmosphere', 'a high dream power' and the 'dangerous pleasure of the private world' – are vivid verbal equivalents of the metaphysic that informs Cornell's art. His emphasis on the power that certain objects exert upon the mind of a child (Cuckoo Clock, an uncle's trunk full of 'curious presents' having returned from a voyage, the turn of an ancient staircase in the evening, a dark labyrinth of wainscotted corridors), what he refers to as levers to set the child's private world to work, is obviously what Cornell was interested in with his story of Bérénice and her pagoda in 'The Crystal Cage'.

An aspect of Pryce-Jones's article that Cornell would have connected with is the replacement/transformation idea lying behind the final sentence of the passage: 'For the Zeppelin was

80 Bérénice gazing into her own past and future, from 'The Crystal Cage', published in *View* magazine, January 1943.

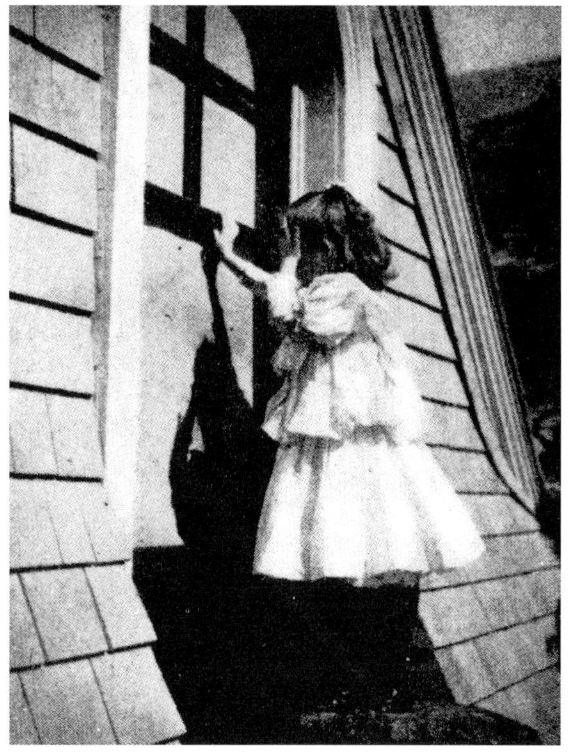

less real than The Cuckoo Clock, and one's mother playing with the violin, and the fun of using saccharin instead of sugar'. Other artists/writers have shown a fascination with this idea – that children's games are invented as a panacea. Nathaniel Hawthorne kept records of the play of his daughter, Una, and in both his notebooks and in *The Scarlet Letter* he shows particular interest in the succession of games through which the real Una and the fictive Pearl act out an imaginative freedom. The child creates a counter-world, a private world in order to gain some understanding of the world at large: Pearl plays imaginative games, savagely uprooting weeds that represent the Puritan children who tormented her, in an effort to understand her own feelings.[183] In Henry James's *What Maisie Knew*, Maisie plays out her own private games with her doll Lisette.[184] With Lisette she 'mimicked her mother's sharpness' and through mimicry learns that she doesn't want to become like either of her parents, the pair of disputants in the adult game of divorce. The six-year-old in Cornell's story, told in the letter excerpt of

16 September 1942 in 'The Crystal Cage', plays a game where the stars fall from the sky onto the beach and Red Indians carve canoes out of 'shining white birch' especially for her. With this game she copes with the unsympathetic rudeness of adults who lay down rules, and of one in particular who orders her to go to bed, and 'no fooling about'. In another Cornell story (contained in the letter of 21 November 1942 in 'The Crystal Cage') a little girl in a tenement block with red brick walls and bare rooms ('a bareness never before observed') plays out games of 'seven league boots' and 'evil ogres' and 'croaking frogs' that usher in the magic of a counter-world and so block out the bleak fact of her immediate surroundings.

In Bérénice's world it is the unexpected combination of elements that strikes the reader: science and poetry, miracle and experimentation, severity and beauty are all brought together in harmony. This leads us to a consideration of the title of the whole project: 'The Crystal Cage'.[185] Here, nouns are connected that, at first sight, suggest incompatible things, with 'crystal' indicating vision/freedom, and 'cage' obviously representing constraint/captivity. When we think of crystal we think of visions: through crystal balls the future is forecast; crystal gazers are those who seek to conjure up what is otherwise unknowable, unseeable. Bérénice's cage is a place of visions and marvels ('rarified realms'), but it is also her prison. Widening the doors of perception signals freedom, and Bérénice can see all the world and create poetry from her crystal cage, but she cannot, from her isolation within the pagoda, experience it.

The idea of perceiving the world from a vantage-point that allows poetry and art to be created but yet which makes direct contact with the real world impossible is the idea behind Tennyson's 'The Lady of Shalott'. The Lady, immured in her tower on the island of Shalott, weaves her extraordinary tapestry, 'a magic web with colours gay'.[186] The reflections from her mirror (an essential item for the craft in which she is engaged) include images from beyond her island world – the river, the highway, travellers on the road to Camelot. The Lady experiences this world only through the 'shadows' of it that weave through her mirror. Like Bérénice, she has no direct contact with the world itself, but from the glimpses of it she gains via the glass, she forms her art: 'in her web she still delights / to weave the mirror's magic sights'. Art and poetry are inspired by a state of confinement.[187]

The doomed heroine of Tennyson's poem finds her imagination reaches its full potential exactly because of her imprisonment. This was an idea that obsessed Cornell. He returned again and again to the image of a female in a box, in a cage, in a tower: Mélisande (illus. 81), for example, is trapped in a tower made from beach materials; another doll, in *Sequestered*

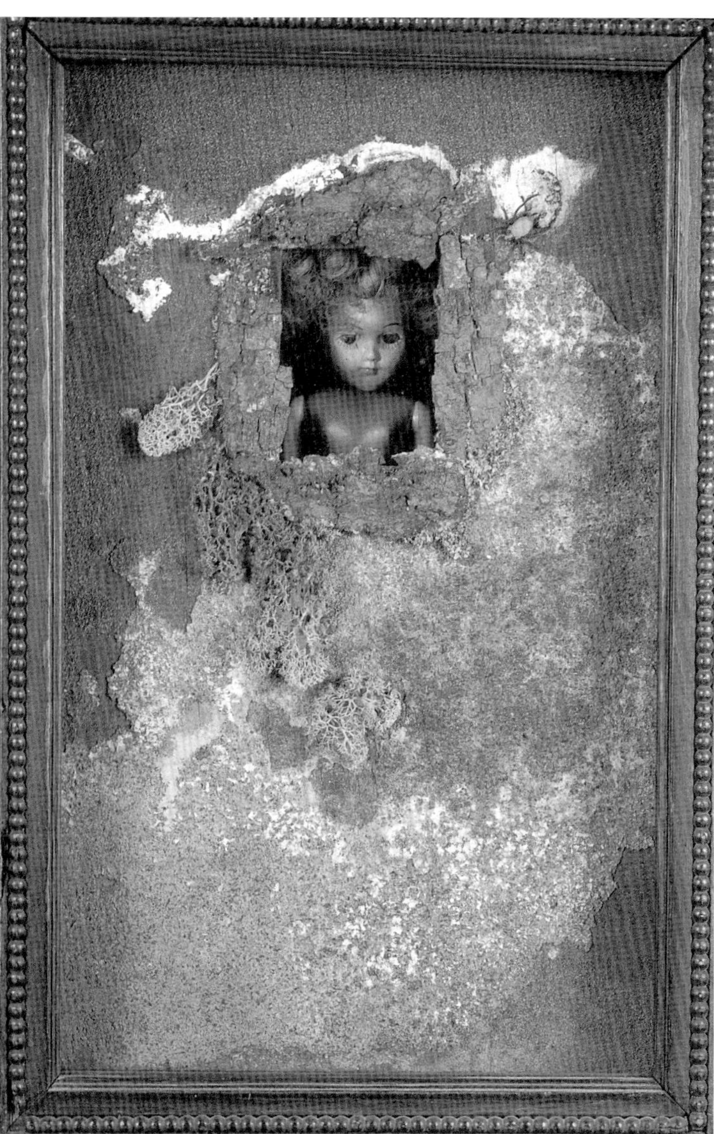

81 *Untitled (Mélisande)*, c. 1948–50, construction.

Bower (1948), is bound by her wrists and ankles within a boxed space.

The idea of physical imprisonment setting free the creative imagination obsessed Cornell because this was the image he had of his own personal situation. Running like a refrain throughout his dossiers and diaries are comments about being in the cellar at Utopia Parkway confined by his domestic responsiblity, and further confined by the chosen form of his boxed art. And yet, the situation seems to have encouraged him to find freedom in his art. If we were to tease out the one strand that runs throughout the diary writings, it would be the one that has to do with the see-sawing nature of his mental state, which swings from conceiving of his art and his circumstances as his prison (and the need to escape to 'life' in the city), to – on other days, when everything is going well in the cellar – the feeling of release, of freedom, a natural flowing that is the result of being at one with his art:

> connection with life as opposed to the confining, aesthetic feeling of limitation experienced too often when working on the boxes.
>
> stimulating feeling of release and perspective that comes from getting into town.
>
> unfoldment, expression, LIFE vs aesthetics
>
> Intense longing to get into the box – this overflowing, a richness and poetry felt when working with the boxes
>
> One of the best days at home (feeling right without having to get away) . . . worked late on owl box in cellar . . . Had satisfactory feeling about cleaning up debris on cellar floor – 'sweepings' represent all the rich cross-currents ramifications that go into boxes.[188]

Leila Hadley spoke perceptively of Cornell and the constraints of the box format: 'the cage is the shell, or the thing around oneself, the magic wall that people don't penetrate, and the box is also very symbolic of security. Everything is within that. Now the round thing is the female symbol and the rectangular is the male, so it is always the male enclosing everything. Its like enclosing the anima, the female side, the mystical female.'[189] This is close to the traditional symbolic interpretation of the damsel trapped in the tower as a representation of the female mind trapped within the male. The image of imprisonment must be linked also to the idea of repression. Cornell's life was so much one of self-denial in any physical sense that he was driven to find ways of expressing and sublimating his sexuality, and the idea of constraint is clearly related to his chosen course of asceticism.

3 The Self in Others

There was an obsession with the ballerina, prima donna image, the untouchable, idealized, de-personalized feminine presence.[190]

THE 'LAUREN BACALL' DOSSIER

Cornell's individual approach to portraiture may be epitomized in a single box construction, *Penny Arcade Portrait of Lauren Bacall* (illus. 83). In 1946 he held a show entitled 'Romantic Museum (Portraits of Women)' at the Hugo Gallery in New York. In addition to the *Lauren Bacall* box, this show included 'The Crystal Cage', 'Pasta', 'Malibran' (portraits of famous nineteenth-century divas); *Taglioni, Portrait of Ondine* (ballerinas); *Garbo* (the movie star) and *Metaphysique d'Ephemera* (which are, Cornell noted, 'Faces seen but once', 'Faces seen in Crowds', 'Girl in Pigtails, New York City'). His subjects in 'Portraits of Women' ran from fictional characters to famous women, and even to 'unknown', unidentified girls or women briefly glimpsed.

There is one dossier that reveals the background to the *Lauren Bacall* box (illus. 82).[191] This dossier reveals the process in Cornell's selection of particular imagery and objects. These were not 'found' objects as with the Surrealists, but sought-after things, deeply cherished and only relinquished and placed in the box after a period of intense, obsessive scrutiny. The objects and images in *Lauren Bacall* – as in every other work – were meticulously sorted and placed to produce an articulated whole that is yet part of a continuous concern, part of a profound affection.

In *Joseph Cornell: Gifts Of Desire*, Dickran Tashjian devotes a chapter to this dossier and the box created from it.[192] Tashjian focuses sharply on several features of the work. He brings out the parallel with Cornell's film *Rose Hobart* (1936) and the purification process that is present in both, and also Cornell's awareness of being in competition with the imagery of a decadent Hollywood. Tashjian also considers the aspect of gender doubling and interest in androgeny as revealed in *Rose Hobart*, in the dossier and in the *Lauren Bacall* box itself. He argues that the aesthetic achievement of the box is part of the inner vision it represents of an unspoilt world beyond childhood and sexual difference. Here, however, I wish to draw attention more to Cornell's associative process, to show what Cornell reveals in the process from dossier to box, and how the box epitomizes his obsessions not just with a particular woman and the cinema but with the processes of his own mind. *Lauren Bacall*, in fact, reveals much more about Cornell than it does Bacall, and in this is more self-portrait than portrait.

The 'Penny Arcade Portrait' is unique among Cornell's dossiers because it has a direct relationship with a single box. The majority of Cornell's dossier files each serve a number of boxes and collages: either they relate directly to a series (for example, 'Medici Prince') or indirectly to numerous art works ('GC 44'). Two other dossiers stand as texts to specific boxes: the 'Caliph of Bagdad' and 'Hôtel Chariot D'Or'. These two can be differentiated in terms of function from the 'Penny Arcade' dossier. They are storage places for raw materials, not for ideas. The 'Penny Arcade' dossier provides for us a link between imagination and execution in Cornell's artistic process. It supplies clues to the relation between the inspiration at source and the features of the finished piece, and therefore points towards the meaning of the box for the artist.

The dossier is, as one might expect, a comprehensive account of the growth of Cornell's fascination with Bacall:

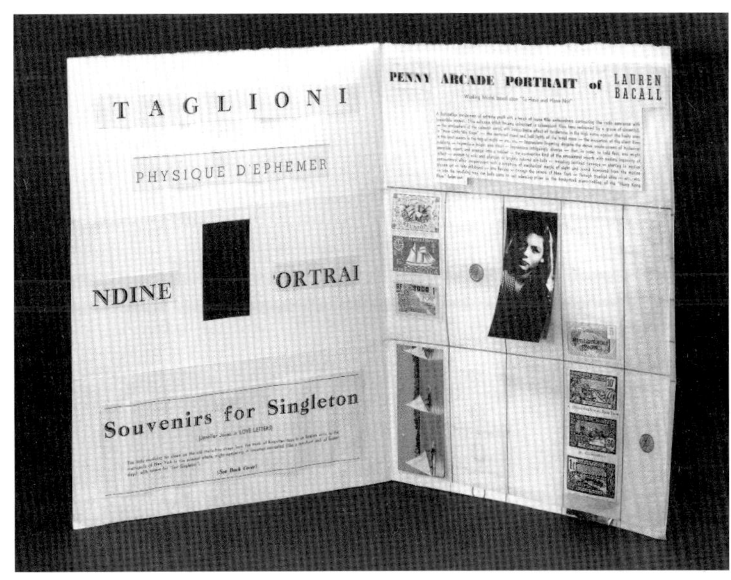

82 The 'Penny Arcade Portrait' dossier for the Lauren Bacall box, 1945–6, (paperboard folder containing photographs and various paper materials).

1. THE IMAGE: Cornell glimpses a reproduction of Bacall's face in a stack of advertising photographs for the film *To Have and Have Not*. It sticks in his memory, particularly the 'different face of interesting Javanese modelling'.

2. KEITH'S OF FLUSHING: Cornell sees *To Have and To Have Not* at 'Keith's' and is deeply impressed.

3. THE QUEST BEGINS: Feeling an 'intense interest aroused', Cornell begins to gather up as much information and imagery as he can muster. He contacts Warner Brothers for stills and begins scouring newspapers and magazines. A search conducted at the New York Public Library on Broadway supplies *Harper's Bazaar, Screenland* and *Mademoiselle,* which contain photos and biographical material. One picture in particular pleases him – Bacall in a 'healthy and unartificial light'; some childhood photographs are 'unexpectedly fresh'.

4. FASHION INDUSTRY: A connection is found (he has freelanced for *Harper's Bazaar* and *Vogue,* contributing illustrations and designing layouts for fashion pages, while she, of course, has modelled). He writes of a 'kindred feeling of wandering', and imagines her toting for work in Manhattan's offices, just as he himself has done.

5. CHANCE ENCOUNTERS AND EXPERIENCES: Various incidents are swept up into the obsession with Bacall: (i) An unexpected opportunity to go to 42nd Street leads to a 'special sense of the city' he gets from a film he sees with 'refreshing childhood stills' and some penny arcade machines he comes across. (ii) Three Christian Science meetings, a memorable experience with a Christian Science Practitioner and a dream result in a 'sense of elation' because of their close proximity to periods of intense absorption with Bacall. (iii) On 9 June 1945 Cornell sees a reproduction of Delacroix's *La Sibylle au Rameau d'Or* and decides to integrate a 'heroic and spiritual quality' with a 'honky-tonk box'. (iv) In July of the same year Cornell comes across a copy of the French magazine *Geographique* in which Martinique (the location for the film *To Have and Have Not*) is placed in the index immediately following Marie, the character Bacall plays in the film. Having 'discovered' Bacall, Cornell decides to do a portrait that has nothing to do with 'cheese-cake' or 'Hollywood artificiality'. He feels the public has misconstrued her:

> As far as the fans are concerned a new slinky, sultry, sexy, siren of the silver screen, but underneath all this cheesecake a girl of Botticellian slenderness, evidently destined to cling to her, accentuating her 'hard boiled' and very honest and sincere qualities to a touching degree. This contrast is evident in another way equally poignant in her startling voice whose huskiness blends perfectly with her almost rude assurance but in the high notes of the song 'how little we know' there is an indescribable effect of tenderness and extreme youth.[193]

He felt committed to the creation of a different image of Bacall – 'one with a shiny clean look, fumigated of Hollywood booze, cigarette smoke and slow-motion mugging'.

We see in this dossier Cornell the artist, but there are Cornell the collector and the archivist too. For example, Cornell carefully dated all his work in progress on Bacall. Inspiration began in the spring of 1945; the earliest specific date logged is 19 April. On 19 August he reassessed the experiences, the ideas and the rich web of associations he had by then assembled. He typed out a summary from the rough notes used to record the incidents and thoughts as they occurred. Apparently, from early spring through to mid-summer he allowed his ideas to flow freely around the obsessive point of Lauren Bacall. This period was a time of expansion and assimilation; during it he felt no need to mould his thoughts into any definite shape. However, by 19 August he had begun to envisage the box construction, wondering which boxes from his past productions he might refer back to, and how this new box might differ in appearance and function. In 1946 he wrote his 'General Working Notes' that outline further the box format. In October of the same year he made a short, late entry, aligning the box and the dossier with his beliefs and with Christian Science ('purity of the original inspiration should be held to – Principle vs Personality').

What we cannot but be made aware of is, within the whole associative process, the importance Cornell attached to chance connections. He used these chance connections and built them into his obsession as if they were somehow symbolically meant. Synchronicity is seen as a signal, a guide to be trusted. All manner of unlikely relationships are thus established. Even so, they are not thought of as fate or as coincidence, which are seen as outside agencies, but as quite the opposite – the mind as director, albeit at times the unwitting director of association. Cornell developed strategies to encourage his mind to make connections, to be in a state of readiness, of receptivity. The mind thus enables the artist to escape from seeming fixities and he is free to establish alternative histories through hitherto unseen connections. Thus Bacall becomes associated with Delacroix and Cinderella, with penny arcade machinery and Christian Science through his receptivity to other associations than the ones Hollywood had impressed upon her.

Two interesting additional points emerge if we look more searchingly at the writing in the 'Penny Arcade' dossier. One is the notion of a highly developed aesthetic acuity, which Cornell uses in the service of a spiritual intent; the other is the awareness he has of two audiences for his 'private' dossiers – himself, and the wider public.

In the notes made in his dossier regarding Bacall's persona in *To Have and To Have Not*, Cornell reveals that he was not so much interested in plot as he was in the mechanics, the tricks and evocation of atmosphere he encountered in the film:

> the atmosphere of the cabaret songs, with an indescribable effect of tenderness in the high notes against the husky ones in 'How Little We Know' – the nocturnal mood and the half lights of the hotel room, the evocation of the silent films in the boat scenes in the fog at night – etc, etc – Impressions lingering despite the dense smoke screen of hysterical publicity – impressions bright and clean – impressions intriguingly diverse.

Atmosphere, effect, mood, evocation and impression are the key words here. Impressions are the substance of what Cornell gleaned from *To Have and To Have Not*. These impressions represent the qualities that Cornell himself would strive to recreate in his own art. Atmosphere and mood stand above all else in Cornell's priorities, but this attention to effects is underpinned by Transcendentalist moral intent. Again the Luminists, with their insistence on the marriage of God and material things within their curiously theatrical landscapes, represent a tradition that Cornell followed here. He understood the importance of attending to minute physical details in order to control the more elusive, remote, dematerialized aspects of visual stimulus – absence, loneliness, pathos.

Another point emerges when we examine the *manner* of Cornell's writing rather than at what he sets down. Some pages are direct impulsive outlines of events and thoughts, put down urgently in order to retain either a quality of feeling or at least the bare bones of some facts. Other pages hint at an uncomfortable voyeuristic feeling, with Cornell chiding himself for over-indulgence with his obsession. Here and there we come across confessions of nervous tension and unstable emotional states. And yet, there is another completely distinct style of writing – a controlled, more polished prose. Sentences are fastidiously punctuated, and organized in paragraphs. He uses poetic devices, alliteration for example (Bacall is a 'slinky, sultry, sexy siren of the silver screen'). Some adjectives have a contrived modishness (Bacall has 'Botticellian slenderness' and 'jeune fille awkwardness'). Many words are charmingly naïve, rather like a species of refined lingo. Sometimes he slips into film journalese, jargon, and employs slightly archaic words. The two modes of writing here – the urgent and the polished – suggest that this dossier was not just for the artist's personal use, that while at some points he was recording impressions for his own immediate artistic purposes, at others he was composing for a future public readership. These two manners – the spontaneous and the selfconscious – seem to marry somehow with his disparate ideas of Bacall as a Hollywood star on the one hand and as a youthful innocent on the other. They also indicate that Cornell was in search of a voice. They reveal uncertainties concerning the appropriate tone, the proper relationship with his readership, the relationship with his subject. What we discover in this dossier is an artist attempting to create an identity for himself with which he will feel comfortable.

THE *LAUREN BACALL* BOX

Penny Arcade Portrait of Lauren Bacall (illus. 83) is constructed from wood, glass, metal, paper and paint. It is just over twenty inches in height. The front panel is comprised of circles, squares and rectangles, and shades of the colour blue. Regularly distributed over the face of the box are cut and pasted collage fragments (their edges softened by being behind a dark-blue tinted glass). An enlarged photograph of Bacall, peering out at us through a window-like rectangle, is the central feature. Smaller images, set into panels, surround her like an edging or border. Framing surrounds isolate and contain each image or set of images, and the various frames sit within the larger frame of the box construction itself. One is struck by the formality of this box, by its scheme of things. It is beautifully ordered: Cornell has contained the images, tied them together in compartmental panels. At the bottom of the box is a back-mirrored transverse corridor, into which a metal chute reaches down. A wooden ball lies at rest there. This is a box that looks like an early slot-machine game.

The mood of this box is difficult to define. It is not glossy, as we might have expected, given that this is about Lauren Bacall and slot machines, but it is sophisticated. It manages an air of sophistication without ostentation. Though dealing with human appearances and concerns, the box is somehow detached. We respond to the geometry rather than the human content (perhaps because of the fact that the central face is fractioned off). The atmosphere is subdued, it suggests mystery. The faces are always obfuscated, either by dissecting lines or the heavily tinted glass. It is night-time in this piece. Night hides and conceals.

A strong feature of this box is its planar subtlety: Cornell worked here with different depths and planes. The central face is behind two frames and a three-dimensional grid of blue glass. The images in the side panels are close to the surface; in the top panel they are spliced in half (half of the image is just under the glass, the other half is lining the back wall of the small compartment); the images at the bottom seem to hover in no fixed position. A row of circular peep-holes disappear into black depths, and elsewhere a mirror works to throw images forwards, out beyond the box to the spectator (who is thus left looking at his or her own features) – the backdrop has fallen away completely here. The intricate geometric and measured construction of the box has set against it the pleasure principle. The box is a game.

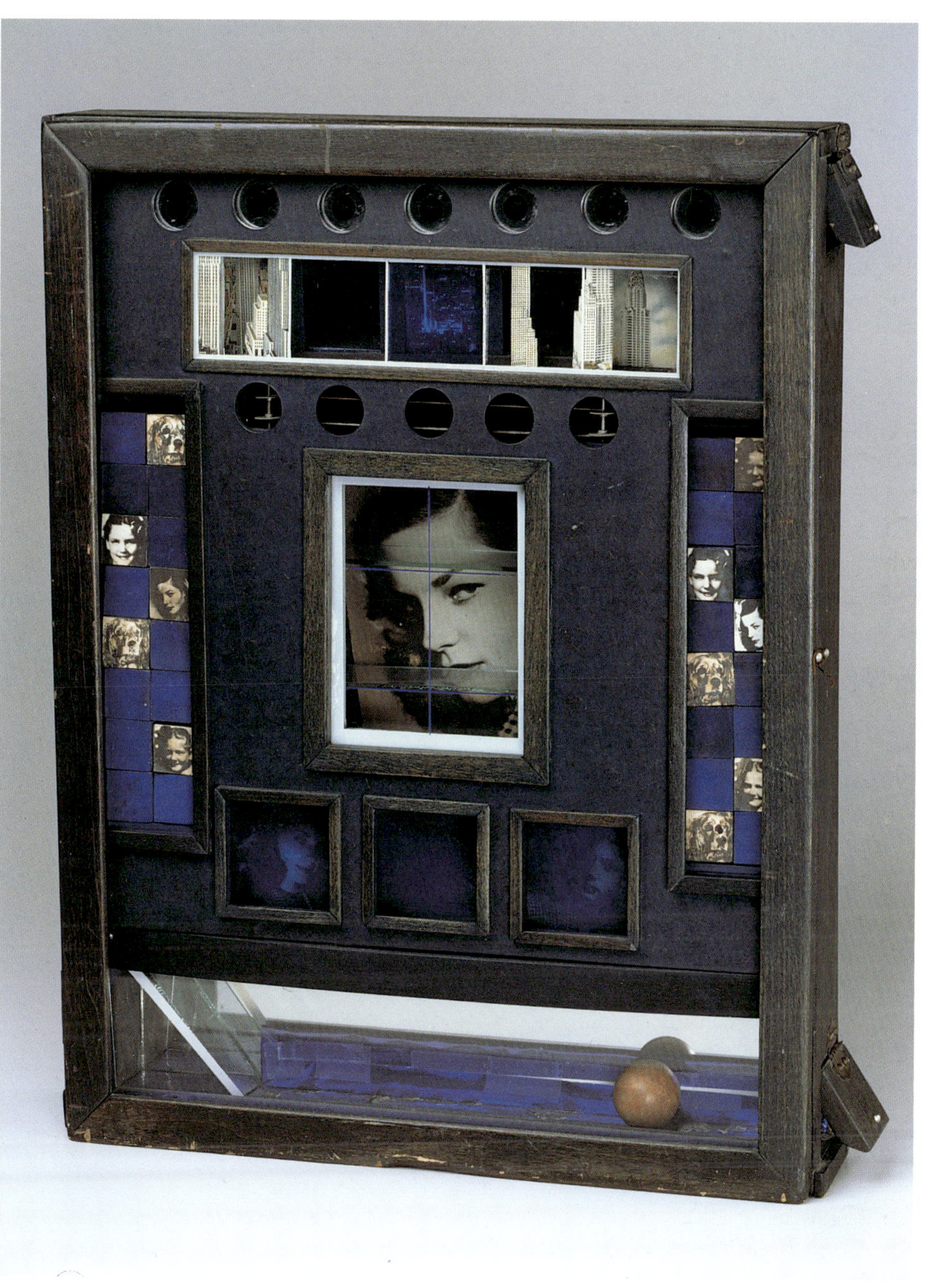

83 *Untitled (Penny Arcade Portrait of Lauren Bacall)*, 1945–6, mixed-media construction.

In the 'Penny Arcade Portrait' dossier Cornell records that he planned to build 'a cabinet – the contraption kind of the amusement resorts with endless ingenuity of effect'. He envisaged the 'peep-show' box as a model: 'A machine reminiscent of the early "peep show" boxes (the first ones, Edison kinetoscopes, were installed in penny arcades)'. He also makes reference to other machines, those 'worked with a coin by plungers': 'this one is controlled (put into motion) by a set of coloured balls that roll on a series of runways down to the receiving tray. Chambers controlled by a set of plungers on side as stops of an organ control the pipes or notes of an organ.'

Cornell's excited fascination for early arcade machinery, which clearly emerges in his writing, almost carries him away with listings and discussions about devices. He dreams of

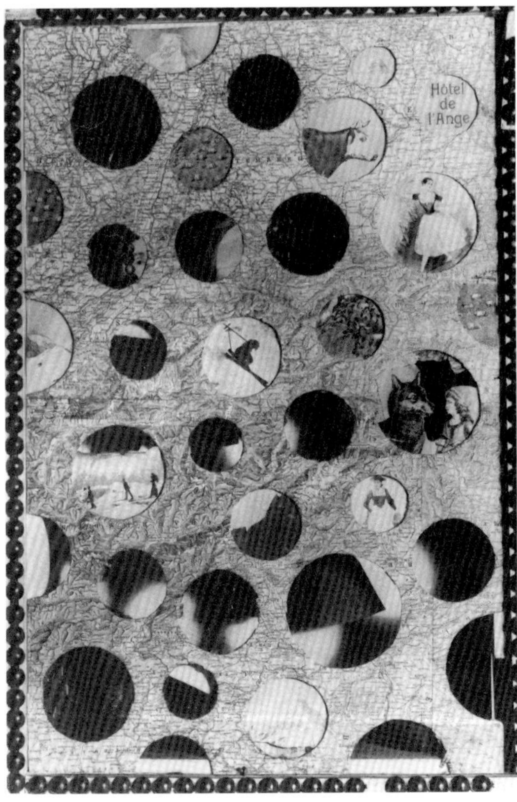

84 *Swiss Shoot-the-Chutes*, 1944, construction.

'miniature steam shovels digging into a pile of candy and prize(s)', of 'musical effects', and of a 'kind of glorified JUKE box'. 'The charm and ingenuity', he notes, 'of old time automata may be added'. However, not all Cornell's ambitions were realized. Perhaps it was at the stage of assemblage that he found it necessary to edit out and discard certain themes and device ideas in order to maintain the 'modern art', the 'simplicity effects from former boxes' that he also desired for the *Lauren Bacall* box, which was to be based on two former boxes from Cornell's repertory – two of an arcade machine format, *Medici Slot Machine* (the first was produced in 1942, but a series of them followed), and *Swiss Shoot-the-Chutes* (1941, with later variants: illus. 84). Cornell took the layout from the *Medici Slot Machine* and the movement mechanism from *Swiss Shoot-the-Chutes*. His dossier records that

> Later, a photo of Bacall in MADEMOISELLE (candid camera) presented a more natural side of her and aroused further interest. Then some unexpectedly fresh (Kodak) pictures of her childhood amongst the posed publicity ones brought the desire to do her portrait along the lines of A Medici Slot Machine. With the added effects of movement of Swiss Shoot-the-Chutes box, runways for a ball to roll throughout, plungers, mechanism, etc. 'as though it worked'. And so a box, a game, a portrait or a machine that belongs in a penny arcade.

In that same set of dossier notes (dated 19 August 1945) Cornell also mentions 'souvenirs in receiving tray, tickets from parrot (stamps)', and in a later dossier note ('General Working Notes', 1946) 'connotation of street vendors of former times white cockatoos, parrots, picking out fortunes on cards from a drawer beneath its cage on a hurdygurdy'.

These two references seem to be the seeds of an idea for another box. The mention of a hurdy-gurdy and street vendors indicates that his thoughts had begun to work along the lines of street entertainment. At an early planning stage for the *Lauren Bacall* box, Cornell must have intended to include something of 'souvenirs' or 'fortunes' in the bottom receiving tray, which, in the final event, was to consist of nothing more than a chute, a ball and a mirror. In the course of manipulating the material for *Lauren Bacall* – putting in the parts first one way, then another, then changing the arrangement again

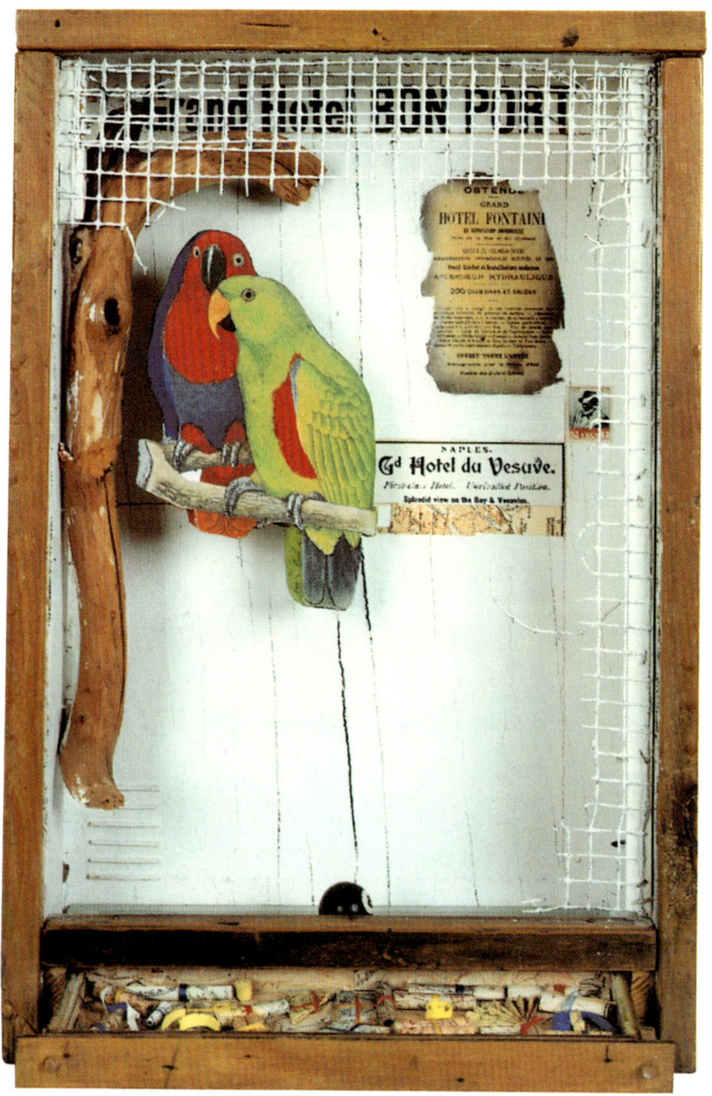

85 *The Caliph of Bagdad*, *c.* 1954, box construction.

to see how that suited – he must have decided on a simple uncluttered appearance. But it is interesting that the germ of an idea should occur in the 'Lauren Bacall' dossier and yet not be physically realized until the *Caliph of Bagdad* (illus. 85), constructed more than ten years later.

In the course of preparing his *Lauren Bacall* box, Cornell discovered something further to celebrate: 'this can be a homage to cinema as much as a personal portrait'. In the dossier, notes concerning the connection with cinema are commonplace: 'blue glass like night blue of early silent movies'; 'compartments become individual silver screens'; 'work out "strips" of film as though they are stored in the back of machine for operation'. It is true that a quality of shimmering luminosity imparted by the heavily tinted blue glass is given to the black-and-white image of Bacall. She appears here (especially in the bottom three compartments) just as she does in the strange, flitting luminous images of the silver screen. The top three images of Manhattan appear as strings of frames within a film strip (and within the images of Manhattan, the buildings themselves also resemble strips of film). Whether intentional or otherwise, other physical elements seem to make reference to the world of the cinema. For example, the staggered display of faces either side of the main portrait are reminiscent of billboard photographs – the stills found outside and within cinema foyers to announce current and forthcoming attractions. (It was, we recall, in just such a context that Cornell first saw Bacall and became captivated by her.) There is, too, the sizings of the images: they are properly cinematic, with tender close-ups, more distant shots, and miniature figurations; in one piece of 'continuity' we see the same face from different angles, and the course of events that might change or age a face.

In the late 1890s, moving pictures and penny arcade machines were one and the same thing. Cinema began in the nickelodeon hall, and was, initially, simply a primitive fairground-style entertainment: comedies and melodrama were the favourite subjects of the slot machine motion picture. Cornell's own family was absorbed from the outset by the novelty of cinema and the developments it rapidly made. Between 1906 and 1910 his mother had written film scenarios for both her own and her family's amusement, and in 1914, when Cornell was aged eleven, he and his sister began regular visits to the local Bayside movie house. Lillian Gish 'meant so much to him', Betty recalls. 'We used to go to the movies on Saturday afternoons and we would see *Broken Blossoms* and these different movies with the Gish sisters and it was magic.'[194] In later years Cornell took Robert with him. Both turned into fanatical film buffs, prizing even the flimsiest scraps of information, for example the fact that Bayside, in the 1920s, had on one occasion served as the location for a shoot by a film outfit from New Jersey, or that the famous Talmadge sisters lived only a few blocks away from the Cornell family house there. In time Cornell established personal connections with a number of successful movie stars. He introduced the family to Tony Curtis, who afterwards became a firm friend of both Cornell and Robert.

Cornell's interest in moving pictures was such that eventually he began, if rather tentatively, to make his own films. In 1933 he wrote a scenario, *Monsieur Phot*, comprising four detailed scenes, an epilogue and five stereopticon images, which was published in 1936 in Julien Levy's catalogue *Surrealism*. And in December of this latter year, his first film, *Rose Hobart*, was screened at the Julian Levy Gallery. (Cornell was a regular participant at the New York Film Society meetings over which Levy presided.) In conjunction with other film-makers, Cornell made approximately 14 or 15 films (several of which are variants). He directed, while Stan Brackhage, Rudy Burckhardt and Larry Jordan undertook the photography. Most of them were made in the mid-1950s, but Cornell was still working in the medium as late as 1965.

At the time of *Rose Hobart*, his first attempt, Cornell was in fact employed at Universal & Columbia Film Studios. His contribution was 'hack montage', as he explained in a letter to an actress friend when he was preparing an advertising campaign for *Diamond Jim*.[195] None the less, during the short time he spent there he learned much about the subtlety, sophistication and versatility of the language of montage, a form of art in which he was already accomplished. For example, the two side panels of the *Lauren Bacall* box (a 'symphony of mechanical style' borrowed from 'the motion picture art'), include a visual pun by means of montage: the face of the adult Bacall, and those of the child and dog, are pasted onto toy building-blocks, and all three become interchangeable. Perhaps this effect succeeds through the tiny proportions of the portraits, through cropping the images tightly around the faces and excluding the necks, and through the sharply contrasted black-and-white tones that depict each face but merge into an even patterning. The top panel of the same box also displays his expert montage work, where the suggestion of streets narrowing into the distance is apparent. Depth is incised by a series of images pasted on flat planes marked off and separated from one another by an 'illusion'. As image trickery it seems all the more suitable in this context, reminding us of the stereopticon image and the wonders of early photography.

BACALL'S PORTRAIT

The central portrait image of the *Lauren Bacall* box is a three-quarters view of the actress's face, masked by a blue-edged glass grid. Our attention is directed to her face simply because it is the largest image, it is placed at the centre, and it has a mount and wood picture frame enclosing it. And yet there are those clear criss-cross markings that obscure it. Bacall's image is repeated ten times in this box: five times as an adult and five as a child. One large reproduction and two small ones are heavily obfuscated by dark-blue ink staining, and seven minute images are pasted onto blocks in the side panels. The slight erasure of the central image pushes us to focus on the shifting images that border the Hollywood face – shifting facets of a personality yet to be revealed.

The portrait tells a story. Even without the information available in the dossier that makes it clear Cornell set out to tell Bacall's life story, the box's narrative element would be unmistakeable. The images of Bacall as a child and those of the dog are probably the Kodak pictures Cornell found (19 August 1945) during his initial research phase. The two images second from the top in the side panels are copies of the 'photo in Mademoiselle magazine showing her [in a] healthy and unartificial light'. The collaged images of Manhattan high-rise buildings relate to the biographical detail Cornell discovered concerning Bacall's early career as a New York fashion model. The large central portrait and the two smaller ones in the lower half of the box are the gratifying 'posed publicity' shots he acquired from Warner Brothers in the same year ('the usual pleasure in all the stills from Warner Brothers').

Cornell's plan was to give Bacall a second life, one composed of traces of her real life: isolated moments caught in photographic images from her past connect and come together in a biography dreamed up by the artist. With everything in place, the story of Lauren Bacall can be told by means of the workings of his machine: as the ball passes by the images set up around the box, a narration emerges and the pieces of her life coalesce.

Lauren Bacall is a portrait about which we have a good deal of information. It is quite unusual in a portrait to know why and how the subject was chosen, the method selected for creating the portrait, and the company it kept on the gallery walls when it was first exhibited. Many people would have known a lot about Lauren Bacall herself from the widely disseminated interviews and profiles published in magazines and newspapers and broadcast on the radio. Even more would have seen her on the silver screen. Even today, everyone has at least heard of Bacall and glimpsed her via photos and stills. This means that almost everyone would have some sort of notion or opinion of Bacall before confronting her in Cornell's box. First exhibited in 1946, the box appeared at a time when she was a rising Hollywood star who enjoyed a lot of media attention, her first successful film having appeared only two years earlier. Cornell, of course, was often inspired by film stars, but in the course of making his boxes he appears to have felt frustrated by high public profiles. In the 'Lauren Bacall' dossier he complains of the 'hysterical publicity' that surrounded Bacall, and when working on his Marilyn Monroe project he declined to 'despatch' his compositions until the media frenzy had died down: 'At all costs it must be kept at the fartherest remove from the inevitable "everybody wants to get in on the act"'.[196]

There is, inevitably, an inclination to consider Cornell's 'portraits' first and foremost as likenesses of his subjects. But when a 'portrait' is actually based on nothing more than a photograph, this tendency should be resisted. Likeness is not an issue here. As Giacometti insisted:

> It's impossible to paint a portrait. Ingres could do it. He could finish a portrait. It was a substitute for a photograph and had to be done by hand because there was no other way of doing it then. But now that has no meaning. The

> photograph exists and that's all there is to it. It's the same with novels, because of the newspapers. A novel like one of Zola's would be absurd today because any daily newspaper is infinitely more alive.[197]

There is no room, Giacometti points out, for Cornell to produce a conventional portrait. We need to look at a range of Cornell's portraits in order to discover his very individual approach to the tradition of portraiture.

Cornell worked exclusively with secondhand material, not from raw material. That is, he made portraits of people who were not present before him – he worked from an image in isolation in his studio. Often he took portraits made by other artists and rehoused them in his own box constructions. He took a boy from Caravaggio, Gilles from Watteau, and various figures from the *Caprichos* of Goya. He cut out a reproduction that pleased him and pasted it in as part of his version of the portrait. Borrowing and remodelling images snatched from Old Masters is one good source for faces; another is illustrated books, for Cornell often resorted to 'portraits' of fictional characters commissioned by publishers from professional illustrators. Thus (from at least third-hand) he gained a 'likeness' of the Robinson Crusoe of Defoe's eponymous novel, and those of the heroes of Dumas's *The Three Musketeers*. He also made use of photographic portraits by Duane Michals and Man Ray and the prints of Hollywood stars that poured forth from commercial photographers. In addition, on occasion he turned to lithographs (for example by Marie Taglioni), to chromolithographs (by Blondon) and to engravings (of Paul and Virginie) and photostats (of Henrietta Sontag).

Thus Cornell seized on portraits of individuals and of types, of real individuals and of fictional characters, while his figures were extracted from high art and from popular culture in equal numbers. His *subjects*, of course, have little in common in themselves, for what links them is only the nature of Cornell's relationship with them, that is, he relates to them in obsessive ways, though from a physical distance. There is not the one-to-one confrontation that invariably occurs between an artist and his sitter when together in a studio. The two-way act of painting (or photographing) and posing is absent. Cornell had to invent – to create – that dynamism within himself, in the process turning what he saw before him (a flat, passive image) into the emerging shapes and ideas of his imagination. His relationship with the world was essentially voyeuristic: he viewed the world from behind windows, from moving vehicles, through curtains – always at one step back from its brute physical presence. He collected images in order to collect the world. It was his substitute for direct experience. And the talismanic use of photographs meant for him the means of acquiring pseudo-presences. These presences were his incitements to reverie. Other artists have warned of the risks taken when dealing directly with models. Delacroix, for one, reckoned that

> T— very rightly says that the model drags the artist who works from him down to his own level; a stupid fellow makes you feel a fool. An artist of imagination strives to raise the model to the ideal of his conception but, in spite of himself, he is drawn towards the vulgarity that besets him on every side, and which he sees in front of his eyes.[198]

In the 1960s Giacometti painted a portrait of a Japanese professor named Yanaihara, who had sat for a number of his paintings and sculptures:

> I came to accept him as the norm because I was with him so much. We are always together in the studio, at the café, at the Dome and the Coupole, in night clubs. We were together so much that one day I had a curious experience because of it. Yanaihara was posing for me and suddenly Genet came into the studio. I thought he looked very strange, with such a round, very rosy face and puffed lips. But I didn't say anything about it. Then Diego came into the studio. And I had the same feeling. His face looked very rosy too, and round, and his lips looked very puffy. I couldn't understand why. Then suddenly I realised that I was seeing Diego and Genet as they must have looked to Yanaihara. I had concentrated so long and hard on Yanaihara's face that it had become the norm for me and during a brief moment – it was an impression that lasted for only a very little while – I could see white people the way they must look to people who aren't white.[199]

The identification of the artist with the model is part of the process. But this intense connection with a subject separate from himself is something Cornell was never to experience.

Whatever the differences in treatment in Cornell's portraits, in each one he attempted an 'unauthorized biography'. He used this very term when commenting on his *Portrait of Ondine*, but if we look at some of his other works we can see that applies equally well there too. In the case of Suzi Wong, for example, a bottle labelled 'Nuyenand Co.' that contains references to boats and the sea (rope, driftwood, sand, shells), as well as her photographic image, tells of Suzi's origins (she is a French Chinese from over the sea discovered at the age of nineteen when on a visit to the States), of her family background (her father was a sailor), and, finally, the object–portrait spells out her real name (Nuyen). In another portrait, a box-portrait of Marie de' Medici, Cornell included references to his subject's childhood (jacks, wooden building blocks, a red ball, a marble, coloured stuck-on stars), to her rank as a princess (lands and territory denoted by cut-out cross-sections of maps) and to her association with a young man (the reproduction of the *Medici Boy* by Pintoricchio).

In all these portraits Cornell constructed a life structure, a biography, around a central portrait image. As a format for portraiture, this one is very familiar. In the early days of the genre this was perhaps the most usual way to indicate the character and status of the sitter. In the works of the younger Holbein, for example, the individual we see in the portrait *George Gisze*, or the pair we examine in *The Ambassadors*, are surrounded by goods and chattels, symbols of their lives and careers. In Van Eyck's *The Arnolfini Wedding* we encounter both narrative and portraits, as we do in the *Penny Arcade Portrait of Lauren Bacall*. The Arnolfini narrative is organized around their wedding-day, though there are indications too of the time before and the time to come, while *Lauren Bacall* is a display of pictures and other items that stand for various moments in the actress's life. And just as Van Eyck sought to say something of the state of marriage in general, so Cornell is concerned with more than just the actress herself. He encodes the past of any young, blossoming film star, or indeed any young girl who has been transported from a routine existence into a world of wealth and glamour.

Both Van Eyck and Holbein express character through the inclusion of accessories, and this is also the method Cornell relied on. But his highly idiosyncratic interpretation of this and other subjects can only be richly appreciated by

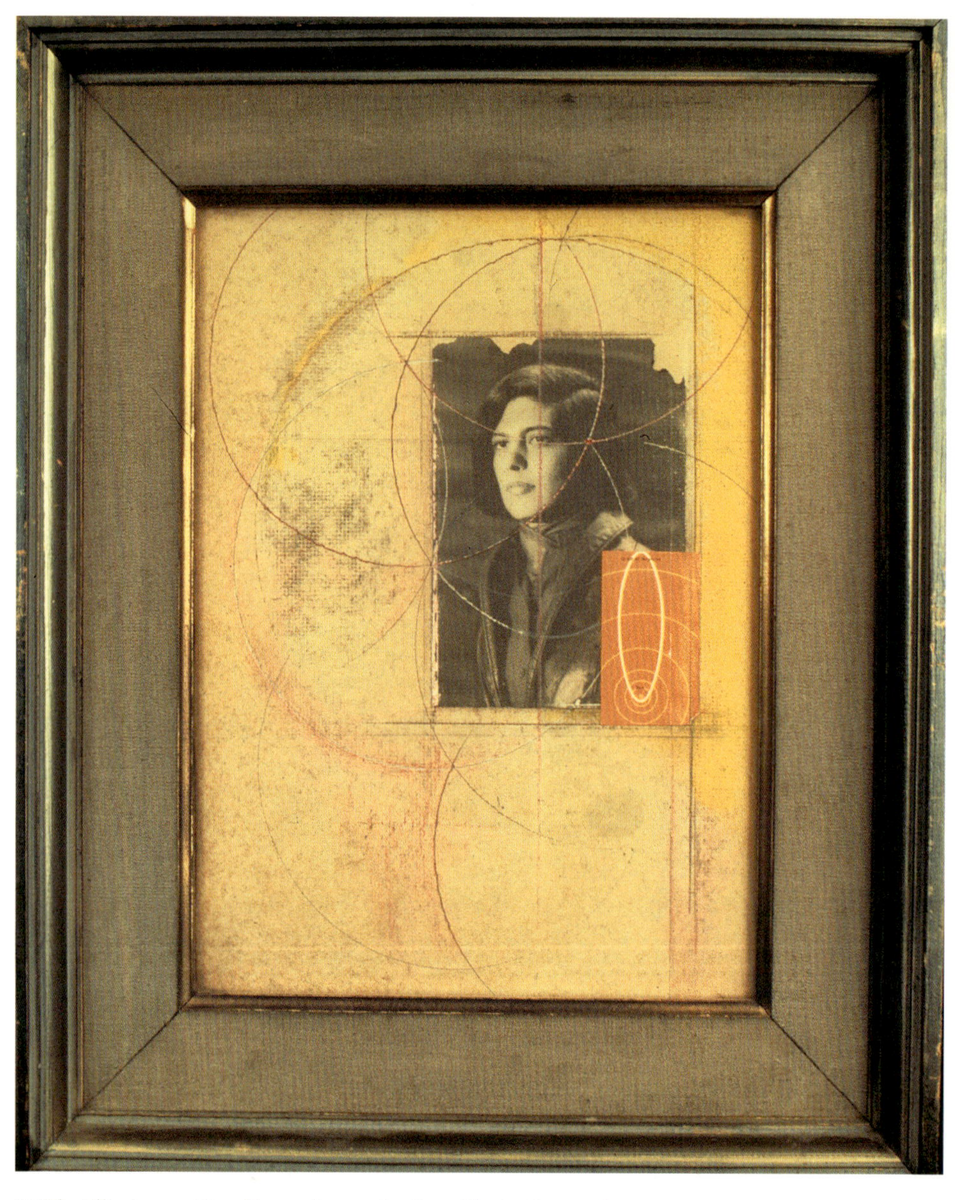

86 *The Ellipsian*, 1966, collage of reproduction, illustration and paper, with pencil, crayon and stain.

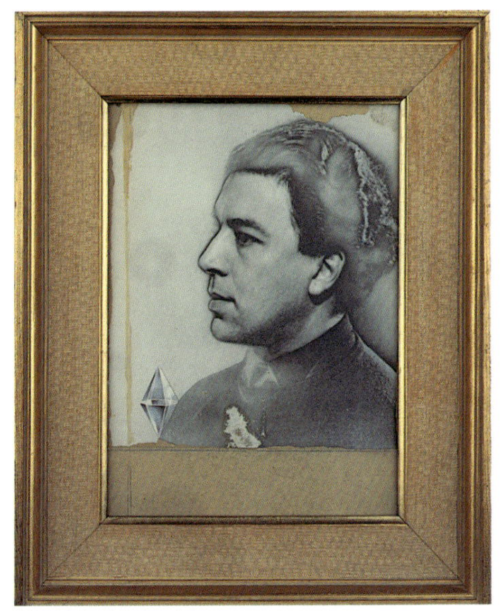

87 *Le Tournesol de Minuit*, c. 1966, collage.

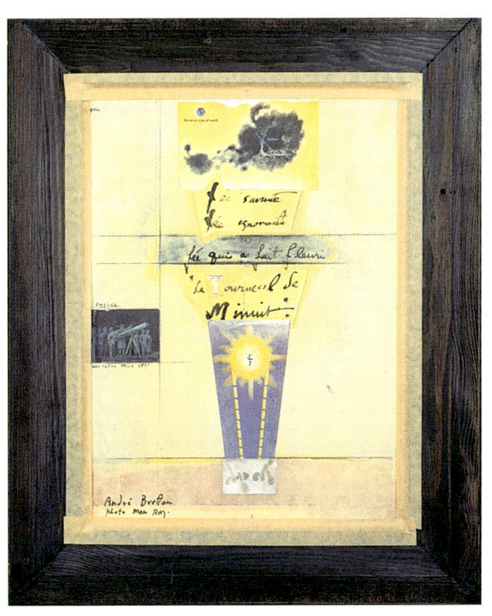

88 *Untitled*, c. 1966, collage, verso of illus. 87.

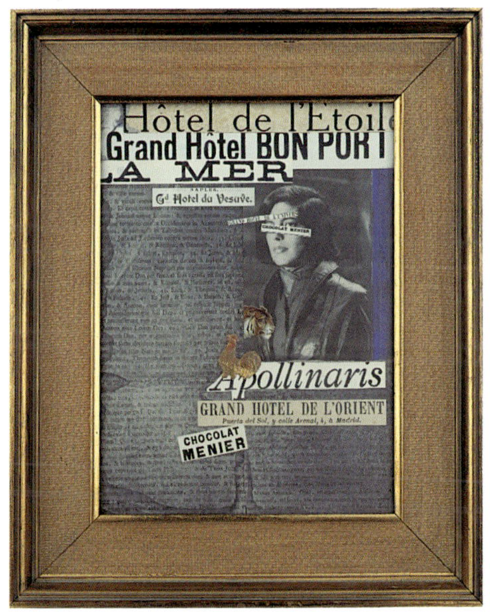

89 *Untitled (Hôtel de l'Etoile, Grand Hôtel Bon Port, Apollinaris)*, c. 1966, collage.

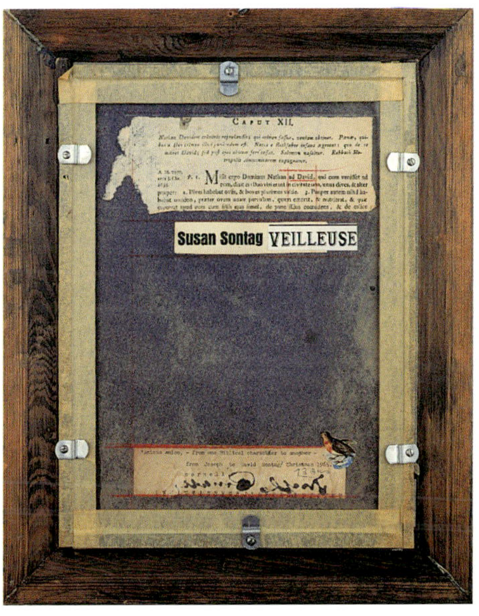

90 *Untitled (Susan Sontag, Veilleuse)*, c. 1966, collage, verso of illus. 89.

examining the relevant dossiers, and, as we might have guessed, his portrait box of Bacall tells us far more about the artist than it can the woman he set out to portray.

SUSAN SONTAG

Cornell's portrait of Susan Sontag is a useful point of comparison with the *Penny Arcade Portrait of Lauren Bacall*, for Sontag, though also well-known and admired, was from a quite different world. Sontag's portrait takes the form of the collage *The Ellipsian*, which has at least three variants (illus. 86). Unlike the source material connected with *Lauren Bacall*, which is mainly to be found in Cornell's dossiers, my background information for this particular work is gleaned from Sontag herself.[200]

Cornell's initial interest in Sontag was aroused by her book review of Maurice Nadeau's *History Of Surrealism* of 1965, which appeared in the *New York Herald Tribune Book World*. He began writing to her, and then phoning that same year, by the end of which he had arranged a meeting at his home at Utopia Parkway. They met only on this one occasion. Cornell certainly associated her with Surrealism: his correspondence with Sontag makes numerous references to members of the movement, particularly André Breton: 'I dreamt that Nadja was an anagram of Don Juan, only to find it wasn't'.[201] Among the three works of art Cornell gave to Sontag is the collage *André Breton* (1966), a portrait based on a photo by Man Ray.

According to Sontag, Cornell 'presumed an interest in Breton and we talked about Breton and how important he was. I had a phrase which I used in something I wrote him about how Breton was a liberating personality.' The more that the link is explored between Cornell and the Surrealists, the clearer becomes the connection – the fact that there could have been agreement here on the way in which Breton is a liberating influence shows that Cornell's debt to Surrealism was as much psychological as aesthetic. *The Ellipsian* makes direct connections with Sontag's first novel, *The Benefactor* (1963). The image of Sontag featured in the collage comes from the photograph on the jacket cover of this book taken when she was 30 years old. Her face is traced over with circles and ellipses, and in the lower right-hand corner – and over the photo of her – Cornell pasted a diagram of the 'Orbit of

Neptune', which includes the planet's relation to the sun. The elongated oval shape of the diagram replaces Sontag's arm: the diagram marks out the shoulder to elbow area.

The name of the main character in *The Benefactor* is Hippolyte, whom the author herself describes as 'an extremely eccentric recluse' who could only have 'imaginary relations with women'. Sontag, unwittingly, invented a character Cornell could recognize as himself. His identification with this fictional character is obvious, as Sontag explains:

> I was a woman in my late twenties, writing in the first-person voice. The autobiography is of an imaginary person in his early sixties who is French, and the book is clearly set in France. I have always been fascinated by the figure of the recluse, and in my own shy way of beginning as a writer, and desperately wanting to avoid anything that was even remotely autobiographical, I invented this character, Hippolyte. He's extremely eccentric and has only the most imaginary relations with women. I invented this character who is a figure of my fantasy and has nothing to do either with my life or anyone I've ever known. And then, a kind of Hippolyte came out of the shadows.

The character of Hippolyte, who has imaginary relations with women, drew Cornell to Sontag. There was, however, some actual basis to the relationship, unlike, for example, in the case of Bacall. They had the one meeting, they exchanged telephone calls, and there was correspondence, though primarily one-sided – from Cornell to Sontag. Sontag has also speculated on the aspects of the situation that drew Cornell to her:

> I wrote this novel and invented this character that he could identify with. I was a glamorous woman as far as he could tell from the photograph, and then after the novel I began to write articles and essays very largely about European, and particularly French, themes.

In this connection Sontag mentions that during their meeting, Cornell played Jacques Brel records because he knew that she had lived in France and spoke French, but when she had asked him about his knowledge of the language his reply was that he didn't understand anything of French. Sontag found this astonishing considering his apparent immersion in the mythology and culture of France, but concluded that it was all a kind of poetry to him. This is quite consistent with Cornell's creative process, in which it is the glimpse, the associations, the eclecticism that leads to the moment of inspiration, and so it was his travels to the Europe of his imagination that kept the magic in.

Sontag was also able to relate the theme of her novel to Cornell's interests:

> The theme of the novel is the theme of dreams. It starts with a parody of Descartes. Instead of 'I think therefore I am', it is 'I dream therefore I am'. The narrative spine of the novel consists of a series of dreams which Hippolyte recounts. He then recounts these preposterous interpretations that he makes out of his dreams which leads him to behave in such and such a way following the dictates of his dreams.

Another connection, this time German, that Cornell applied to Sontag was that of Henrietta Sontag, a soprano, one of two or three great divas of the nineteenth century:

> She spelt her name with one 'n', which is unusual because it is a German name obviously, and it's spelt with two 'n's. Indeed, my father says 'Of course we're related to Henrietta Sontag'. But I'm sure we're not. Cornell quickly made that association, and so anything to do with Henrietta Sontag became another way of referring to me.

(Apparently, this famous diva was christened Henriette Gertrud Walpurgis Sonntag.) So Susan Sontag began to receive letters from Cornell addressed to 'Henrietta Sontag'. He would not have missed the visual parallels: both women have large dark eyes with strong dark eyebrows. The resemblances can be clearly seen in the collages executed in the same year, 1966: *The Ellipsian* (illus. 86) and *The Uncertainty Principle* (illus. 91), the latter being a double portrait of the great diva. Both collages have similar markings – circles and tracings – which make reference to principles and mathematical laws.

Another more minor association Cornell made with Sontag was with Emily Dickinson. He connected the S's in her name with 'Sweet Sister Sylph', the term of endearment Dickinson used for her sister-in-law, Susan Gilbert. Cornell gave Sontag the unfinished work titled *Chocolat Meunier* because Dickinson wrote one of her poems on a *Chocolat Meunier* wrapper.

As with Lauren Bacall, Cornell created for Sontag an alternative biography. She, however, was in a different situation to most of the other women who were the subjects of Cornell's infatuations. As a writer and an intellectual, Sontag had a very high regard for Cornell's art, and to some extent she could intellectualize the relationship he sought with her. But even she was taken aback by the strangeness of it all.

Initially Cornell sometimes communicated with her through her son, David, who was thirteen at the time. Cornell would write 'Amicus, Amico – from one Biblical character to another', and he would address letters to David, and sometimes drawings by the artist's brother Robert, when they were clearly meant for Sontag herself. She had received mail from all sorts of strange people over the years, and presumed that Cornell was one of these. 'I was getting letters from a lunatic, and this lunatic happened to be a great artist.' Of her relationship with him, she confesses to having felt 'very moved and disconcerted to play this role, but I felt shy. It seemed to be

91 *The Uncertainty Principle*, 1966, collage.

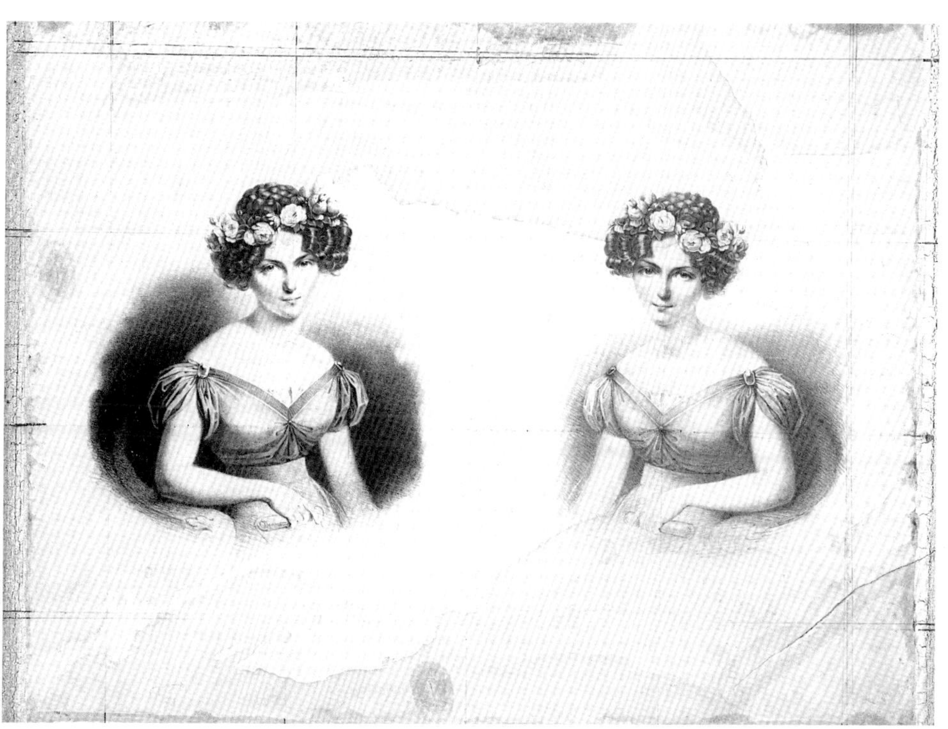

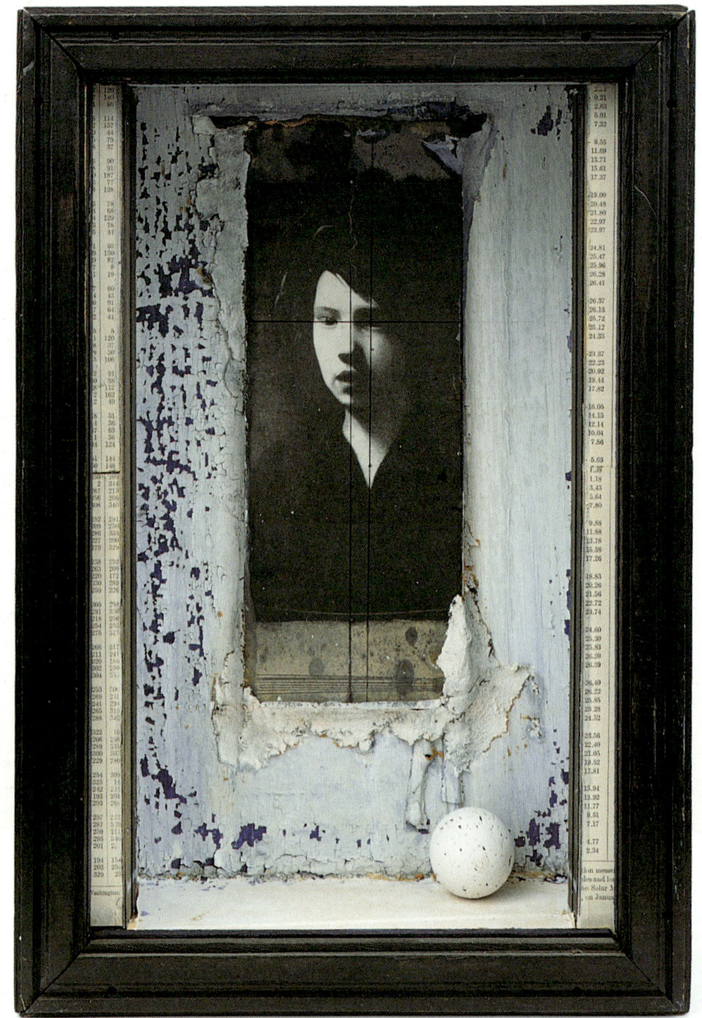

92 *Portrait*, c. 1955, box construction.

This portrait possesses qualities Cornell particularly admired – a face that is both haunting and mysterious, that is shadowy, dark, solemn and androgynous. 'The Caravaggio Boy' and Susan Sontag share this look.

something that was going on in his own imagination and I didn't want to interfere with that'. Indeed, 'although I was in my early thirties, I think I was very girlish at that time. I think had I been a litle older I might have thought this is his way of communicating with people. I would have seen it less as the gesture of an artist, a very eccentric artist, and more of the gesture of a human being reaching out for contact.'

LEILA HADLEY: LIKE MINDS

A very different kind of portrait emerges from the relationship that Cornell had with Leila Hadley. Whereas the relationship with Bacall was conducted within Cornell's own imagination, and the relationship with Sontag *almost* wholly so, his relationship with Hadley was a direct and very personal one. It began in 1964, when, in the course of a visit to Jean De Menil's home, she encountered a work of art by Cornell (an *Apothecary* box) for the first time: 'I wanted to just take it and put it into a shopping bag and run away with it and just be alone with it, like a lover'.[202] She wrote to Cornell, telephoned him, sent him some little African trading beads . . . and then he telephoned her. (He 'liked that long distance conversation', for on the phone 'you can talk stream of consciousness, we always talked that way. He'd say a word, and then I'd say a word, and then we'd just be off in making associations . . . it was like a universal unconscious that you could plug into with Joseph.') Their first face-to-face meeting took place that same year at Utopia Parkway. Brian O'Doherty advised her to go equipped with cookies and pastries, and Hadley continued to take gifts of this kind on subsequent visits: 'cadeau de fée', wrote Cornell, 'huge marzipan box (too generous) arriving 11:10'.[203]

Hadley's intuitive initial response to Cornell's work was indicative of a shared sensibility. She herself certainly felt this. They became firm friends, and he met her daughters, Caroline and Victoria. Cornell and Hadley both had a deep appreciation for the world of nature, even as it existed in the city – pigeons in the park, dead leaves piling up. Hadley's mother was a Christian Scientist, and this background gave Hadley herself an insight into Cornell's grasp on life. They both set great store by symbols of all sorts, and sympathized with the view that creativity and sexuality were closely allied. And they loved word-games:

> We joked about Victoria who said 'I'd like to be the sea, the jungle or else a cloud, so then of course we called her Elsa Cloud. And then we made a joke about Elsa Cloud, Elsa Nouage and then Elsa New Age. And that was the way it was with Joseph. It was just words, playing on words, you

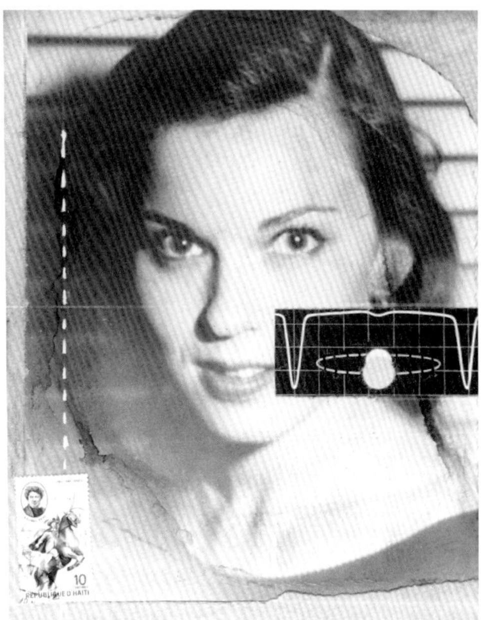

93 *Untitled (Leila Hadley with Haiti stamp)*, c. 1960s, collage.

could understand what he was thinking, and then he would come forth with an anecdote, or you could ask anything and then he would do his associations, or a remembrance. When he was with you he would be involved with you, so there was a partial merging. He would merge with you and you would merge with him.

They were both avid readers, sharing their books and also their reveries, particularly those involving fantastical travels: 'We used to make up places we would go, great fantasy palaces, hotels we'd stay, all sorts of wild places. He didn't like to travel really. Joseph just travelled in the imagination – the mind's time is so much faster . . . he, like the shamans, could make journeys in the mind.'

Cornell also began to correspond with Hadley's two daughters, and to attend their birthday parties, sitting cross-legged on the floor or running the funny films by Chaplin and others that he had brought. He particularly appreciated the automated bird in a cage he encountered there, a souvenir from Switzerland that Hadley would produce as part of the birthday ritual. 'He loved being around children', she recalls. 'He always wanted to have photographs of people as children – I know, I sent him about a dozen of myself as a child. I think he much preferred the child selves of people, the curious and fresh and honest and open.'

Henry Geldzahler and Betsy von Furstenburg were both taken to Utopia Parkway by Hadley to meet Cornell. Geldzahler gave the artist a small multiple of Warhol's flowers, and spoke about art in a convoluted and didactic manner, 'nothing from the heart'. Cornell was visibly discomfited by academic 'art' discussions, for he 'just responded to feelings, he didn't respond to intellect like that. Joseph loved nature and birds or trees and flowers or stars and French. It wasn't an academic appreciation, it was just a feeling, like dancing, like a whole other world.' The visit made by the actress Betsy von Furstenburg was a success, however, and Cornell became friendly both with her and her young daughter, Gay-gay. Cornell prized a photo he obtained of Gay-gay ('she shows so marvellously in it. I am so proud to have this picture'[204]). Betsy and her friend Leila Hadley were 'the

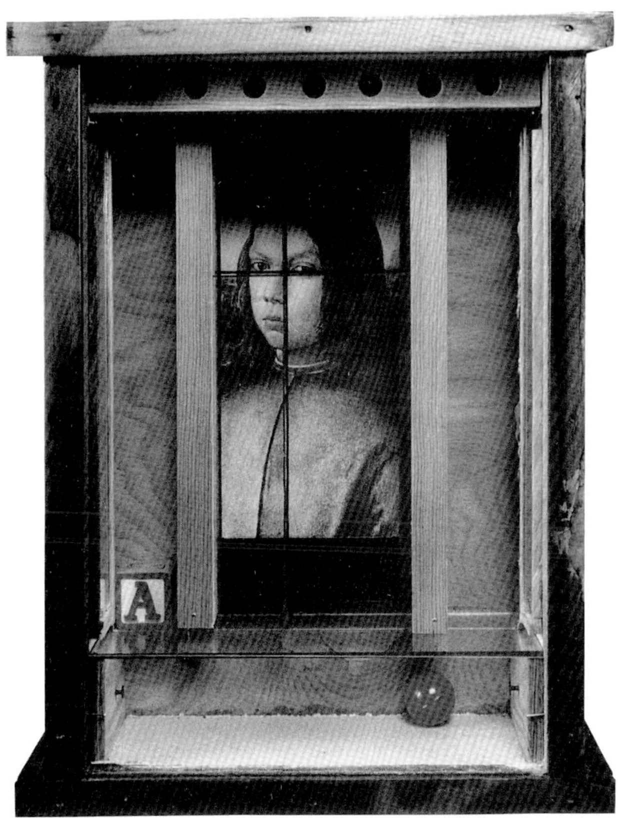

94 *Untitled*, c. 1964, mixed-media construction.

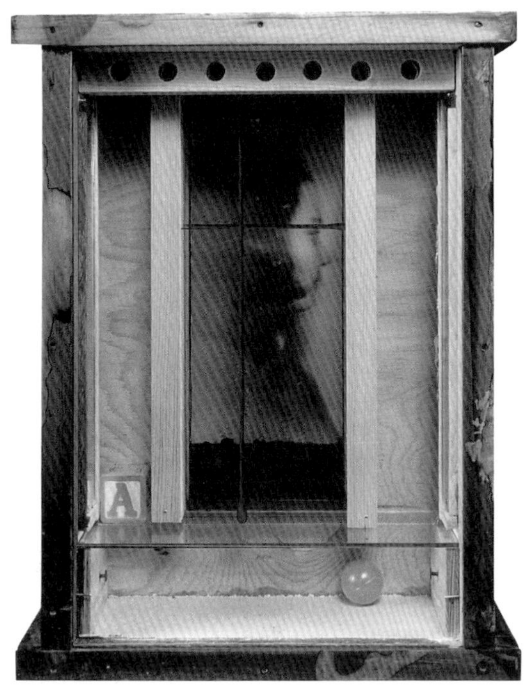

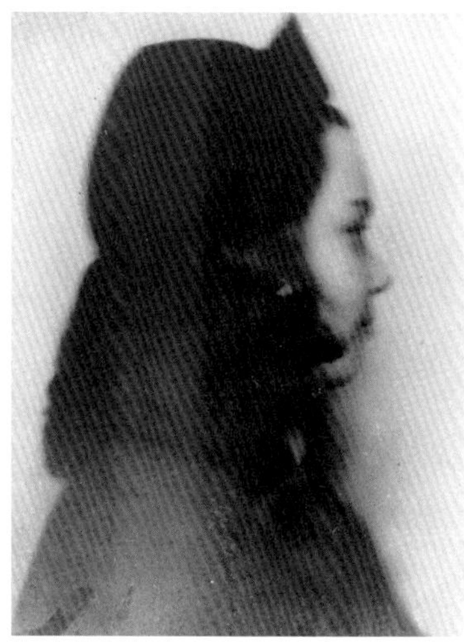

96 The automat photo of Leila Hadley seen in illus. 95.

95 *Untitled*, *c*. 1964, construction.

peach' and 'the plum', as Cornell liked to call them. He sent them images of star constellations that included the Gemini twins, and pointed out that these were the two of them.

The box that features Hadley's side-view portrait is a Medici Machine, one of the later varieties. It is quite bare, and includes a simple wooden framing, circular peep-holes (at the top), a bottom panel containg a red plastic ball, a child's toy brick with a red letter *A* stamped on it in a side panel, and a central panel that features her portrait. The *A* may have its origin in Hawthorne's *The Scarlet Letter*, a novel Cornell knew well; if so, then *A* stands for *Adulterer*, possibly hinting at the relationship between the page-boy of the box and the Medici Princess of other Medici Machines. Blue ink sightlines are etched into the glass, slicing through the eyes and nose of the page. What is notable about this box, though, is the fact that the central portrait image of this page-boy (illus. 94) can be removed, allowing a second image to be slotted into place – the photo of a young girl (illus. 95). She also wears a hat, and has shoulder-bobbed hair. She is seen side-on. This girl is Leila Hadley aged twelve ('Girl in the Breton Hat . . . the profile! . . . one does not have to have recourse to a prototype

– it is imagined more graphically in the heart & chambers of imagery' Cornell wrote[205]).

When this photo was taken, Hadley had been out with her father, and they had stopped at a photomat machine (illus. 97). (Three photos, in fact, issued forth from this *ur*-machine, and Cornell was to use two of them in his works.) In the course of that same outing Hadley had been introduced to a well-known heavyweight boxer of the time, Jack Dempsey, who immediately responded to a request for his autograph but misheard her name and signed the card 'to Lillian'. This slip amused Cornell, who often referred her in his correspondence as 'Lillian', and he pasted the autographed card onto the back of one of his collages, the one featuring the *frontal* view of the twelve-year-old face from the photomat machine.

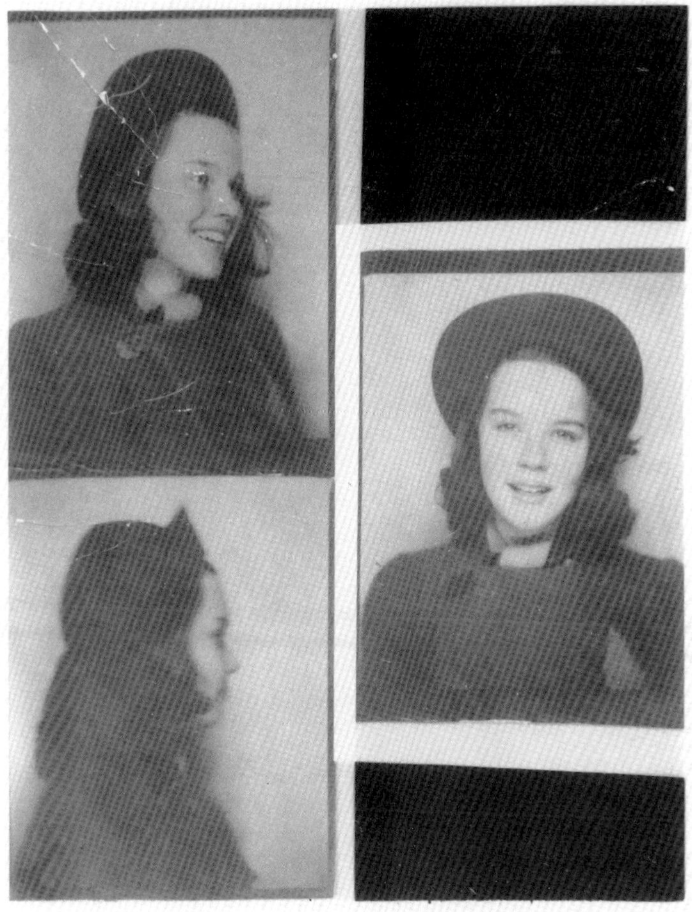

97 The three automat photos of Leila Hadley aged twelve.

These collages 'he would colour . . . with ink, or put a stamp on . . . or make little marks. They were extraordinary when he got finished.'

In these photos Hadley wears her 'Breton hat'. A month before he died in late December 1972 Cornell wrote 'but there's little Lillian in A Breton's chapeau. La premiere demoiselle surrealiste indigine? qui peut dire? Dire consequences? Work on it. After all, she discovered Hercule de Funambule!'[206] He was keenly interested to know the details of her clothes on particular days:

> If he knew what I was wearing then he knew how I was feeling, because he felt that, subconsciously or unconsciously, everything was an extension of oneself. So he loved it if I would wear blue stockings and be 'bas bleu'.

If we glimpse her in this box wearing her Breton hat it would be easy to mistake her for the page-boy from the Renaissance era. 'Faces seen but once', 'Faces from the past', Cornell had written in his guide to the exhibition 'Portraits of Women' of twenty years before. It remained an enduring passion with him, to find faces that reflected the past. He liked to bring to life the faces that haunted his studio cellar. And swopping the gender – the boy becoming a girl – is another recurring feature of his vision.

The profile image of Leila's face is worth dwelling on because it reveals much about Cornell's approach to portraiture. The angle of the face is revealing for what it does not reveal, for that which is left out. The angle of the head, the general shape of the profile takes precedence over the personality of the sitter. A portrait usually reveals something about the sitter. But Cornell goes out of his way to conceal or obscure the image we have of this sitter, thus making it difficult to penetrate into her character. Even the cheek, hair edging and hat all work to hide crucial features – eyes, nose, mouth. If we examine the *Penny Arcade Portrait of Lauren Bacall* and Cornell's dissection of the facial features there, and then the heavy blue-ink staining that lies over them, we can see that this is the pattern of procedure. A face glimpsed, rather than a face penetratingly searched into, is what the artist presents. Leila's face had reminded him of another face from the past – that of his own mother:

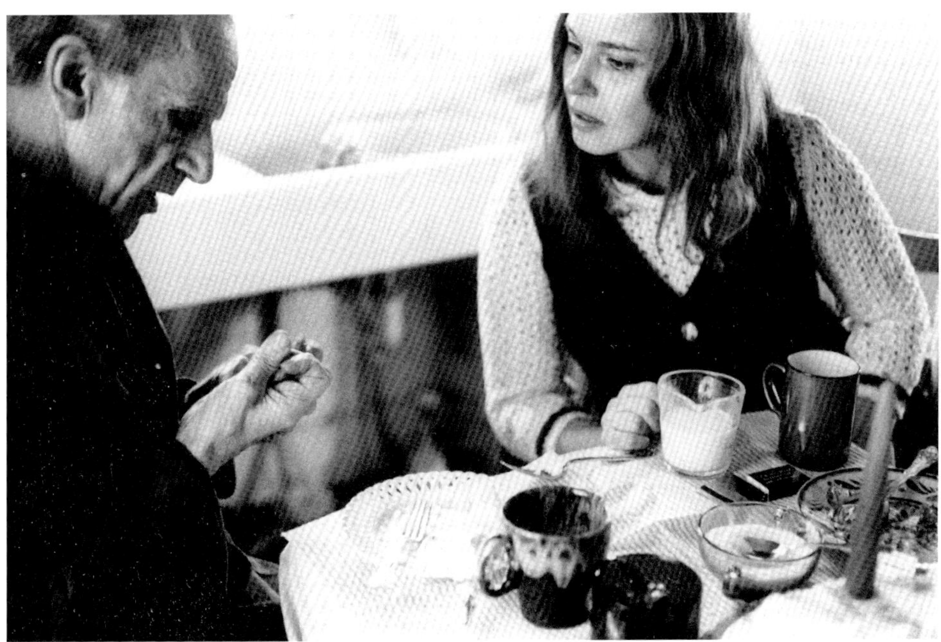

98 Cornell and Leila Hadley having tea at the kitchen table, Utopia Parkway, 1971.

> It wasn't really about me, it was just that somebody was like the key to a door to another private world of his, and I was lucky enough to be a key. I think it was because I looked like his mother . . . He felt so tremendously about his mother. And he gave me a photograph of his mother standing before the bureau and the mirror. I think he was searching for his mother after she died and I think there were pictures of me as a child that looked like his mother. You can see the resemblance. It's like knowing somebody in another incarnation. It's like having your mother as a child come back in someone else.

'It wasn't really about me . . . I was lucky enough to be a key.' This is the same understanding Sontag had of the situation, that really for Cornell the images of the two women were props that allowed him to recover a private world and make art. They are less portraits than they are revelations of his own obsessions and preoccupations. In Hadley's case, Cornell's own mother – the source of his beginning – comes into play. We know that he twisted and turned in every which way in the hope of finding out more about his own origins and earliest years. He took Hadley on a nostalgic trip to a restaurant he had visited as a child with his mother, the *Korn*

Kobbler in New York, perhaps in the hope of erasing the sludge from his memory and thus to recapture more of his past. Indeed, given that he had the right setting and stand-in, perhaps he hoped to get a glimpse of that same mother.

Although Hadley was only acquainted with Cornell for the last six years of his life, she seems to have touched on it in profound ways:

> moment of clearing up
> " " awareness etc
> obsession Leila-wise assuaged
> a strange day to begin with –
> expecting Leila request – possible phenomenon of having to
> keep cherished one at a distance for something to work,
> imagined reality outrunning the 'reality'. Visit of Leila
> extremely meaningful, rich, but in new and unexpected ways –
> 1 hour earlier her arrival, bringing naturalness to environment.[207]

During 1972, when Cornell was in hospital (he compromised his religious beliefs while there, by having surgery), she visited him. He made a funny little drawing, and made a collage out of her name. He assembled a box from the bricks one of Hadley's daughters had put together. The reciprocal flow of energy between Cornell and Leila was constant, and they marked this fact with frequent gifts. They both understood the need to protect the creative self, for cherishing the ability to create, and in Cornell's case it resulted in a truly detached personality, which as Hadley points out, 'means you don't need people around you. Joseph's own mind was a complete world.' And as she makes clear, Cornell compartmentalized things, both in his life and his art: other people he knew rarely knew one another; they were kept separate.

> The nest, the eggs, the male bird, the male bird and the female nest and the cage, that's also the compartmentalizing. The cage also is the shellfish, the thing around oneself, that magic wall that people don't penetrate, the box is also symbolic of security, security, security. We used to joke about shellfishness or selfishness . . . it's the living of one's life hermetically sealed in one's own ego, the mind

> expanding and self realization and self aggrandizement all the time . . . Totally in his own world but with the ballet, and these wonderful books, beautiful ancient books, history in the eighteenth century, it was the refinement of things, a perfect dance, very pure, very spiritual, very mystical.

Although Cornell's relationship with Hadley was an unusually close one for him, it is interesting to see that in the various ways they came together – through conversation, through her children, through his art – he was relentlessly pursuing his own journey, his own self-description or exploration. The way in which the image of the twelve-year-old girl is made interchangeable with the Medici page-boy shows how interchangeable she is in Cornell's mind. Hadley was assigned an identity within Cornell's vocabulary of images. She was an inspirational muse, certainly, the artist's model perhaps, but to an artist like Cornell she was much more a channel to the self he was tirelessly pursuing.

4 The Cosmological Search

CORNELL'S SCIENCE BACKGROUND

For Cornell nature was not something to do only with surface and synthesis, it was about substance and structure. He took an interest in the laws of nature as well as nature's appearances. Geology, geography, physics, chemistry, geometry and, most important, astronomy were all subjects he investigated. It may be that what fascinated him within these areas of study was as much to do with the methods (experimentation), the equipment (mechanical devices and instruments), the aims (discovery), the associations (suggestive of arcane knowledge: keys to unlock the mysteries of the world) and the form scientific answers take (order, balance, sequence, harmony, precision and regularity) as with any desire to amass real knowledge of the sciences or any desire to answer specific scientific questions to do with aerodynamics, gravity, volume and so on. Victorian-style experiments around the kitchen table, the wonders of the world, the strangeness of scientific instruments and the didactic aspect of scientific representation made more impact on Cornell than contemporary scientific discoveries. As with all of his interests, it is difficult to separate out his interest in science from his absorption in other disciplines – literature, philosophy, theology, history, art history and music. What we do see when we look at his more science-orientated boxes is how all his strands of exploration are drawn together to make a coherent formal statement.

The source of Cornell's interest in, and continuing fascination with, science is connected to a number of factors: the associations carried over from childhood and schooldays; his reading in scientific books; the influence of other artists; and America's pivotal role in technological progress. The part traditionally played by astronomy as inspiration was another source of fascination. Cornell's immediate family – his father, mother and sisters – were not involved in scientific pursuits, but Cornell did hear stories of his maternal grandfather, Commodore William R. Voorhis, who was involved in science and engineering.[208] Voorhis founded Nyack's water company, was influential in connecting Nyack to New York by rail (via the Erie railroad system), and experimented with modes of water transport, for example even inventing a steam-operated passenger catamaran. 'Cousin Bill' was of Cornell's own generation, 'living up in Nyack in one of the old sandstone Dutch houses'. He was, apparently, a protégé of Edison.[209] At school at Phillips Academy, Cornell chose a science course rather than classical studies, and as a result studied algebra, plane geometry, physics and general science. He was never particularly interested in sports, and his reading matter was often about 'discovering the universe'. His sister explains:

> I would hear mother say 'Joe will you . . . I wish you would please go out and get some fresh air and do a little exercise'. This was mainly in the winter because his nose would be buried in a book. But they weren't all intellectual books. They were Thomas Hardy, and, you know, the Alger books . . . but it was very important to him – the

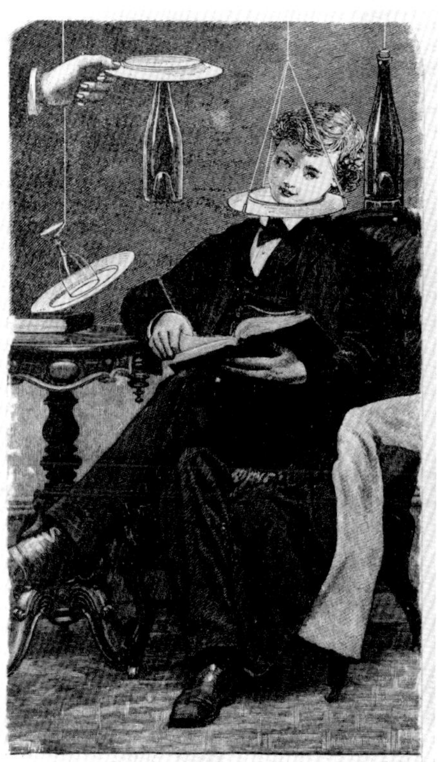

99 *Untitled (after La Pression Atmosphérique)*, *c*. 1932–9, collage of engravings and photomechanical reproductions on paper and cardboard.

> Book of Knowledge, and there's a good many of those. And he learned a lot . . . He and I would discuss: is a sound a sound if there's nobody to hear it? They would have a picture of a tree falling in a wood and it said: 'Would that make a noise if your ears weren't there?' Well, those kind of things fascinated him.[210]

Betty also tells of how the young Cornell had 'one of those first little steam engines'. As an adult he frequently visited the Hayden Planetarium at the American Museum of Natural History in New York, and subscribed to its periodical *The Sky Reporter* (excerpts from issues in 1959 feature in his dossier 'The Celestial Theater', *c.* 1944–58). He bought new copies and tracked down antique copies of *The Scientific American*.[211] Other books in his collection he either cherished from childhood or acquired later included Camille Flammarion's *The Wonders of the Heavens* (1871), three editions of Elijah Burrit's *The Geography of the Heavens* and the *Class Book of Astronomy* (1838, 1853, 1873), and O. M. Mitchell's *The Planetary and Stellar Works: An Exposition of the Discoveries and Theories of Modern Astronomy* (1859).[212] Science books that were attacked with scissors for Cornell's early collages of the 1930s included *La Science Amusante* (1890) and *Popular Diagrams* (1850). The

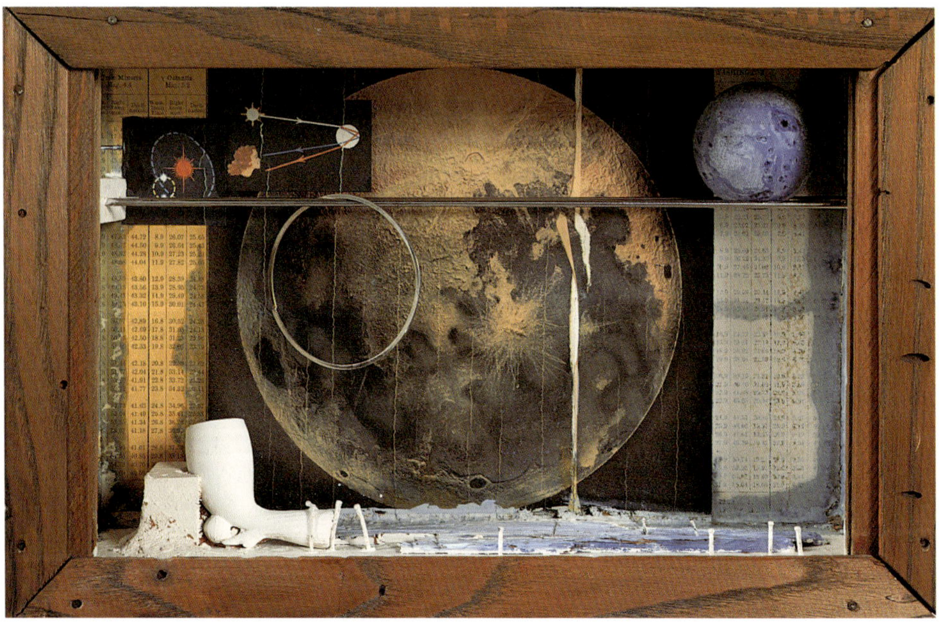

100 *Soap Bubble Set (Lunar Rainbow) (Space Object)*, an undated box construction.

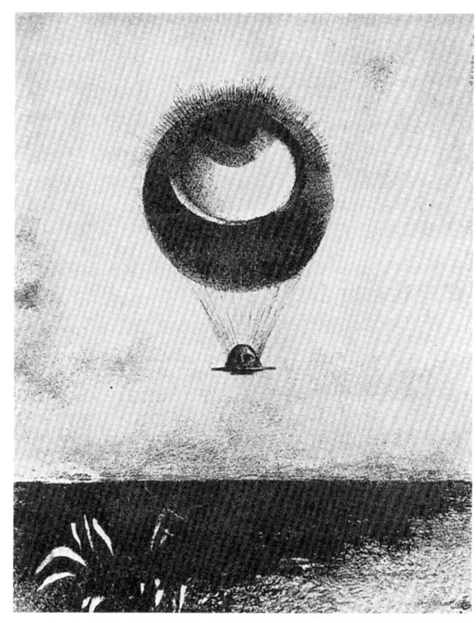

101 Odilon Redon, *The Eye like a Strange Balloon wafts itself towards the Infinite*, 1882, lithograph.

Irving Adler science books designed for children in the 1950s provided image sources for Cornell's 'Mathematics in Nature' series of collages executed in the 1960s.[213] He also used Otto Binder's *The Moon, Our Neighbouring World* (1959). Many of these titles were early Victorian scientific books, not modern accounts: Cornell's interests recall his childhood fascinations.

A particular family ritual took place on the 4th of July every year. Rituals and occasions were sacred ceremonies to the family, and together it upheld and treasured them. They punctuated the year, and allowed the family's orderly rhythms to be maintained. On the 4th of July the Cornell family would troop up to the top of their large mansion house, climb out onto one of the little rooftop towers, and watch the celebrations from this spectacular vantage point. In Nyack, at that time, balloons would be sent upriver: 'They used to have a form of balloon with a light inside and it must have been something burning . . . they were huge balloons . . . They had set them loose some place south of us and then they'd go floating up the Hudson River . . . Joe just loved those balloons'.[214]

The illuminated balloon, the floating sphere with a burning inner core moving over the landscape, is a familiar image in Cornell's frame of reference. It looked like an eye,

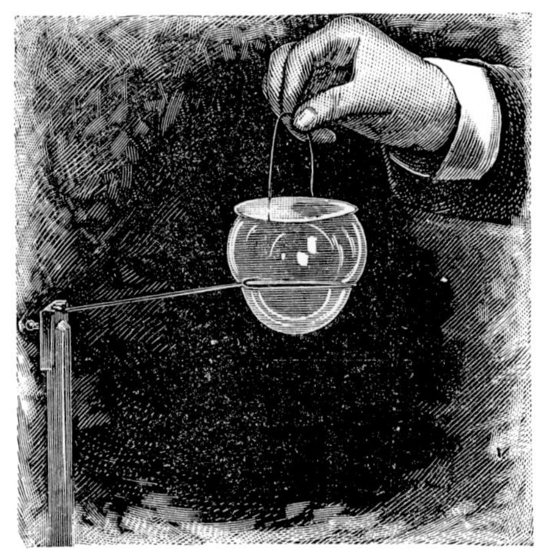

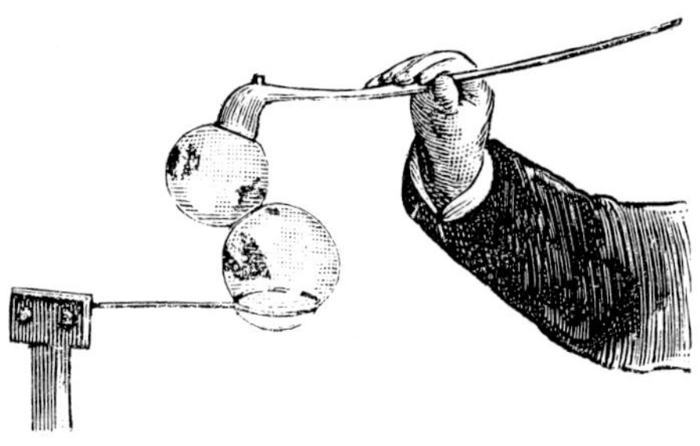

102 and 103 Illustrations from C. V. Boys, *Soap-Bubbles, and the Forces which Mould Them*, London, 1902.

surveying the world below. As a young adult Cornell became interested in the French Symbolist artist Odilon Redon. Most especially Cornell was influenced by Redon's lithograph *The Eye like a Strange Balloon wafts itself towards the Infinite* (illus. 101). So familiar was Cornell with this image that he affectionately refers to it in his diaries as 'Redon's L'Oeil'.[215] The eye was a much favoured image within American Transcendentalist thinking, another important influence on Cornell, as this excerpt from Emerson's 'Nature' indicates:

> Standing on the bare ground – my head bathed by the blithe air, and uplifted into infinite space – all mean egotism vanishes. I become a transparent eyeball; I am nothing; I see all; the currents of the Universal Being circulate through me; I am part or parcel of God.[216]

This statement, with its explicit spiritual subjectivism, finds an echo in Cornell's Christian Science sympathies. The sphere floating above the landscape – the transparent eyeball seeing all, and the self being consumed by spirit – this was a most potent symbol for Cornell, representing scientific discovery, a visionary element besides.

JOURNEY TO THE STARS

One of the most influential books in Cornell's childhood, and later on in terms of imagery and his approach to science and astronomy, was *Soap Bubbles and the Forces which Mould Them* by C. V. Boys, first published in 1896 (close to the year

Cornell was born) by the Society for the Promotion of Christian Knowledge.[217] It was part of a 'Romance of Science' series. The author, a British scientist, was particularly interested in engaging children's interest in the world of science. The book was developed from a series of three lectures Boys had delivered to an audience of children at the London Institute in the winter of 1889–90.

Boys was able to bring science together with art, literature, history, music, nature, religion and matters of everyday life. He opens *Soap Bubbles* with references to Millais's famous painting *Bubbles* (1886), a work widely known via late nineteenth-century posters and magazines as the advertisement for *Pears Soap*. (Cornell, characteristically, slipped a scrap of paper with one of these adverts on it inside the front cover of his own copy of the book.) Boys goes on to explain how, perhaps unexpectedly, there is a long history of children's fascination with bubble pipes, and he mentions an antique Etruscan vase in the Louvre that bears an illustration of this activity. Later Boys connects science with nursery rhymes, specifically Edward Lear's *Book of Nonsense* and the 'Book of Proverbs'. He connects experimentation with spiders' webs, and shows how a water fountain can be interrupted by sound and how to construct a musical water-jet. The material Boys used enabled children to try things out at home, where they could readily put their hands on candlesticks, wine glasses, clay pipes, wire rings, glass sheets, lanterns, mirrors, chains and so on. These items on Boys's list are the precise materials that Cornell used to make up his vocabulary of objects in the Soap Bubble Sets. Also, Boys's train of thought – which moves easily in reference from science to art, to religion, to cosy gather-round family entertainment – parallels the train of thought that Cornell was to develop as an artist.

Boys makes clear the inevitability of science, but he also indicates the aspects of science that are so often missed out – the beauty, the wonder, the magic of science:

> I do not suppose there is anyone in this room who has not occasionally blown a common soap bubble, and while admiring the perfection of its form and the marvellous brilliancy of its colours, wondered how it is that such a magnificent object can be so easily produced.
>
> I shall show you one or two experiments first, which I

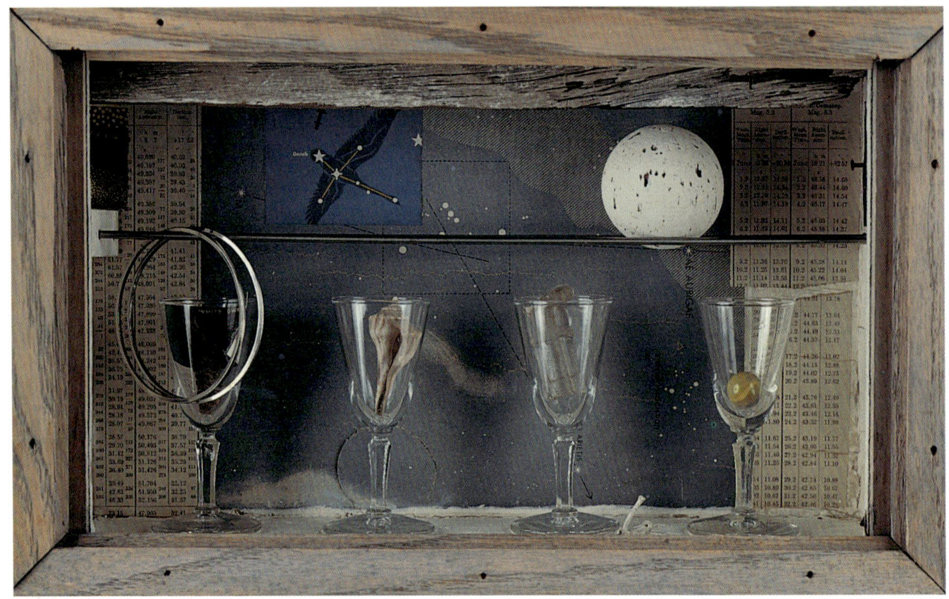

104 *Untitled*, an undated box construction.

> think you will agree are so like magic, so wonderful are they and yet so simple, that if they had been performed a few hundred years ago the rash person who showed them might have run a serious risk of being burnt alive.[218]

The connections Boys makes remained with Cornell for life. Cornell's work in his first Soap Bubble Set takes further the connections between art and science, and science and magic (or illusion). Cornell would have digested the technical as well as the more abstract issues of Boys's account. We know, for example, that Cornell used an aniline dye called 'Soluble Blue' as recommended by Boys in his chapter 'Practical Hints'.[219] But another interesting point in direct connection with the box constructions is the equation made by Boys when demonstrating a particular experiment, originally done by Plato, between bubbles of liquid and the heavenly bodies. The soap bubble is not just a carrier of dreams and reverie and magical revelations, it is, as Boys reveals, something that can provide answers to questions we might ask of nature, and it is an example of the perfections within nature – the soap bubble is the perfect sphere, and is thus a manifestation of the perfection of God's created universe.

The clay pipe is part of the visual vocabulary in Boys's book (illus. 103). It plays its part in the experiments and in the science of soap bubbles. For Cornell the clay pipe has other connotations. He was a frequent visitor to the World Trade Fair held in Flushing Meadow in 1939, sharing with Robert many experiences, and managing to collect on one visit a substantial number of Dutch clay pipes to put into store. As well as the fact that everything to do with the World Fair held special significance for Cornell, the discovery that the pipes were Dutch enabled him to make the association with the Voorhees, his own Dutch ancestors on his mother's side.

Cornell's own compilation of two-dimensional paper work in a book-like form on the heavenly bodies is *The Celestial Theater* (*c*. 1940–56). This was a project that remained

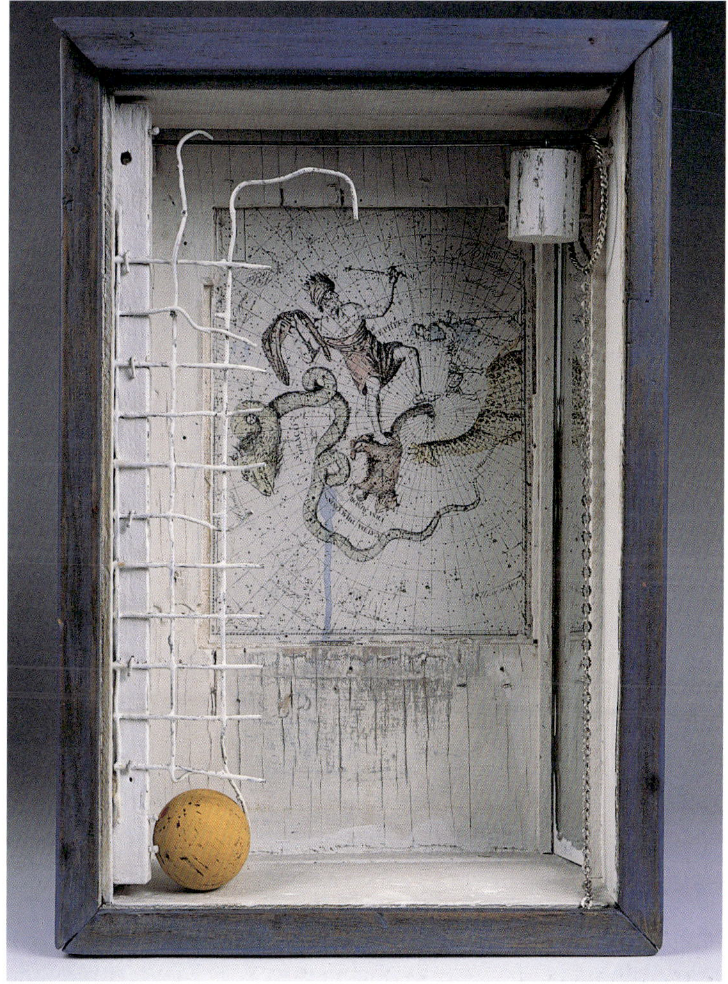

105 *Untitled*, an undated box construction.

unresolved. He had hoped it would be a 'visual exploration' along the lines of *Portrait of Ondine* (1945–6). Charles Henri Ford, the editor of *View* magazine, announced it in 1944 as a forthcoming attraction for the magazine's December issue. It was announced, also in 1944, in *Dance Index* as a special number on the 'Celestial Ballet and Heavenly Spectacle'. In 1952 Cornell attempted to revive the material, mounting and staging it for an installation at Wittenborn bookshop in New York. But instead he put up his *Portrait of Ondine* 'exploration' (first shown in 1945–6 at the Museum of Modern Art). There were in total three failed attempts to bring the material into the public sphere, although Cornell also wrote about 'shadow box treatment', a 'travelling unit' with a definite educational bent for museums, galleries and schools. The material was so important to him that he angled it in numerous ways to try and bring it out.

The reason for the dossier's dormant state is discussed within the dossier. Exhibitions, recent book and magazine publications, Cornell felt, had rather exhausted the subject of astronomy at that time (1944 through to 1952). Another reservation was that *The Celestial Theater* may be thought to be 'unrealistic, escapist', with, as he remarks, 'world tension at an unprecedented high in the aftermath of the terror and destruction of World War II and the threat of the atom bomb'.[220] In another notation Cornell records that the project was 'too ambitious in its extended relationships and in the acceleration of scientific advances'.[221] However, at the same time as discussing his failure to bring the project out, he clarifies the values that he was searching for, while revealing his own awareness of the rarified nature of his speculations:

> May it not constructively supplement the more serious aspects of current star-gazing . . . may it not bring reminders from times when the majesty of the heavens inspired poets, astronomers, musicians and thousands of the less articulate . . . As a foil to the monotony of atomic scares and high percentage of useless bomb scares, against the commercially inspired endless flow of speculative space-ship literature . . . The CELESTIAL THEATER. . . offers many tonic reassurance, stimulation and inspiration.[222]

Among the papers of Cornell's 'feuilleton devoted to the enjoyable aspects of the heavens' is a wide array of images

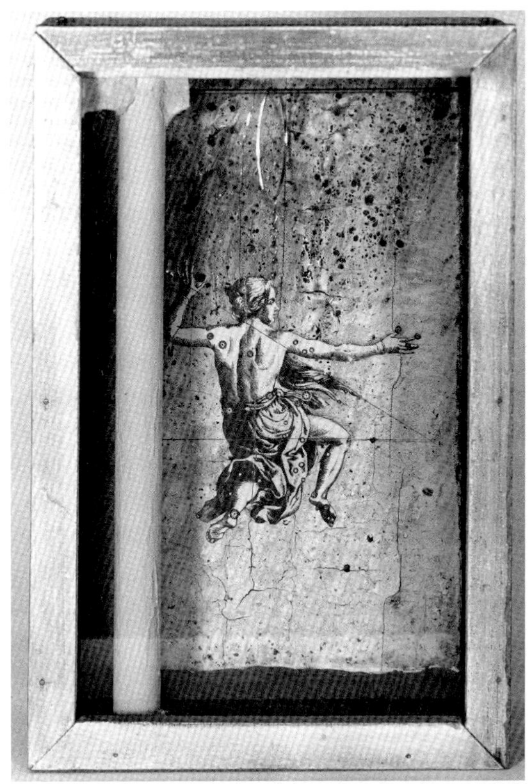

106 *Untitled (Hote)*, an undated construction.

and clippings.[223] They were what Cornell saw as the less familiar paths and by-paths he had hoped to open up 'into the future'. One, for example, was 'correlated to Beethoven':

> Our worship is all the more deep, the more clearly we recognize the creation and its greatness. Indeed how many songs did David sing, the true servant of the true God! He received the idea for his songs from the admiring observation of the skies. 'The heavens declare the glory of God'.[224]

And on Beethoven (Cornell is again quoting):

> let us consider only a few high points, such as the majestic calm and wide sweep of the Motto adagio of the 2nd Rasoumoffsky in E minor. Czerny says that the theme of this movement occurred to Beethoven one evening 'as he gazed at the firmament and thought about the music of the spheres'. We know that astronomy fascinated the Master. He owned a copy of Bode's Guide to Knowledge of the Starry Heavens. In his copy of the Odyssey he scored the

line about the Pleiades. And in one of his diaries he wrote with emphasis: 'The moral law within us, and the starry sky above us – Kant.[225]

Romantic ideas proliferate in Cornell's chosen quotations. In this dossier we read about musicians, poets, the Japanese, an American G.I. talking on television, Rimbaud and so on – people who have significantly changed their view of the world, their personal vision, because of a relationship, momentary or otherwise, with the stars. The fact that Beethoven was inspired by the heavens, and was interested in astronomy to the extent of owning books on the subject, even jotting down quotations in his diary on the subject, fascinated Cornell. This is another example of what Cornell's called 'parallel biography', as he had in relation to *Le Grand Meaulnes*. But the link between music and the heavenly bodies is one that was taken up in much of his art, perhaps most overtly in his collages, for example the undated *Mozart–Cassiopeia*. Here, an image of an automated toy Mozart playing a harpsichord accompanies a porcelain image of Cassiopeia on a snowy landscape. The collage is a variation of *Eine Kleine Schnee-Musik* (*c.* 1962), its title a pun on Mozart's *Eine kleine Nachtmusik*, and the title Cornell had chosen for the 'WITT. project feuilleton' that never materialized, that is, 'The Celestial Theater', in the form that it was to take for the bookshop gallery in 1952. *Mozart–Cassiopeia* shows how Cornell's sources can be difficult to discuss, because of – as he put it – the 'rich cross-indexing and cross-references'. This work connects strongly not only with *The Celestial Theater*, but also with the dossier 'GC 44'. *Eine Kleine Schnee-Musik* refers to Dorothea Tanning and her exhibition of 1944 at the Levy Gallery, and her subsequent influence on Cornell's work and thoughts. Tanning had a painting in her exhibition with this same title as Mozart's composition, and Cornell's oblique reference to her lies in the snowy landscape that serves as a backdrop to the toy Mozart, a landscape snipped and saved from a copy of the magazine *Arizona Highways* dated 1944.[226]

The inter-connectedness of man and the Created Universe was what captivated Cornell as he became more and more absorbed in the stars. It is the magical suggestiveness of science and the world of astronomy that opens everything up to him. In 'The Yale Student File' dossier we learn of his

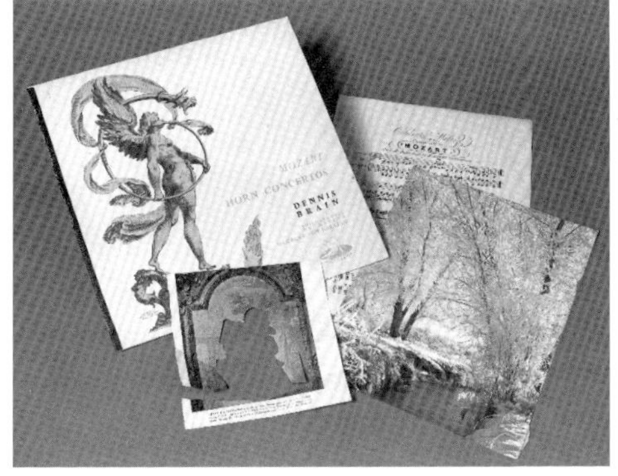

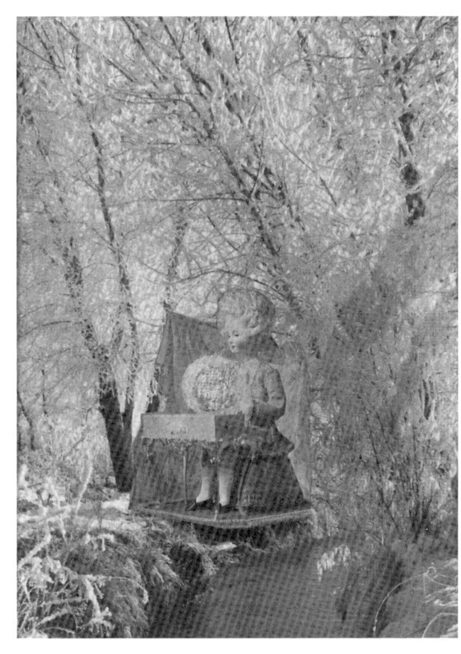

107 Source materials for the collage *Eine Kleine Schnee-Musik* including landscape illustration from *Arizona Highways* and cutout of a Mozart automaton, *c*. 1962.

108 *Eine Kleine Schnee-Musik*, *c*. 1962, collage.

approach: 'My experience was apart from any conscious study . . . A natural and informal response to beauty in a broad and general way'. In rough drafts of reply letters stored in the file, he records the fact that if, in his work, any bona fide contact was established with the source of his inspiration (be it Mallarmé's poetry or the heavenly bodies) then this was because of a 'kind of fool's luck intuition of a sort too elusive to consciously shape up into words for my own or another's enlightenment'. This statement may be usefully connected to his comment on the aim being to reach a final distillation wherein the subject is almost lost to sight.[227]

A MUSEUM INSTALLATION

In 1936 Cornell contributed his very first *Soap Bubble Set* (now in the Wadsworth Atheneum) to the Museum of Modern Art's 'Fantastic Art, Dada and Surrealism' show (illus. 109). One is immediately struck by the vastness encapsulated in this very small construction – the world, it seems, is in a box. The formal elements also quickly catch one's attention: the moon, egg, head, the planet Saturn and the bowl of the clay pipe make visual puns. The sphere, oval, cylinder and circle

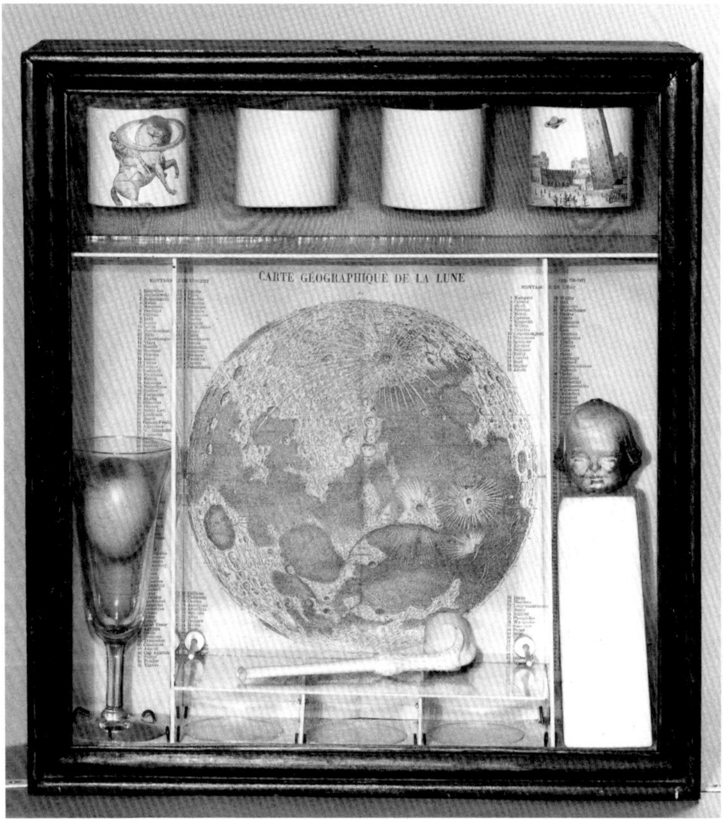

109 *Soap Bubble Set*, 1936, box construction.

are distinctive geometric forms. This could have been a box of large abstract concerns and formal, almost mathematical shapes if Cornell had not placed a small head within it. The head puts a different construction on the work: it suggests meanings that would otherwise lie outside the box's circumference. It suggests that the box concerns man's place within the universe, with the symbol of the egg (the beginning) to the small image of man (development) to the diagram of the moon (the place he dreams of conquering). Cornell's main subject with the *Soap Bubble Set* is man's exploratory urge and man's attempt to order the vastness that he finds in the universe that surrounds him.

The situating of things is all-important within this work. Cornell demonstrates a fascination with what holds things in their places: the egg is contained in a glass, the head rests on a plinth, the map of the moon is lodged at the back of the box, and the planets (in the shape of wooden cylinders) hover in mid-air suspended above the whole scene. Cornell can engineer a wide variety of ways of securing elements, but perhaps what he is driving at is the gravitational pull that holds all things in place and thus establishes order for the universe.

As for the balance of colour and tone in the *Soap Bubble Set*, the sombre, muted colouring suggests a seriousness not always present in Cornell's work. The buff colour of the map is picked up in the low-key colouring of the picture diagrams on the cylinders in the top two corners. Either side of the box the same muted green of the egg keeps the box in an even balance; the box is balanced, not symmetrical. The milky white of the wooden cylinders and the plinth and pipe is intermittently spaced around the edges of the box. The balance throughout suggests a highly schematized approach to the world and implies the idea of a grand design imposed on things. That his artwork was imbued with a selfconscious harmony may be inferred from a short notation in his diaries from a later date. In September 1951 he wrote, 'the expansiveness of the heavens, the song of nature, the breezes, the fragrances of the grasses – like great breathing, deep, harmonious, elemental, cosmic.'[228]

There is a preponderance of glass that, once again, draws our attention to the way we see things. Glass, we notice, holds up the egg, it divides the miniature world within the box, it supports the pipe, it rests on the base of the box in the shape of three round lenses, and it is glass that ultimately houses the elements within the box and completes the four walls of the construction. Just as Cornell brought together all sorts of unexpected things by reason that they shared the same spherical shape, so by drawing our attention to the different properties of glass – that is, its transparency, its capacity to distort, magnify and distance – he achieves a unity and creates a formal artistic order within the box. Finally, everything within is partitioned or supported by glass, which suggests, besides, the fragility on which many of our conceptions of the world are based.

Closer examination of the *Soap Bubble Set* reveals an interest in lines carved or etched on surfaces. The lines on the large central map of the moon supposedly record facts, they trace the forms of the planet. The lines on the face of the miniature human being (lines moving into a little depth with light relief), are signs of what is underneath. The egg has vague tracings on its surface. The pipe is carved in a craftsmanlike way, and the cylinders in the top corners carry linear designs. The fascination with carving, tracery, engraving, marks on the surface and what they represent is the concern of the map-maker and the concern of the artist. This leads to the question of representation: Cornell chose objects and images that are moulded, painted, carved, lacquered, sculpted or, in the case of the map, drawn. Through the placing of objects or images, through the kinds of objects chosen from different worlds (scientific, domestic, cartographic, artistic, decorative) Cornell created a complex synthesis in his representation of reality that also indicates the limitations of two and three dimensions and points us towards the possibility of a fourth dimension – time.

In addition to the *Soap Bubble Set*, which I think we can take to have been the main feature of the installation, there are also ten small glass bell-jars with ephemera, a large free-standing photo of a heavily fenestrated building with an elaborate railing bordering it, and a wooden chest containing small glass phials filled with various substances, all with cork stoppers and labels (illus. 110). Collaged onto the lid of the chest is a picture of what appears to be a rock formation. Some of the glass phials from the chest spill out onto the floor of the larger glass display cabinet that houses the whole installation: the phials stand upright among a scatter of more glass (either strips or tubes), and these reach across to the photo of the windowed building, thus bridging a gap between the larger pieces of the installation and working to connect the individual elements.

Looking at this installation – *The Elements of Natural Philosophy* – face-on, there are three pictorial images: the rock pictures within the chest, the building with the windows, as in the photo, and the diagram of the moon at the centre of the *Soap Bubble Set*. Propped up around and about these two-dimensional images are small round objects and loose substances within containers. Again, in the installation we can see a preponderance of glass. Again, we can see lines on the surface of things being of particular interest – from the carving of the clay pipe (noticed in the *Soap Bubble Set*) to the elaborate carving of the building and its railing, to the natural carving of the rock as it has been eroded by the elements weathering the earth. There are three aspects to the installa-

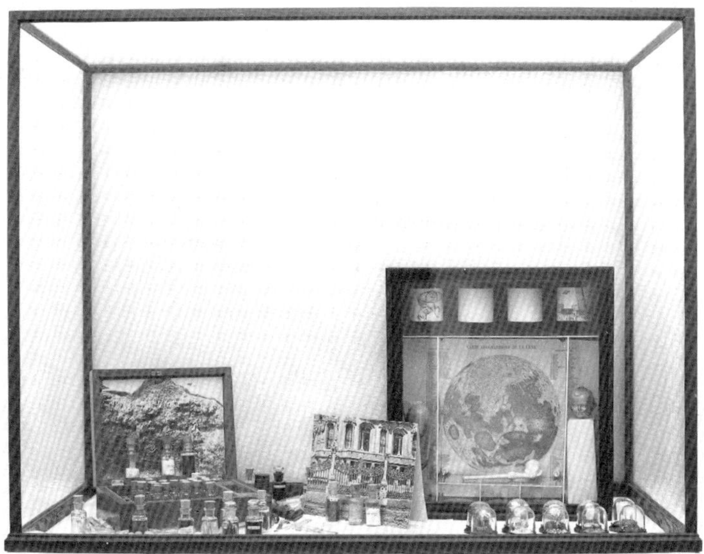

110 Installation view of *Elements of Natural Philosophy* and *Soap Bubble Set*, shown as part of the exhibition 'Fantastic Art, Dada, Surrealism' at the Museum of Modern Art, New York, 7 December 1936 – 17 January 1937.

tion. The *Soap Bubble Set* concentrates on the search: looking into things, what the world looks like, how far man can see. It demonstrates man's attempt to understand and then represent the universe. Second, the wooden chest holds raw substances and chemicals; it penetrates to what cannot be seen, to what lies beneath the surface. And third, the photo demonstrates man's use of his imagination: the placing of lines, rhythms and motifs to make new and unexpected shapes in the environment of his own creation. The incorporation of the rock and the raw substances alongside an image of fantastic architecture emphasises how far man has travelled as a creator, where his imaginative vision has taken him.

George Platt Lynes's photo (illus. 111) immediately tells us why attention to arrangement, order and form must be primary in any study of Cornell's methods. Lynes's arrangement loses the sense, created by Cornell in his box, of the world encapsulated in formalized constraint. It loses the immediate power and tension of the world in miniature – the tension created by containing so much in so little a space. The large diagram of the moon has been replaced in Lynes's arrangement by a strip of serial photos of a planet passing through an eclipse. Two faces are new to the arrangement – one on a dark background, the other on a light one; one seems modern and

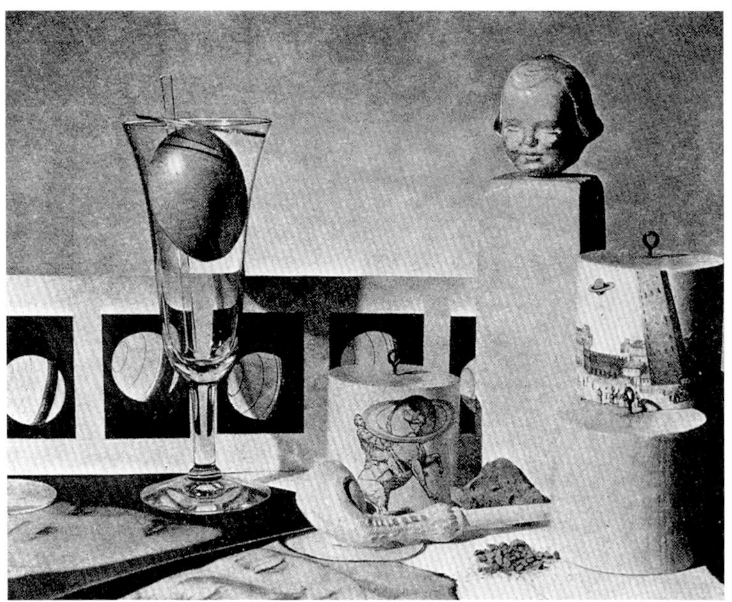

111 George Platt Lynes's re–arrangement of Cornell's installation: *Soap Bubble Set, Composition of Objects*, 1936.

the other (perhaps a Renaissance) rendering of a face. The planets are no longer suspended, they rest on a surface, and some of the loose substance (sand or earth) has tumbled out from its glass phial and sits in a pile on that same surface. Lynes's photo (in black-and-white) of the installation was taken with strong light flooding in from the left. The shadow effects are accentuated by the lack of colour. The planet in the serial photo eclipses away from the light source in Lynes's photo, and so the disappearance of the edges of the other round objects – egg, head, cylinders – echoes the disappearance of the edge of the planet. Something has happened to the scale of things in Lynes's image that affects the relationship between objects. The head is placed closer to the egg, without the interruption of the huge sphere of the moon (as in Cornell's box). The planets, as symbolised by the wooden cylinders with pasted imagery, are now standing below the head and loom large beside it, and yet seem small when seen alongside the bowl of the pipe. The order of things that seems to make so much sense in Cornell's box is here topsy-turvy. The egg and the head stand out like skyscraper buildings towering above the surrounding constructions. They diminish the effects of the heavenly bodies.

A sensuous tactile quality is brought out in Lynes's image. He squashes together the spherical shapes rather than dividing them out by glass sheeting. (The base of the wine glass is utilized to the full as a mirroring medium: it carries all the reflected and refracted curves from the surrounding objects.) He introduces faces with glossy lips and somnambulant eyes. He adds the mound of earth and lump of rock. The photo is a still-life display of arranged objects, a *nature-morte*. Cornell's box is a small world encapsulated: it is more alive, more dynamic, because of the inference of larger forces at work. Lynes's photo is more naturalistic: by putting in the faces and the pile of earth and piece of rock we are aware more of things as they are rather than of a created world. When Cornell's formal arrangement and encasement is altered, the metaphysical dimension is removed.

THE SOAP BUBBLE SETS

Soap Bubble Sets appear in one or other shape or form from 1936 to the 1960s. Other series of box constructions were concentrated within shorter periods: the Pharmacy series, for example, belongs to the 1940s, the Hotel boxes to the 1950s, the Observatories to the early 1950s, the Dovecotes to the mid-1950s. Much can be learned about Cornell's working method by tracing the development of the Soap Bubble Sets.

The white clay pipe occurs time and again although we cannot take it as a necessary ingredient to a Soap Bubble Set composition. A box from the 1940s – *Spirit Level*, which was included in an exhibition at Copley Galleries, California, in 1948 as a Soap Bubble Set – is one example of a bubble set minus its pipe (illus. 112). But by the end of the 1940s admirers of Cornell's work would have come to expect the pipe as the motif/signature of this particular series.

Each box, although it may ostensibly be a Soap Bubble Set, and therefore concerned with the heavens, seas and earth – the 'created Universe' – also has an individual story to tell. With a limited range of props Cornell was able to create a Soap Bubble Set that is like a lunar landscape, a beach scene, a planetarium or a circus. In the choice of props he did not differentiate between sources: between bric-à-brac and high culture, between rare impressions of French engravings and step-by-step popular guides for American schoolchildren. He consistently identified combinations of objects whose linked associations break down the complacency of the beholder's stock responses.

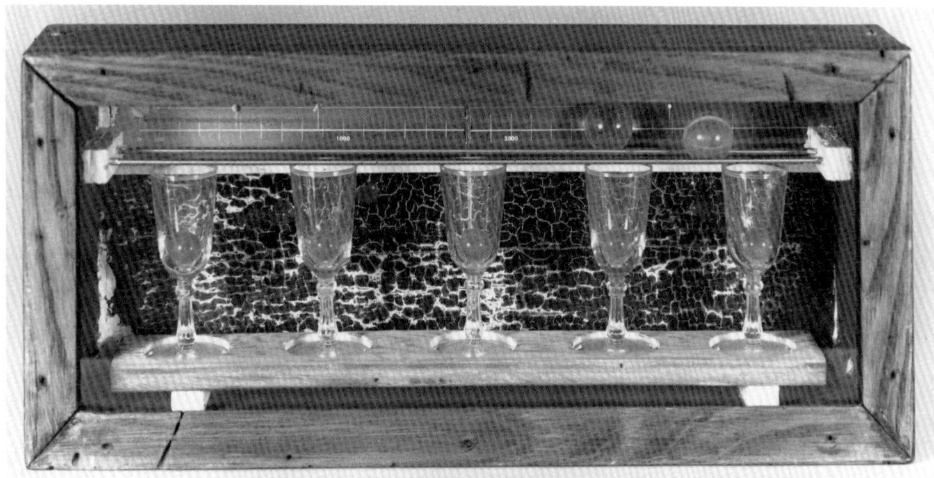

112 *Spirit Level*, 1940s, box construction.

The early Soap Bubble Sets are similar to the box of 1936 in that they are balanced, compartmentalized and selfconsciously formal arrangements. Many of them have a map or diagram covering the back wall; they have side compartments, objects placed at floor level and a thin narrow top compartment (often containing the wooden cylinders we have encountered in the 1936 box, though even if there are no cylinders or upper compartment there is still some sort of demarcation symbolizing the heavens). The vocabulary Cornell made constant use of includes wine-glasses (or cordial or sherry glasses), sea-shells, cork balls or stoppers, glass marbles, natural sea-sponge, driftwood and wooden cylinders, while the pipe is invariably doubled up in the box, flanking either side of the central map. Sometimes, in addition to the back wall displaying a printed map or diagram, the side walls carry print in the form of tables or written text or additional diagrams. Again, as in the 1936 construction, there are compartments of wood and glass dividing up the whole space. And we see Cornell has carefully and imaginatively fixed the elements; he built wooden niches for objects to stay in place on the base of the box, and he looped and threaded cord through the cork balls to suspend them from the ceiling.

The compartmentalized Soap Bubble Sets of the 1940s and 1950s that follow the basic format of the 1936 version progress to a stage of greater variety, intricacy and density (illus. 113). But Cornell was also producing boxes of a very different character in the 1940s, such as the *Soap Bubble Set* of 1947 (illus. 116) and the one that followed in the next year. Here the bubble pipes appear in an open plan space with fewer props and no diagram or printed matter on the back wall facing the viewer. The most immediate difference between these Soap Bubble Sets and the others we have been discussing is that the pipe now stands out against a self-coloured dark backdrop. These boxes have a completely different atmosphere: they have the high dramatic quality of the stage, where the stark contrast of white on black suggests the platform of a conjurer's magic show. Motherwell commented on this feature of Cornell's art, likening it to that of

> the old vaudeville acts which I myself saw in America as a small boy, where, for example, the performer would blacken a white enamel tray with the soot of a candle, and then begin to draw on it with his finger various scenes which, as the soot was more and more erased, would become a snow scene in its whiteness, and at that moment paper snow flakes would slowly float from above. There was a lot of that sense of illusion – come to think of it, in every sense of the word – in Cornell. Illusion is a more accurate word than magic, or perhaps better still, illusion that was indeed magical when he succeeded.[229]

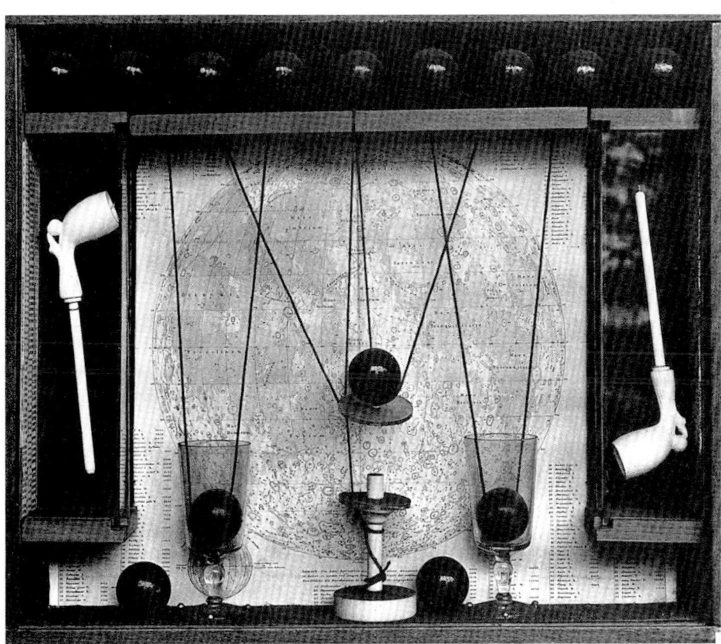

113 *Soap Bubble Set*, 1942, box construction.

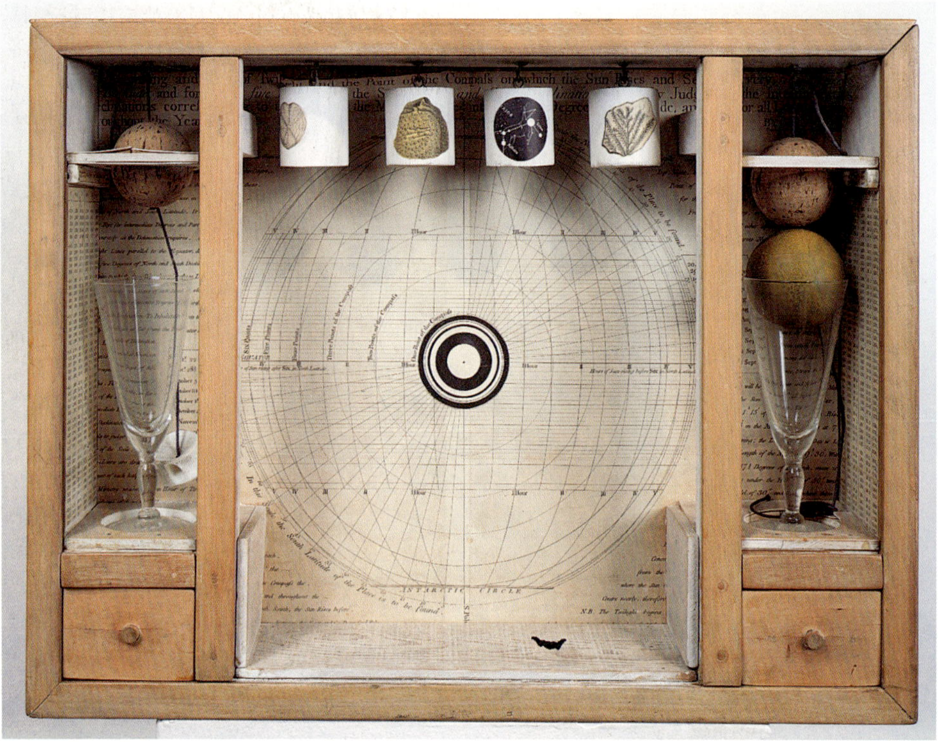

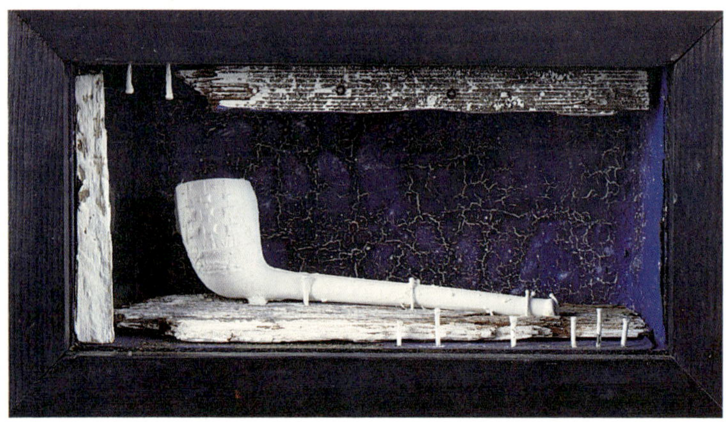

114 *An Analemna, Shewing by Inspection the Time of Sun Rising and Sun Setting, the Length of Days and Nights*, 1948–50, box construction.

115 *Untitled*, 1950, box construction.

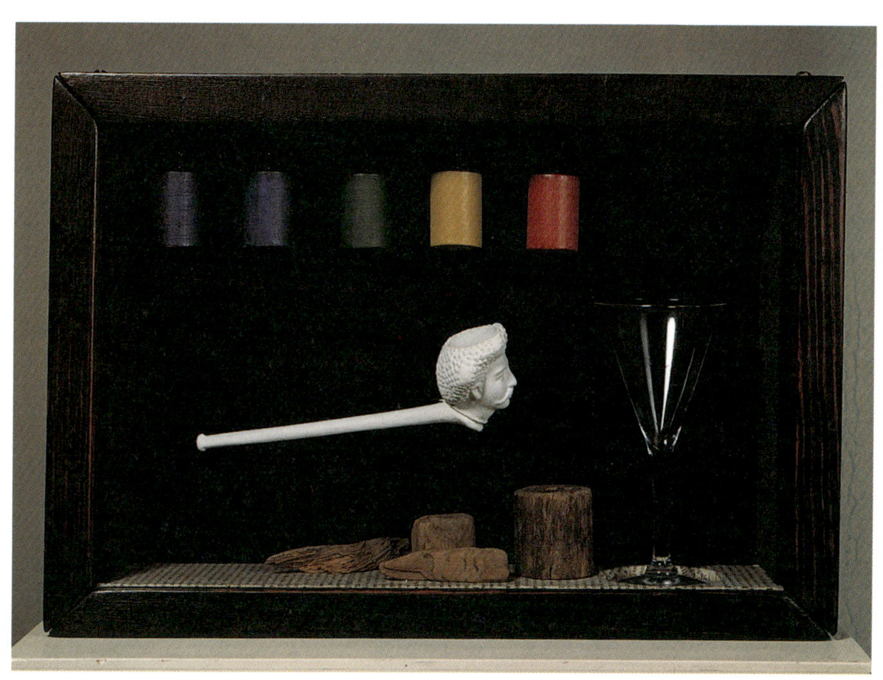

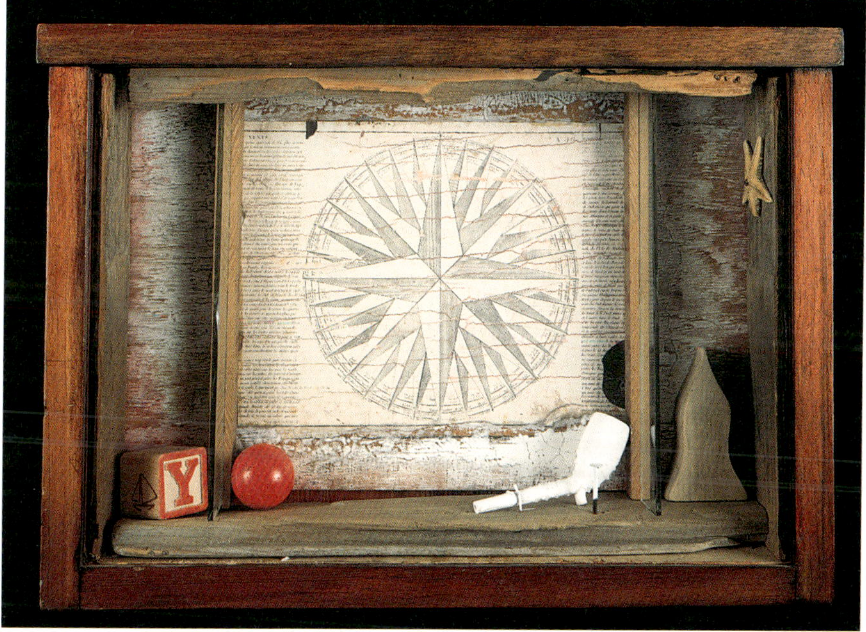

116 *Soap Bubble Set*, 1947, box construction.

117 *Rose des Vents*, *c*. 1966, box construction.

The pipe takes the centre stage and appears in these boxes almost as a presence rather than as an object (the two pipes have respectively a head and a hand sculpted onto each bowl). The other elements in the box pale in significance against the brilliant, glowing white of the pipe (Cornell included either coloured or decorated wooden cylinders rather than the white ones used in the 1936 construction). Both the wine-glass and driftwood also appear in these boxes – in one of which the theatrical emphasis is reinforced by the way the driftwood is made to resemble sweeping curtains drawn back for the show to begin. A carved hand holds out the bowl of the pipe in a gesture of heightened expectancy. These two Soap Bubble Sets of the late 1940s seem aptly to fit the description of the series Cornell wrote for the Copley Galleries catalogue in 1948:

> Shadow boxes become poetic theaters or settings wherein are metamorphosed the elements of a childhood pastime. The fragile, shimmering globules become the shimmering but more enduring planets – a connotation of moon and tides – the association of water less subtle, as when drift-

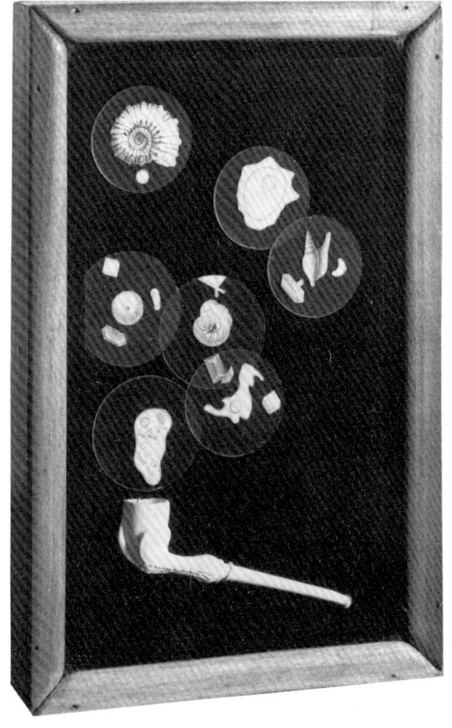

118 *Soap Bubble Set*, 1939, construction of wood, glass, fibreboard, clay, velvet and photomechanical reproductions.

wood pieces makes up a proscenium to set off the dazzling white of sea foam and billowy cloud crystallised in a pipe of fancy.

Even in this description it is impossible to ignore the self-descriptive element or implicit self-portraiture of Cornell's purpose: these poetic theatres lead the maker and the viewer not through the arch of experience but through a proscenium into the past. The formal precedent to this 'strain' of the Soap Bubble Sets could be the *Soap Bubble Set* of 1939 (illus. 118) and *Object* (1940). These were early box/objects that stand vertically and are much shallower constructions than the 1936 assemblage. They contain, besides the pipe, only flat discs and collage. They fit, perhaps, in terms of classification, somewhere between a two-dimensional collage and a three-dimensional assembled construction (they are only 2 5/8 inches wide as opposed to 5 7/16). However, what links these Soap Bubble Sets/Objects to the 1947 and 1948 boxes is the simple, bare layout of a minimal amount of 'things', and the black-and-white tonal scheme that is used. What is curious regarding the subject-matter of these pieces is the scope that may be inferred with so few objects and images. What the glass discs (the bubbles) hold are fossils and amoeboid forms – references to the origins of the world. Clay links the object (the pipe) to the images (the fossils). The dark velvet background of the boxes refers to the depths of the sea, to clay beds and fossils. The bubbles move towards the sky, thereby also symbolizing the heavenly bodies; thus the opposite ends of nature are drawn together and the whole cosmos implied with the bubble pipe at its centre.

Cornell's use of collage was to alter in the Soap Bubble Sets of the late 1940s and the 1950s and 1960s. In some he did away with picture imagery altogether, sometimes suggesting the heavenly bodies or particular planets by other formal means. For example, Saturn could be present within a box by the inclusion of a wooden (or cork) ball and a brass ring. Instead of using a map or diagram, the moon might be represented by a thick layer of cracking white paint or gesso, as when Cornell creates the texture of the surface of the moon in *SA Correspondence Astronomique* (undated). When he did include collage he endeavoured to integrate the collage into the whole. The sun's beams radiate out further than the pasted image, or the rhythms of the winds permeate beyond the picture – Cornell would pick them up on the back wall or in other parts of the box. Sometimes he added markings or used ink staining on the glass, or even embedded nails into the thick paint in order to suggest these radiating lines and rhythms, as in *L'Humeur Vagabonde* (illus. 119) and *The Magnetism of the Sun* (illus. 122).

These boxes are more atmospheric: a weathered, time-worn look prevails. The pipe no longer appears always in pristine condition: often the stem is broken and the carving on the bowl may be worn or chipped. The pipe in some boxes holds a less prominent position – it merges with the uneven, broken surfaces of the back wall and the floor of the box, and maybe also with the knobbled, whitewashed cork ball, or a piece of ravaged driftwood or a smashed and abandoned wine-glass. Instead of each of the elements representing something in itself that contributes to the concept of the whole (the created Cornell world), in these boxes the elements are part of a modest scenario. Although Cornell continued to separate off the upper area for the heavens and the lower part for the seas and earth, the boxes are no longer divided up into compartments, so that the pipe and the moon occupy a more 'naturalistic' space. Some boxes have a circus mood – balls in the air or running through hoops, a tightrope, a trapeze with ladder – but although all the paraphernalia is in place, no acrobats or clowns are to be seen. The absence of the awaited protagonist makes time stand still. In another Soap Bubble Set an African–American's head is sculpted onto the bowl of the pipe, and this head is bound by string to a post in the form of a nail sticking into a piece of driftwood.

On the whole, a lightheartedness abounds in the later Soap Bubble Sets: there are more light backdrops than dark ones, and a smiling tin sun appears much more often than a serious diagram or map of the moon. (The source material for the sun was provided by cans of *Il Sole Antipasto* bought in a delicatessen near Bloomingdale's,[230] whereas the image used for the moon was extracted from a rare copy of a scholarly nineteenth-century guide to the heavens.) Cornell often punned on titles to boxes, as in *Lunarscape* or *Spirit-Level*, and in *British Guiana* (undated) he revealed a schoolboyish sense of humour – once blackening the teeth of a smiling tin sun.

There are certain essential differences between the early

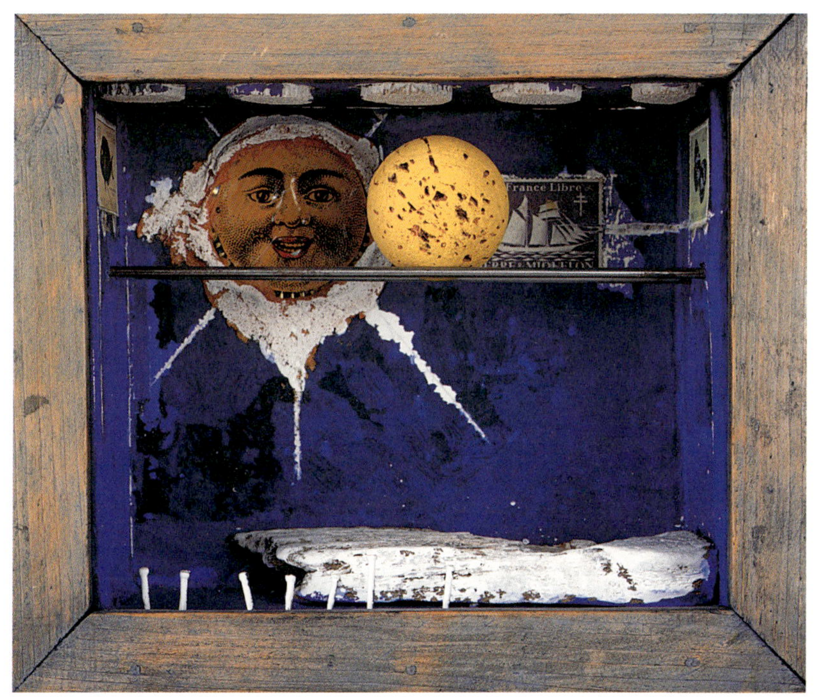

119 *L'Humeur Vagabonde*, late 1950s, box construction.

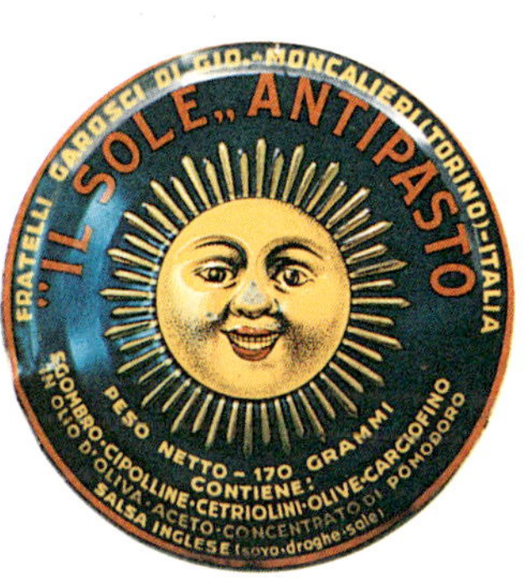

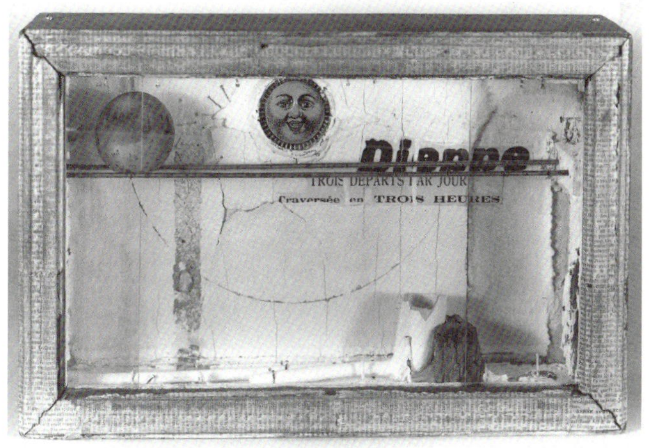

120 The lid from a can of *Il Sole Antipasto*, 1964.

121 *Dieppe*, an undated box construction.

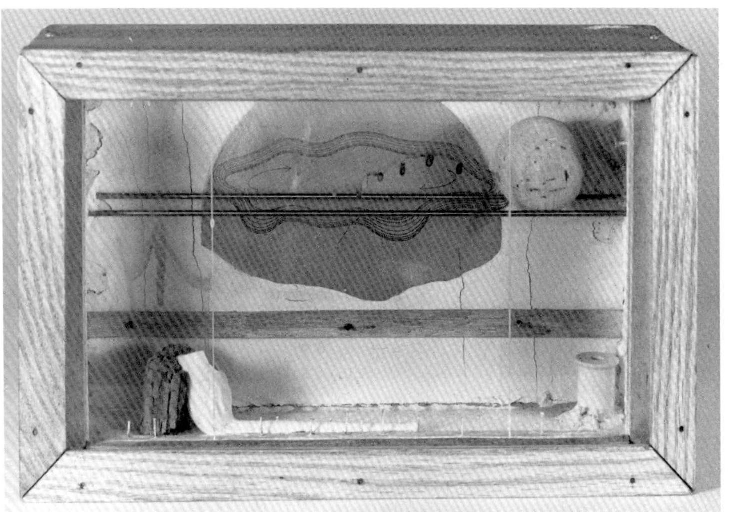

122 *The Magnetism of the Sun*, an undated box construction.

and late Soap Bubble Sets. In the earlier boxes the items had their own aesthetic qualities and a distinct identity in themselves (Cornell collected together a laboratory lens, a Victorian doll's head, and a nineteenth-century map of the moon in one box). The fact that they were placed adjacent to one another is unexpected, but this incongruity is offset by their formal relations within Cornell's created world. In the early boxes objects and images are set out as though they were part of a specimen box, a window display, a museum display cabinet or a salesman's sample case.[231] In the later boxes there are fewer objects, more space and an important change in scale. In *Dieppe* (illus. 121) the relationship of the small sun to the pipe and driftwood below suggests the spatial relationship of a conventional landscape, whereas in the early boxes a huge moon might fill the whole central space of the box and be surrounded by small accessories. There is a suggestion of perspective in *Dieppe* through the way the two bars at the top of the box create a perspective line: they are set into a piece of wood at the side that obviously moves back into space, and there is the hint of a horizon line at the back of the box at the bottom, with extra cracking for emphasis. The box resembles a seaside scene: a broken clay pipe indicates the sort of debris that is washed up on the shore; the sun shines, the harbour sign announces 'Dieppe'; the nails are like the timber struts that hold a sandy shore in place; and the overall whiteness of the background suggests

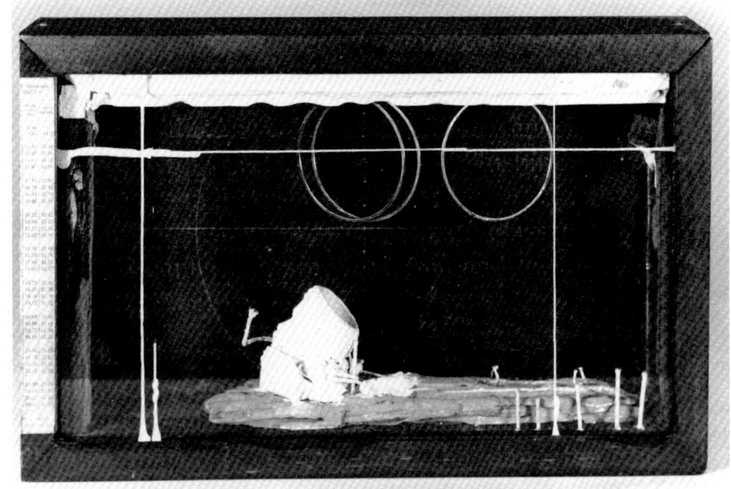

123 *'Sono un caro, e riverito foglio di . . . illustris'*, an undated box construction.

the bleached appearance of buildings in a seaside town. Another important change is the treatment of time. In later boxes time is present in the frayed edges and cracked surfaces; time is represented in two dimensions – the broken line of the pipe, the blurred edges, the uneven cracking, the tears in the paper, the crumbling plaster at the side or the unevenly dotted, almost lost, line of a circle drawn onto the surface of the box. In the early boxes time is indicated diagrammatically, thus a diagram of amoeboid forms is combined with diagrams of the sun rising and setting. One further point of difference is that demarcation in the early boxes is of a formal, rigid nature (wooden shelves, or compartments or drawers, or glass sheeting or plinths), whereas in the later boxes lines of demarcation are indicated through cracks or tears or other marks of wear or staining.

In the later Soap Bubble Sets the 'things' are more suggestive. Cornell preferred to let the materials speak for themselves as materials. There was a move away from the emphasis on the manmade to the found object. If we think of the 1936 box, for example, the map was drawn by man, the pipe sculpted and the head moulded, while the wooden cylinders representing planets are miniature art works in themselves. Everything in the box was designed. In later boxes the objects Cornell chose are not 'crafted' ones, nor was there any attempt to disguise their 'ordinariness'. Their functional purpose was not subordinated to artistic purpose to the degree they were in previous ones. For example, in *The Magnetism of the Sun* (illus. 122) the cotton reel and cork ball are allowed to speak in the box context as cotton reels and cork balls, as well as echoing the cylindrical, spherical shapes Cornell always included in his Soap Bubble Sets. It is the same with the parallel bars and bits of wood. He could have attempted to disguise what these things actually are, but he chose not to. He wanted to allow different kinds of association to be provoked by the objects he selected. In the early boxes the objects were crafted and specialist, and because of their rarified quality they draw attention to the function they had before they entered his created world. A map drawn by a cartographer is precise in its rendering, it has been used by travellers or explorers through time and it displays a known and specific way of depicting the world. An object like a cotton reel or a piece of driftwood allow, by being more everyday, the possibility of a different range of associations entering into the assemblage.

Conclusion

Comments by Cornell's family, friends and others make it clear that Cornell was a hugely repressed individual. Self-obsessed, he was impossible to relate to except on his own terms, a person who was much more comfortable when communicating by telephone or mail than he was in face to face situations, who hardly ever paid even lip-service to social convention, who frequently refused to be photographed or allow for his voice to be taped. He drew on Christian Science as well as Surrealism to support his innate subjectivism, and, to a lesser extent, on American Transcendentalism, nineteenth-century Romanticism and Chinese art and philosophy. His works of art largely mirror his elusive and obsessional nature in their borrowings from a diffusion of sources, in their child-like vision and mature sophistication, in their nostalgic accents and Modernist leanings, in their origins in complex classifications and use of collage and juxtaposition.

The study of his working method, however, allows us to see that Cornell's endeavour is a remarkable yardstick in the history of art's attempts to bring more of the mind to consciousness. He worked purposefully and relentlessly on the subjects that obsessed him, and the very strictness of this regime often afforded others glimpses into a self that was consistently submerged. This is evident in the way he followed preferred routes – his wanderings in Manhattan, his observations in the backyard, his journeying to the Europe of his mind and his persistent dredging up of his own and his family's memories. His was a method that used discipline and structure almost like a strategy to encourage deviance. The films, the collages and the boxes all reach for an element of surprise, or what he referred to as white magic, the magic that would reveal to the artist in a flash of recognition the secret hiding-places of his mind.

Cornell's dossiers reveal the antithetical nature of his sources, and the variety of definitions of his work offered by contemporary and more recent artists and critics show that, so far at least, he has successfully eluded easy categorization.

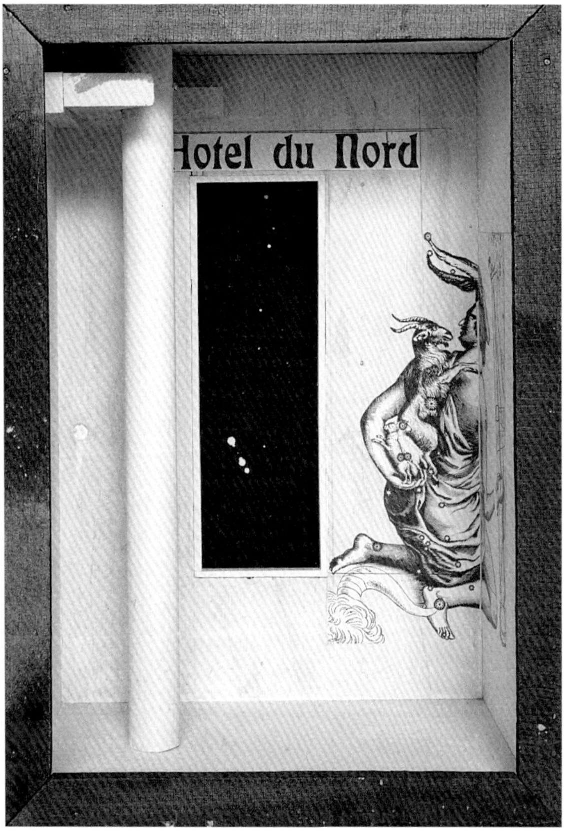

124 *Untitled (Hôtel du Nord)*, c. 1950–51, box construction.

Even the boxes themselves have that ambiguous quality. They are distillations, apparently, yet they are clearly part of a process; they exude stillness, timelessness, yet are manifestly stages in a voyage. Cornell's contradictory attitude to his art is revealed in the juxtaposition of the statement he made to David Mann – 'you don't know how terrible it is to be locked into boxes all your life' – with the instructions he left on certain dossiers to 'destroy in toto'.[232] That he poured himself into his art is certain, but no more certain than that he was a master of concealment. Motherwell's anecdote concerning Cornell's refusal to touch alcohol – he explained that he never wished to risk revealing something about himself – again reinforces the idea that self-revelation of an unedited nature would have been unthinkable to Cornell.

'GC 44' epitomizes Cornell's relentless gaze and his desperate attempts in this, his most expansive dossier, to find a method for 'crystalizing experience'. When he writes of the final distillation, where the original inspiration is almost lost sight of, we see again the paradox. He wanted something that was precise and crystallized, but which yet would conceal its origins (in the self). 'The Floral Still-Life' (an episode kept in the 'GC 44' dossier') shows, however, that the self is never lost sight of. Ostensibly a description of the way an image is transformed by the imagination, the episode is more tellingly an account of the way Cornell applied his will to mastering external realities by means of the subjective vision. With *Le Grand Meaulnes* we find Cornell linking himself to a character he referred to as the seeker of visions. This is the pull of the parallel biography, where Cornell's sense of his own life was to be reinforced or defined through association with a revered figure in literature.

Cornell's links with the Surrealists, but especially with Dorothea Tanning, are revealed in his fascination with dreams. Like the Surrealists he saw dreams as a source of precise images that could open the door to the mind. For Cornell the dream could confirm the worth of an image resting in the unconscious, and the dreams experienced by members of his family, and especially by Robert, could bring out images that had been buried in his own memory. Again, though, Cornell had his disagreements with the Surrealists: he had no time for their automatic writings, and insisted, like Nerval, on the need for a 'classical sense of form and genius of expression'.[233]

Cornell's approach to science confirms the personal nature of his response to his subject. His was not essentially an interest in contemporary discoveries but, instead, a form of nostalgia for the scientific books and experiences of his childhood. His Soap Bubble Sets tell us little about science, but quite a lot about Cornell's lifelong fascination with classification. He was concerned not only to find new ways to break up representations of the elements of the universe but ways also to classify his own representations: the questions we are left wondering about are those that reflect Cornell's obsession with museums and classification systems.

It is childhood, though, that was the central subject for Cornell. Dossiers, films, collages and boxes abound with images, and there is ample record of his relations with children. The importance of the memories of his childhood are inestimable – this was the most inextinguishable source of wonder for him. His choice of young girls and androgynous

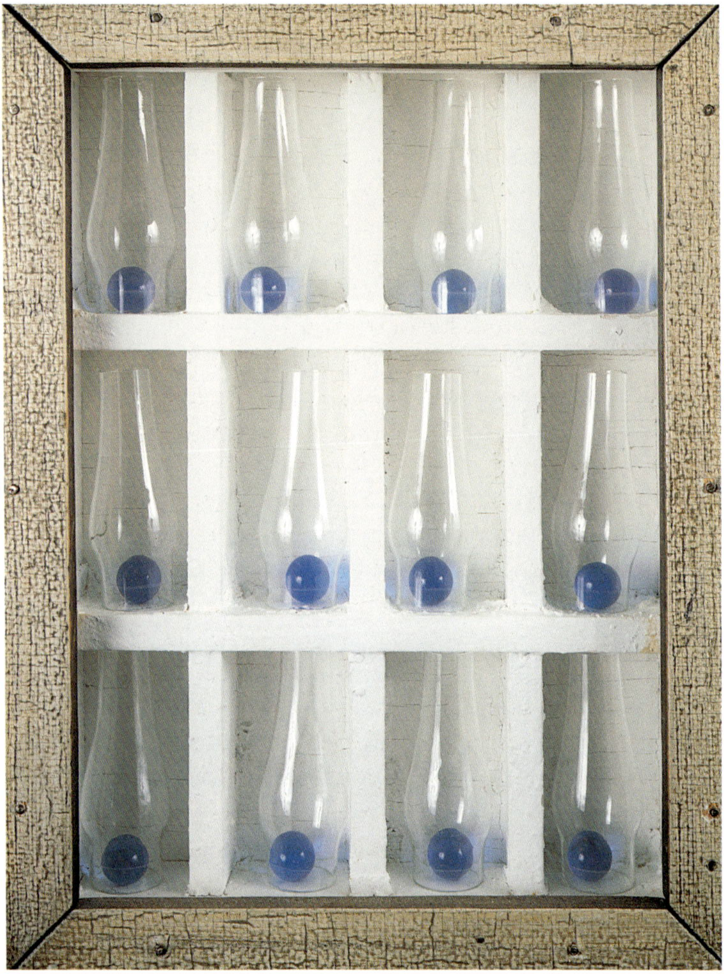

125 *An Image for 2 Emilies*, c. 1954, box construction.

images and the way that these are presented prompts again the speculation that he was able to entertain two separate notions of childhood, the first being the nineteenth-century ideal centring on the child's natural wisdom, and the second the use of the child/heroine as a surrogate for the artist himself, especially in the way that the child/heroine represents the rejection of real sexuality in the interests of creativity.

In the *Penny Arcade Portrait of Lauren Bacall* we can see how Cornell moved away from his subject to produce in the movie star a symbol (of purity and innocence), an icon that is housed in an architecture both formal and evocative. We find here Cornell linking himself to his subject as he had done in the case of Alain-Fournier's Meaulnes. In his relationships with women we see many of Cornell's characteristic obsessions, vagaries of behaviour and peculiarities of correspondence. His relation to the subjects of his 'portraits' is so patently – as Sontag noticed – to do with his own idea of that subject, that he consciously edits out what does not fit with that idea. In addition to this idea of control over his subjects is the very strong sense of identification he had and the idea of a second life that could be given by the artist as a gift to his subjects. The sense of the subject is much weaker than is the sense of the artist in dialogue with his obsessions: in this, all his portraits tend to belong to the genre of implicit self-portraiture.

May Tabak's story (see page 107) concerning Cornell and the packages seems to epitomize Cornell's way of discovering things. He planned out the way to surprise himself, and within the elaborate contrivance that he set up, he succeeded. Everyhing about this peculiar story reveals Cornell: his strange tangential relationships with people, where he sets the rules, the establishment of a ritual, the anticipation and the surprise. The dramatic shape he creates about this series of incidents reflects so much of his working method, as he sought with his arcane scenarios to create alternative worlds that would arrest him from his everydayness; in which he could free himself from the fixities about him, link himself to another enchanted wanderer, and find the self/spirit that would release him from his bodily concerns and physical limitations.

References

My research for this book has been greatly facilitated by access to the Joseph Cornell Papers, Archives of American Art, Smithsonian Institution, Washington, D.C., Gift of Elizabeth Cornell Benton. In the References that follow, this major archive is cited as Cornell Papers, followed by the microfilm reel and the frame number and/or date.

1 For further biographical details see Lynda Roscoe Hartigan, 'Joseph Cornell: A Biography', in *Joseph Cornell*, exh. cat., New York, The Museum of Modern Art, 1980, p. 100; and Deborah Soloman, *Utopia Parkway: The Life and Work of Joseph Cornell* (New York, 1997).

2 My interviews with Betty (Elizabeth Cornell Benton), were held on four occasions: 22 January 1982, 18 January 1983, and 16 March and 11 April 1984. All took place at her home at Westhampton on Long Island. These interviews have been crucial for my research, not least because she was close to her brother in sensibility, they shared a creative awareness (she studied art with Edward Hopper), the same spiritual beliefs and, of course, many childhood experiences. The information here was given in the course of my first interview, 22 January 1982.

3 See Julien Levy, *Memoir of an Art Gallery* (New York, 1977), p. 77ff.

4 See Dawn Ades, 'The Transcendental Surrealism of Joseph Cornell', in *Joseph Cornell*, exh. cat., MoMA, 1980, pp. 15–42.

5 Cornell Papers, reel 1058, frame 231.

6 Reprinted in André Breton, *Manifestoes of Surrealism*, trans. R. Seaver and H. R. Lane (Ann Arbor 1969), p. 26.

7 Ades, 'Transcendental Surrealism', pp. 38–9.

8 Interview with David Mann, 26 January 1982. All comments by Mann published here derive from this interview.

9 Soloman, *Utopia Parkway*, p. 336.

10 Early confessional modes and their influence on more recent artistic strategies are usefully discussed in Robert Rehder, *Wordsworth and the Beginnings of Modern Poetry* (London, 1981), chapter 1.

11 Cornell Papers, reel 1061 (9 March 1959).

12 Although almost all the dossiers are in the Smithsonian's archive (Joseph Cornell Papers) in Washington, D.C., a few are in other museums or private collections, for example 'Penny Arcade: Portrait of Lauren Bacall' (Lent to the Art Institute of Chicago by Lindy Bergman), 'Portrait of Ondine' (in a private collection in South America) and 'Portrait of Suzi Wong' (Collection of Anthony and Marie Peluso).

13 Benton interview, 22 January 1982.

14 Cornell Papers, reel 1072, frame 106.

15 The phrase 'museum without walls' was borrowed by Cornell from André Malraux.

16 'The Yale Student File', for example, is labelled 'Destroy All', while the 'Cherubino/Fountain of Youth' dossier is inscribed 'Not to be opened until 10 years after my death'.

17 Interview with John Bernard Myers, 19 January 1983. All comments by Myers first published here derive from this interview.

18 'I do not share in the dream theories of the Surrealists. While fervently admiring much of their work I have never been an official Surrealist, and

I believe that Surrealism has far healthier possibilities than have been developed. The constructions of Marcel Duchamp who the Surrealists themselves acknowledge bear out this thought, I believe.' The letter to Alfred Barr (Archives of The Museum of Modern Art, New York) is dated 13 November 1936, and is quoted in Ades, 'Transcendental Surrealism', p. 19.

19 Cornell wrote to his sister in 1932 to tell her of his discovery of a store – a Catholic icons shop – selling small glass domes.

20 Diane Waldman, *Joseph Cornell* (New York, 1977), p. 31.

21 Mary Ann Caws (ed.), *Joseph Cornell's Theater of the Mind: Selected Diaries, Letters, and Files* (New York, 1993), p. 33.

22 Cornell Papers, reel 1072, frame 162.

23 Michel Foucault, *The Order of Things: An Archaeology of the Human Sciences* (London, 1986), p. xviii.

24 Barbara Novak, *American Painting of the Nineteenth Century: Realism, Idealism and the American Experience* (New York, 1979), p. 110.

25 Interview with David Hare, 27 March 1984. All comments by Hare published here derive from this interview.

26 Interview with Robert Motherwell, 13 January 1983. All comments by Motherwell published here derive from this interview except for those made in his letter to to Jim Cohan and Arthur Greenberg (26 July 1981), credited in Reference 229.

27 Charles Simic, *Dime-Store Alchemy: The Art of Joseph Cornell* (Hopewell, NJ, 1992), p. 28.

28 See Ades, 'Transcendental Surrealism', p. 25, for an illustration of *Cit-Git Giorgio de Chirico* (1928) and a brief discussion of it.

29 Quoted in Siegfried Giedion, *Mechanization takes Command (A Contribution to Anonymous History)* (New York, 1975), p. 363.

30 Different links, formal links, between Duchamp and Cornell have been noted by Ades (in 'Transcendental Surrealism'), by Waldman (in her *Joseph Cornell*) and by Anne d'Harnoncourt ('The Cubist Cockatoo: A Preliminary Exploration of Joseph Cornell's Homages to Juan Gris', *Philadelphia Museum of Art Bulletin*, 321, 1978, pp.2–17).

31 Cornell Papers, reel 1058, 15 August 1945.

32 Motherwell interview.

33 Motherwell interview.

34 Cornell Papers, reel 1072, frame 436.

35 Cornell Papers, reel 1072, frame 229.

36 Cornell Papers, reel 1072, frame 229.

37 Cornell's notion, recorded in 'The Yale Student File'.

38 Interview with Donald Windham, 5 January 1982. All comments by Windham published here derive from this interview.

39 Cornell Papers, reel 1072, frame 125.

40 Cornell Papers, reel 1072, frame 389.

41 'He had a pad of yellow paper and a box of magic markers. He was writing, in this scribbled large handwriting, arcane notes'. Interview with Steve Wood, 9 December 1982. All comments by Wood published here derive from this interview. See also Dore Ashton, ed., *A Joseph Cornell Album* (New York, 1974), p. 2.

42 Cornell Papers, reel 1058, frame 269.

43 Cornell Papers, reel 1072, frame 339.

44 Cornell Papers, reel 1072, frame 123.

45 Cornell Papers, reel 1072, frame 389.

46 Windham interview.

47 Cornell Papers, reel 1072, frames 436, 437.

48 Cornell Papers, reel 1072, frame 148.

49 Cornell Papers, reel 1072, frame 163.

50 Cornell Papers, reel 1063, 9 September 1968.
51 Cornell Papers, reel 1072, frame 389.
52 Cornell Papers, reel 1072, frame 123.
53 Cornell Papers, reel 1072, frame 125.
54 Cornell Papers, reel 1074, frame 644.
55 Loy's relationship with Cornell was mostly based on their exchange of letters. She also sent him drafts of her poems (Cornell Papers, reel 1055, frame 1267). See also Mina Loy, *The Last Lunar Baedeker* (Manchester, 1985), p. 300.
56 Cornell Papers, reel 1072, frame 121.
57 Cornell Papers, reel 1072, frame 121.
58 An extract from De Quincey's 'The Glory of Motion' also appears in 'Portrait of Ondine' (1940s, 1950s). 'The Glory of Motion' is section I of De Quincey's essay 'The English Mail-Coach', first published in three parts in *Blackwood's Magazine* (October and December 1849).
59 Cornell Papers, reel 1072, frame 121.
60 Cornell Papers, reel 1072, frame 160.
61 Cornell Papers, reel 1072, frame 121.
62 Cornell Papers, reel 1072, frame 316.
63 Cornell Papers, reel 1072, frame 317.
64 Cornell Papers, reel 1072, frame 436.
65 Cornell Papers, reel 1072, frame 148.
66 Cornell Papers, reel 1072, frame 436.
67 Cornell Papers, reel 1072, frame 437.
68 Cornell Papers, reel 1072, frame 316.
69 Cornell Papers, reel 1072, frame 436.
70 Cornell Papers, reel 1072, frame 161. Cornell wrote to Mina Loy in 1943 to tell her he had just read *Le Grand Meaulnes* 'under the most ideal conditions. What an experience!'
71 Cornell Papers, reel 1072, frame 123.
72 Noted by Cornell in Cornell Papers, reel 1072, frame 123. See Alain-Fournier, *Le Grand Meaulnes*, trans. Frank Davison (Harmondsworth, 1974), chapters 8-11 inclusive, for Meaulnes's journey.
73 Simic, *Dime-Store Alchemy*, p. 11.
74 Cornell Papers, reel 1072, frame 161.
75 *Le Grand Meaulnes*, trans. Davison, p. 48.
76 *Le Grand Meaulnes*, trans. Davison, p. 43.
77 *Le Grand Meaulnes*, trans. Davison, p. 66.
78 A quotation from Andersen, used by Cornell in his 'Hans Christian Andersen', *Dance Index*, IV/9 (September 1945), p. 146.
79 Cornell Papers, reel 1072, frame 219.
80 Benton interview, 22 January 1982.
81 Written on a page 'borrowed' from 'GC 44' that is inserted in 'The Yale Student File'.
82 Subsequently published: Donald Windham, 'Things that Cannot be Said', in *Joseph Cornell: Collages, 1931–1972*, exh. cat., New York, Castelli, Feigen, Corcoran Gallery, 1978, p. 12.
83 Cornell Papers, reel 1072, frame 288.
84 Cornell was entirely a self-taught artist, and Betty has made it clear that he learned a great deal from listening to the radio. Inserted in the 'GC 44' dossier is Cornell's script, transcribed from memory, of the radio discus sion of *Swann's Way* in which André Malraux, Huntington Cairns and Allen Tait participated.
85 Boxes with wooden beading include *Untitled (Mélisande)* (c. 1948–50), *Untitled (Medici Prince)* (c. 1952–4), *Untitled (for Sheree North)* (1953–9), *An Owl for Ondine* (summer 1954), and *Untitled (Caravaggio Boy)* (October 1955). His sister explains that 'At the back of this place [the

Garden Center] there was one of the big houses in Flushing being torn down. He asked the man in charge if he could have any of the wood. He carted the wood home in a wheelbarrow. And some of the boxes . . ., any thing you see with the little beading, are from the wood of that house.' The big house Betty refers to here she later identified as Willet Mansion (Willet being the owner's name): Benton interview, 16 March 1984.

86 Motherwell interview.
87 Cornell Papers, reel 1072, frame 264.
88 Cornell Papers, reel 1072, frame 158.
89 Wood interview. Wood has since told Deborah Soloman (see Soloman, *Utopia Parkway*, p. 357), that Cornell claimed his 'mystical days' were Wednesdays rather than Thursdays.
90 Interview with Dorothea Tanning, 17 December 1982. All comments by Tanning published here derive from this interview.
91 Interview with Kathryn Kuh, 2 February 1983. All comments by Kuh published here derive from this interview.
92 Betsy von Furstenberg and Linda Scott were two of the young women that received mail from Cornell that included explicit sexual references and drawings.
93 Interview with Rudy Burckhardt, 7 December 1982. All comments by Burckhardt published here derive from this interview.
94 John Bernard Myers, *Tracking the Marvellous: A Life in the New York Art World* (New York, 1983), p. 73.
95 Motherwell interview.
96 Motherwell interview.
97 Motherwell interview.
98 Interview with Linda Scott, 19 January 1983. All comments by Scott published here derive from this interview.
99 For the 'cause' and the 'evidence', see Mary Baker Eddy, *Science and Health, with Key to the Scriptures* (Boston, 1934), p. 377 and p. 386.
100 *Joseph Cornell: Art and Metaphysics*, exh. cat. by Sandra Starr, New York, Castelli, Feigen, Corcoran Gallery, 1982, p. 1.
101 *Art and Metaphysics*, p. 4.
102 *Art and Metaphysics*, p. 5.
103 *Art and Metaphysics*, p. 4.
104 Cornell Papers, reel 1072, frame 257.
105 Cornell Papers, reel 1058, frame 208.
106 Cornell Papers, reel 1072, frame 136.
107 Cornell Papers, reel 1072, frame 125.
108 Cornell Papers, reel 1063, 17 February 1966.
109 Cornell Papers, reel 1072, frames 210, 257.
110 Windham interview.
111 'The Yale Student File'.
112 'The Yale Student File'.
113 Cornell Papers, reel 1072, frames 123, 106, 76.
114 Ashton, *A Joseph Cornell Album*, p. 10.
115 Ades, 'Transcendental Surrealism', p. 24.
116 Cornell Papers, reel 1072, frame 163.
117 In the dossier 'Portrait of Ondine', begun in the 1940s and revised through to the 1960s.
118 Cornell Papers, reel 1058, frame 241.
119 Benton interview, 22 January 1982.
120 Cornell Papers, reel 1058, frame 332.
121 It was in a letter to Alfred Barr (13 November 1936) that Cornell dissociated himself from Surrealist dream theories.
122 Cornell Papers, reel 1058, frame 231.

123 Gérard de Nerval, *Selected Writings*, trans. Geoffrey Wagner (New York, 1957), chapters 1 and 3.
124 Dawn Ades, *Dada and Surrealism* (London, 1974), p. 33.
125 Tanning interview.
126 Letter from Tanning (3 March 1948). Cornell Papers, reel 1055, frame 509.
127 Tanning interview.
128 Cornell Papers, reel 1058, frame 232.
129 Cornell Papers, reel 1072, frame 134.
130 Cornell Papers, reel 1055, frame 509.
131 Cornell Papers, reel 1055, frame 509.
132 Benton interview, 16 March 1984.
133 Wood interview.
134 Interview with Barbara Somers, 6 January 1983. All comments by Somers published here derive from this interview.
135 Cornell Papers, reel 1072, frame 288; reel 1072, frame 264 (5 October 1945).
136 Benton interview, 16 March 1984: Cornell often 'went fishing with daddy. They used to catch trout, and then they would have them mounted if they were especially nice. We always had this rainbow trout, very colourful, not big, no prizewinner, but very pretty – we *always* had that in our house.'
137 See Lynda Roscoe Hartigan, *Joseph Cornell: An Exploration of Sources*, exh. guide, Washington, D.C., National Museum of American Art, Smithsonian Institution, 1982, p. 8.
138 Benton interview, 16 March 1984.
139 Roger Shattuck, *The Banquet Years: The Origins of the Avant-Garde in France, 1885 to World War I* (New York, 1968), p. 31.
140 Benton interview, 16 March 1984.
141 Cornell Papers, reel 1072, frame 253.
142 Interview with Leila Hadley, 13 December 1982. All comments by Hadley published here derive from this interview.
143 Levy, *Memoir of an Art Gallery*, p. 77ff.
144 Howard Hussey, 'Music in the World of Joseph Cornell', *Keynote: A Magazine for the Arts*, III/3 (May 1979), pp. 7–12; John Ashbery, 'Cornell's Sublime Junk', *Newsweek* (8 December 1980), pp. 110–11.
145 Robert Morris, 'American Quartet', *Art in America* (December 1981), pp. 93–104.
146 Cornell Papers, reel 1058, frame 550.
147 The first 'Children's Page' to appear in View was in Cornell's own special issue, and it was probably he who instigated this feature of the magazine.
148 Windham, 'Things that Cannot be Said', p. 11.
149 Interview with Howard Hussey, 9 September 1981. All comments by Hussey published here derive from this interview.
150 A comment by Proust, cited in Tony Tanner, *The Reign of Wonder* (Cambridge, 1965), p. 15.
151 Interview with May Tabak, 24 January 1983. All comments by Tabak published here derive from this interview.
152 Cornell Papers, reel 1061 (3 March 1958); reel 1061 (27 May 1956).
153 Benton interview, 22 January 1982. After Cornell's death the Bébé Marie doll was returned to Ethel's nephew, Morgan, who inherited her belongings. Later, negotiations were entered into with the Cornell Estate and the box was sold to MoMA, New York.
154 Interview with Duane Michals, 2 July 1991. All comments by Michals published here derive from this interview.
155 This photo, taken by Ernst Beadle, appeared in David Bourdon, 'The

Enigmatic Bachelor of Utopia Parkway', *Life* (15 December 1967), pp. 52–61, 63, 66A.

156 Rosalind Krauss, 'Photography in the Service of Realism', *L'Amour Fou: Photography and Surrealism* (exh. cat by R. Krauss and Jane Livingston, Washington D.C. The Corcoran Gallery of Art, 1985), p. 74.

157 A potential confusion explored by E. Jentsch in 1906; see Sigmund Freud, 'The Uncanny' [1919], in *Art and Literature*, The Pelican Freud Library, vol. XIV, ed. Albert Dickson (Harmondsworth, 1985), p. 347.

158 Freud, 'The Uncanny', pp. 359-60.

159 *Cherubino* Source Box # 2 (undated), Cornell Study Center, National Museum of American Art, Smithsonian Institution, Washington, D.C.

160 Source Box # 3 (verso for 29 June 1960, 'Grad day, Wednesday'), Cornell Study Center.

161 Source Box # 3.

162 Source Box # 3 (7–8 June 1960, 'midnight into morning').

163 Source Box # 2 (20 July 1961).

164 Source Box # 2 (26 August 1959).

165 Source Box # 2 ('little dark haired girl at counter 2 days ago *smile*').

166 Source Box # 2 (26 August 1959).

167 Source Box # 2 (26 August 1959).

168 Source Box # 2 (28 August 1959); Source Box # 2 (undated).

169 Hadley interview.

170 Cornell Papers, reel 1072: 'Invitation to Learning (radio broadcast) 1943'.

171 Hadley interview.

172 Source Box # 2 (verso for 28 August 1959).

173 Source Box # 3 (29 June 1960, 'Wednesday, muggy day').

174 Source Box # 3 (6 June 1960).

175 See André Breton, 'Mad Love (excerpts)', in *What is Surrealism? Selected Writings*, ed. Franklin Rosemont (London, 1978), pp. 160–68.

176 Julien Levy, in *Surrealism* (exh. cat, New York, 1936), pp. 98–9.

177 Caws, in *Joseph Cornell's Theater of the Mind*, p. 35.

178 'The Crystal Cage' was the main feature of Cornell's contribution to this issue of *View*, entitled 'Americana Fantastica'. For this issue he also designed the front and back covers; supplied a photo of an assemblage of objects (a lit candle, a book, fragments of glass, wood, sand), which he entitled 'Spent Meteor / Night of Feb. 10, 1983 (For E. A. Poe)'; a reproduction of *Medici Slot Machine* (1943); a collage for Tamara Toumanova to accompany a poem by Charles Henri Ford; and, on the 'Children's Page', a photo of the doll Bébé Marie before it was encased.

179 See John Bernard Myers, 'Cornell: The Enchanted Wanderer', *Art in America*, LXI/5 (September/October 1973), pp. 76–81, republished in Ashton, *A Joseph Cornell Album*, pp. 150–53. See also the essay by Sandra Starr in *Joseph Cornell: The Crystal Cage (Portrait of Bérénice)*, exh. cat., Tokyo, Gatado Gallery, 1987; Helen H. Haroutunian, 'Joseph Cornell in "View"', *Arts Magazine*, LV/7 (March 1981), pp. 102–8; and Stanley Kunitz, 'The Crystal Cage', in Ashton, *A Joseph Cornell Album*, pp. 121–3. Appreciations of 'The Crystal Cage' were published in the 'Letters' section of *View*, no. 1, series IV (Spring 1944), including one from Marianne Moore ('I am indebted to *View* for making me somewhat closely acquainted with the work of Joseph Cornell') and one from John Bernard Myers ('Several of my friends and I have also wondered when you were going to have another picture story by Joseph Cornell. The Crystal Cage was surely one of your most exciting contributions'). Mina Loy sent her congratulations directly to Cornell: 'I was very happy to get your Crystal Cage. There was one star left in the next morning sky, and truely you had done something to that star' (Cornell Papers, reel 1055,

frame 1264). It inspired Charles Henri Ford to make a film with his niece Shelley – *Bérénice Come True* (Cornell Papers, reel 1055).

180 Blondin's exploit at Niagara Falls is cited by Mary Baker Eddy as an example of the mind's power over matter: 'The feats of the gymnast prove that latent mental fears are subdued by him . . . Had Blondin believed it impossible to walk the rope over Niagara's abyss of waters, he could never have done it'. Quoted in *Joseph Cornell and the Ballet*, exh. cat. by Sandra L. Starr, New York, Castelli, Feigen, Corcoran Gallery, 1983, p. 3.

181 One of Cornell's sources for 'The Crystal Cage' was this description: 'A little girl had just one great desire – to find God and His loveliness, whenever she heard anything particularly lovely, or saw anything particularly beautiful, there welled within her heart a great yearning to understand better the source of all beauty'. It appeared under the title 'The Heavenly Homesick' in a newspaper article for Tuesday 13 June 1939.

182 This article was extracted from Alan Pryce-Jones, *Private Opinion* (London, 1936).

183 Nathaniel Hawthorne, *The Scarlet Letter* (New York, 1962), chapter 5.

184 Henry James, *What Maisie Knew* (Harmondsworth, 1975), p. 37.

185 'Crystal' appears in a number of Cornell's titles for his works during this period: the Greta Garbo portrait is *The Crystal Mask*, and a bird-box in *Aviary* (exhibited at the Egan Gallery, New York, in 1949–50) is *Crystal Palace*.

186 Christopher Ricks (ed.), *The Poems of Tennyson* (London and Harlow, 1969), item 159, line 38.

187 Cornell was fascinated by towers – his childhood home at Nyack had one, and *Centuries of June*, a film he made in 1955, was originally entitled 'Tower House'. A dossier was labelled 'Towers', and one of the names he applied to 'GC 44' was 'Tower of Visions'. De Chirico's paintings frequently include towers, and the Italian artist was an inspiration to Cornell.

188 Cornell Papers, reel 1061 (14 October 1956); reel 1058 (14 October 1950); reel 1059 (15 April 1946).

189 Hadley interview.

190 Motherwell interview.

191 The dossier is now part of the Bergman Collection in the Art Institute of Chicago.

192 Dickran Tashjian, *Joseph Cornell: Gifts of Desire* (Miami Beach, 1992), pp. 119–37.

193 This is an extract from the 'Romantic Museum' publication for the Hugo Gallery, and contains the essence of the dossier notes.

194 Benton interview (11 April 1984).

195 Letter to Ruth Ford (21 May 1941), cited in Hartigan, 'Joseph Cornell: A Biography', p. 102.

196 Cornell Papers, reel 1062.

197 Giacometti, in James Lord, *A Giacometti Portrait* (2nd edn, New York, 1980), p. 10.

198 Eugène Delacroix, *The Journal*, ed. Hubert Wellington and trans. Lucy Norton, 3rd edn (London, 1995), p. 68. Delacroix is one of the few artists Cornell acknowledges by name (in 'The Yale Student File') as having influenced him.

199 Giacometti, in Lord, *A Giacometti Portrait*, p. 35.

200 Interview with Susan Sontag, 10 April 1984. All comments by Sontag published here derive from this interview.

201 Correspondence in the Collection of Susan Sontag.

202 Hadley interview.

203 Letter from Cornell to Betsy von Furstenburg, in her collection.
204 Letter from Cornell, in the Von Furstenburg collection.
205 Cornell Papers, reel 1064.
206 Cornell Papers, reel 1064 (26 November 1972).
207 Cornell Papers, reel 1064 (7 March 1971).
208 See Hartigan, 'Joseph Cornell: A Biography', p. 92.
209 Benton interview, 22 January 1982.
210 Benton interview, 22 January 1982.
211 For example, the steel-engraved image of a piano in a warehouse in Untitled (1930s – see *Joseph Cornell: Collages, 1931–1972*, plate 11) is from a copy of *The Scientific American* dated 1881.
212 See Ades, 'Transcendental Surrealism', p. 32.
213 The recto and verso of the collage *Vue par Tina (Mathematics in Nature)* uses images from science books by Adler.
214 Benton interview, 22 January 1982.
215 Cornell Papers, reel 1058, frame 185. Cornell learned about Redon in the 1920s through contemporary publications, such as the yearbook *Ganymed* (Munich, 1919–25) edited by Meier-Graefe. He also read Marsden Hartley's *Adventures in the Arts* (1921) – 'a beautiful and sensitive book of appreciation . . . to which I owe an eternal debt of gratitude . . . Redon . . . many others all came in for aesthetically stimulating appraisals.'
216 Novak, *American Painting*, p. 110.
217 Cornell was particularly interested in scientists who had religious links – Kepler and Max Planck, for example.
218 C. V. Boys, *Soap Bubbles and the Forces which Mould Them* (London, 1902), pp. 19, 85.
219 Cornell Papers, reel 1072, frame 229 ('August 15 1944, used aniline dye for the first time on boxes').
220 Cornell Papers, reel 1070, frame 256.
221 Cornell Papers, reel 1070, frame 238.
222 Cornell Papers, reel 1070, frame 256.
223 Cornell Papers, reel 1070, frame 256.
224 Cornell Papers, reel 1070, frame 261.
225 Cornell Papers, reel 1070, frame 266.
226 In 1944 Tanning and Max Ernst were living in Arizona.
227 Cornell Papers, reel 1074, frame 644 (undated, but c. 1956).
228 Cornell Papers, reel 1059, frame 352 (21–22 September 1951).
229 Letter from Robert Motherwell to Jim Cohan and Arthur Greenberg (26 July 1981), citation courtesy of Jim Cohan.
230 The *Il Sole Antipasto* cans were collected by a young artist, John Willenbecher, and delivered to Cornell at Utopia Parkway. Interview with John Willenbecher, 12 April 1984.
231 In this context we should bear in mind Cornell's commercial background: while employed as a fabrics salesman in 1921–31 he daily worked on presentations, and he often undertook jobs for Columbia Studios as well as *Vogue, House and Garden* and other magazines, where glamour, style, design and colour coordination were important for the sales of products. His father, too, had been involved in the business of displaying and selling textiles.
232 Mann interview.
233 Cornell Papers, reel 1058, frame 231 (undated).

Select Bibliography

Dawn Ades: 'The Transcendental Surrealism of Joseph Cornell', *Joseph Cornell*, exh. cat. ed. Kynaston McShine; New York, MoMA, 1980, pp. 15–42

L'Amour Fou: Photography and Surrealism, exh. cat. by Rosalind Krauss and Jane Livingston, with an essay by Dawn Ades; Washington, D.C., The Corcoran Gallery of Art, 1985

John Ashbery: 'Cornell: The Cube Root of Dreams', *Art News* (Summer 1967)

—— : 'Cornell's Sublime Junk', *Newsweek* (8 December 1980), pp. 110–11

Dore Ashton, ed.: *A Joseph Cornell Album* (New York, 1974, reprinted 1989)

Aviary by Joseph Cornell, exh. cat. by Donald Windham; New York, Egan Gallery, 1949

David Bourdon: 'The Enigmatic Bachelor of Utopia Parkway', *Life* (15 December 1967), pp. 52–66

André Breton: *Manifestoes of Surrealism*, trans. Richard Seaver and Helen R. Lane (Ann Arbor, 1969)

Mary Ann Caws, ed.: *Joseph Cornell's Theatre of the Mind: Selected Diaries, Letters, and Files* (New York, 1993)

John Coplans: 'Notes on the Nature of Joseph Cornell', *Artforum* (February 1963), pp. 27–9

Joseph Cornell: '"Enchanted Wanderer": Excerpt from a Journey Album for Hedy Lamarr', *View*, I/9–10 (December 1941–January 1942), p. 3

Alexandra Cortesi: 'Joseph Cornell', *Artforum* (April 1966), pp. 27–31

Dorothea Tanning, exh. cat. by Max Ernst; New York, Julien Levy Gallery, 1944

Dovecotes, Hotels and Other White Spaces: Joseph Cornell, exh. cat. with an essay by Brian O'Doherty, New York, The Pace Gallery, 1989

Mary Baker Eddy: *Science and Health with Key to the Scriptures* (Boston, 1934)

Fantastic Art, Dada, Surrealism, exh. cat. ed. Alfred H. Barr, Jr; New York, The Museum of Modern Art, 1936

E. C. Goossen: 'The Plastic Poetry of Joseph Cornell', *Art International*, III/10 (1959–60), pp. 37–40

Anne d'Harnoncourt: 'The Cubist Cockatoo: A Preliminary Exploration of Joseph Cornell's Homages to Juan Gris', *Philadelphia Museum of Art Bulletin*, 321 (1978), pp. 2-17

Helen H. Haroutunian: 'Joseph Cornell in "View"', *Arts Magazine*, LV/7 (March 1981), pp. 102-8

Lynda Roscoe Hartigan: 'Joseph Cornell: A Biography', *Joseph Cornell*, exh. cat. ed. Kynaston McShine; New York, MoMA, 1980, pp. 91–120

Marsden Hartley: *Adventures in the Arts: Informal Chapters on Painters, Vaudeville, and Poets* (New York, 1921)

J. Hobernian: 'The Strange Films of Joseph Cornell', *American Film* (January/February 1980), pp. 18–19

Walter Hopps: 'Boxes', *Art International*, VIII/2 (20 March 1964), pp. 38–42

Edouard Jaguer: *Joseph Cornell* (Paris, 1989)

Ellen Johnson: 'Arcadia Enclosed: The Boxes of Joseph Cornell', *Arts Magazine* (September/October 1965), pp. 35–7

Joseph Cornell, exh. cat. by Diane Waldman; New York, Solomon R. Guggenheim Gallery, 1967

Joseph Cornell, exh. cat. with an essay by John Bernard Myers; New York, ACA Galleries, 1975

Joseph Cornell: Collages, 1931–1972, exh. cat. by Donald Windham and Howard Hussey; New York, Castelli, Feigen, Corcoran Gallery, 1978
Joseph Cornell, exh. cat. ed. Kynaston McShine; New York, The Museum of Modern Art, 1980
Joseph Cornell: An Exploration of Sources, exh. guide by Lynda Roscoe Hartigan; Washington, D.C., National Museum of American Art, Smithsonian Institution, 1982
Joseph Cornell: Art and Metaphysics, exh. cat. by Sandra L. Starr; New York, Castelli, Feigen, Corcoran Gallery, 1982
Joseph Cornell and the Ballet, exh. cat. by Sandra L. Starr; New York, Castelli, Feigen, Corcoran Gallery, 1983
Joseph Cornell Portfolio–Catalogue, exh. cat. by Sandra L. Starr; New York, Castelli, Feigen, Corcoran Gallery, 1976
Joseph Cornell: The Crystal Gaze (Portrait of Bérénice), exh. cat. by Sandra L. Starr and Takahiko Okada; Tokyo, Gatado Gallery, 1987
Joseph Cornell: Cosmic Travels, exh. cat., with essays by Charles A. Whitney and Angela Kramer; New York, Whitney Museum of American Art, 1996
Marjorie Keller: *The Untutored Eye: Childhood in the Films of Cocteau, Cornell, Brakhage* (Rutherford, NJ, 1986)
Thomas Lawson: 'Silently, by Means of a Flashing Light', *October*, 15 (Winter 1980), pp. 29–60
Julien Levy: *Memoir of An Art Gallery* (New York, 1977)
Mina Loy: *The Last Lunar Baedeker* (Manchester, 1985)
Richard Martin: 'Some Lobsters, Some Elephants: Surrealist Reflections on Joseph Cornell's "A Pantry Ballet (for Jacques Offenbach)"', *Arts Magazine*, LX/6 (February 1986), pp. 30–32
Annette Michelson: '"Rose Hobart" and "Monsieur Phot": Early Films from Utopia Parkway', *Artforum*, 10 (June 1973), pp. 47–57
Robert Morris: 'American Quartet', *Art in America* (December 1981), pp. 93–104
John Bernard Myers: 'Cornell: The Enchanted Wanderer', *Art in America*, LXI/5 (September/October 1973), pp. 76–81
— 'Joseph Cornell: It was his Genius to Imply the Cosmos', *Art News* (May 1975).
— *Tracking the Marvelous: A Life in the New York Art World* (New York, 1983)
Gérard de Nerval: *Selected Writings*, trans. Geoffrey Wagner (New York, 1957)
Brian O'Doherty: *American Masters: The Voice and the Myth* (New York, 1974)
David Porter: 'Assembling a Poet and her Poems: Convergent Limit – Works of Joseph Cornell and Emily Dickinson', *Word & Image*, X/3 (1994), pp. 199–221
Fairfield Porter: 'Joseph Cornell', *Art and Literature* (Spring 1966), pp. 120–30
Carter Ratcliff: 'Joseph Cornell: Mechanic of the Ineffable', *Joseph Cornell*, exh. cat. ed. Kynaston McShine; New York, MoMA, 1980, pp. 43–68
Harold Rosenberg: 'Object Poems', *The New Yorker* (3 June 1967), pp. 112, 114–18
Charles Simic: *Dime-Store Alchemy: The Art of Joseph Cornell* (Hopewell, NJ, 1992)
P. Adams Sitney: 'The Cinematic Gaze of Joseph Cornell', *Joseph Cornell*, exh. cat. ed. Kynaston McShine; New York, MoMA, 1980, pp. 69–90
Deborah Soloman: *Utopia Parkway: The Life and Work of Joseph Cornell* (New York, 1997)
Surrealism, ex. cat. by Julien Levy, New York, Julien Levy Gallery, 1936
Dorothea Tanning: *Birthday* (Santa Monica & San Francisco, 1986)
Dickran Tashjian: *Joseph Cornell: Gifts of Desire* (Miami Beach, 1992)
Donald Windham: 'Things that Cannot be Said: A Reminiscence', *Joseph Cornell: Collages, 1931–1972*, exh. cat. by Donald Windham and Howard Hussey; New York, Castelli, Feigen, Corcoran Gallery, 1978, pp. 11–13
Jane Wodening: *From the Book of Legends* (London, 1993)

List of Illustrations

21 Cornell's own late-nineteenth-century stereoscope. Collection of Elizabeth Cornell Benton. Photo: the author
22 Viewing slide for a stereoscope. Collection of Elizabeth Cornell Benton. Photo: the author
23 *Untitled (Ludwig II of Bavaria)*, c.1940–55, boxed dossier: a hinged wooden valise covered in faux leather paper with brass fittings and sepia–toned photograph mounted inside the lid. Photo: Graydon Wood
24 *Untitled (Object)*, c. 1933, box construction. © The Joseph and Robert Cornell Memorial Foundation. Photo: Bevan Davies
25 Robert Cornell smiling. Photo: Joseph Cornell Study Centre (Gift of Mr and Mrs John A. Benton) / National Museum of American Art (Smithsonian Institution), Washington, D.C.
26 'GC 44' notations, 1962 and 1964. Collection of the author, gift of Elizabeth Cornell Benton. Photo: Ken Lee
27 Duane Michals, *Joseph Cornell in a Bedroom at Utopia Parkway*, 1970, photograph. Photo: courtesy of Duane Michals
28 Hans Namuth, *Joseph Cornell by Woof's Burial Site at Betty Benton's in Westhampton*, 1971, photograph. Photo: © 1991 Hans Namuth Estate, Collection of the Centre for Creative Photography, The University of Arizona
29 *L'Abeille*, 1966, collage. Art Institute of Chicago (Lindy and Edwin Bergman Joseph Cornell Collection). Photo: © Art Institute of Chicago 1996; all rights reserved
30 Detail of *Hôtel de la Pomme d'Or*, c. 1954–5, box construction. Private collection. Photo: Pace Gallery / © Ellen Page Wilson 1969
31 A detail (lower central panel) from Jan van Eyck's *Ghent Altarpiece*, completed 1432. Cathedral of St Bavo, Ghent, Belgium
32 *A Swan Lake for Tamara Toumanova (Homage to the Romantic Ballet)*, 1946, box construction. Private collection. Photo: Janet Woodard
33 *Setting for a Fairy Tale*, c. 1942–6, box construction. Collection of Mr and Mrs Robert Lehrman, Washington, D.C.
34 *Untitled (Dovecote)*, c. mid–1950s, box construction. Private collection. Photo: Pace Gallery
35 *Untitled (Juan Gris)*, an undated box construction. Private collection. Photo: Pace Gallery / Bill Jacobsen Studio
36 A pair of book illustrations of cockatoos – cut and inscribed by Cornell – from his files on Juan Gris, c. 1953 – early 1960s. Joseph Cornell Study Centre, National Museum of American Art, Smithsonian Institution (gift of Mr and Mrs John A. Benton).
37 *Untitled (Bird and Corset)*, 1930s, collage. © The Joseph and Robert Cornell Memorial Foundation. Photo: courtesy of C & M Arts, New York
38 *Toward the Blue Peninsula (for Emily Dickinson)*, c. 1953, box construction. Private collection. Photo: Pace Gallery
39 *Untitled*, c. 1970, collage. Private collection. Photo: Pace Gallery
40 *Untitled*, an undated box construction. Private collection. Photo: Pace Gallery / Bill Jacobsen Studio
41 *Pleiades as seen with Unaides' Eye*, c. 1945, driftwood, nails and white china figure. Private collection
42 Cornell's notation on a paper bag from the King Karol music store. Collection of the author, gift of Elizabeth Cornell Benton. Photo: Ken Lee
43 Hans Namuth, *Joseph Cornell*, 1970, photograph. Photo: © 1991 Hans Namuth Estate, Collection of the Centre for Creative Photography, The University of Arizona
44 *Untitled (Young Sparrows in a Basket)*, 1967, collage. © The Joseph and Robert Cornell Memorial Foundation. Photo: Richard L. Feigen & Company
45 *Untitled*, 1959, box construction. Private collection. Photo: Pace Gallery

46 *Untitled*, *c.* 1960s, collage. Collection of the author. Photo: Ken Lee
47 *Satie and Ravel*, *c.* 1960, collage composed of cut and pasted commercially printed papers, with graphite on untempered masonite (including Robert Cornell's rabbit drawing). Art Institute of Chicago, gift of Lindy and Edwin Bergman, in memory of Robert Cornell. Photo: © Art Institute of Chicago 1996; all rights reserved
48 *Untitled (American Rabbit)*, 1945–6, box construction. Collection Mr and Mrs E. A. Bergman, Chicago
49 Duane Michals, *Cornell in his Garden*, *c.* 1970, a photograph taken at Cornell's request. Photo: courtesy of Duane Michals.
50 Harry Roseman, *Rabbits in Snow: Joseph Cornell's Backyard*, 1970. Photo: © Harry Roseman, 1970
51 *Untitled (Woodpecker Habitat)*, 1946, box construction. Collection Mr and Mrs E. A. Bergman, Chicago
52 *Untitled (Young Lady in Blue, Paul and Virginia)*, *c.* 1960, collage. Art Institute of Chicago (lent by Lindy and Edwin Bergman). Photo: © Art Institute of Chicago 1996; all rights reserved
53 *Untitled (Paul and Virginia)*, *c.* 1946–8, box construction with hinged door. Collection Mr and Mrs E.A. Bergman, Chicago
54 Cornell and his sister Betty in a box pram at Nyack, *c.* 1905. Photo: collection of the author, gift of Elizabeth Cornell Benton
55 Cornell and the quince tree, 1964. Photo: collection of the author, gift of Elizabeth Cornell Benton
56 *Untitled (Great Horned Owl with Full Moon)*, *c.* 1942, box construction. Private collection. Photo: Castelli Feigen Corcoran/Malcolm Varon
57 Carton of cutouts from hand–coloured lithographs, etchings, engravings and aquatints from John James Audubon's *Birds of America* (1840–4). © The Joseph and Robert Cornell Memorial Foundation
58 Cornell's toy Ferris-wheel. Collection of Elizabeth Cornell Benton. Photo: the author
59 Cornell and his niece, Helen Jagger Batcheller, in the early 1930s. Collection of Elizabeth Cornell Benton, gift to the author
60 *Untitled*, *c.* mid-1960s, collage. Private collection. Photo: Pace Gallery
61 Hans Namuth, *Joseph Cornell with his record collection, 'listening' to a book*, *c.* 1970, photograph. Photo: Hans Namuth © 1991 Hans Namuth Estate, Collection of the Centre for Creative Photography, The University of Arizona
62 Assemblage of brown paper bags from music stores with Cornell's handwitten notations on them. Collection of the author, gift of Elizabeth Cornell Benton. Photo: Ken Lee
63 *Untitled (Bébé Marie)*, early 1940s, construction (papered and painted wooden box, with painted corrugated cardboard floor, containing doll in cloth dress and straw hat with cloth flowers, dried flowers, and twigs, flecked with paint). Museum of Modern Art, New York, acquired through the Lillie P. Bliss Request. Photo: © 1997 Museum of Modern Art, New York
64 Duane Michals, *Joseph Cornell with Bébé Marie*, *c.* 1970, photograph. Photo: courtesy of Duane Michals
65 Cornell with Bébé Marie before she was encased, 1930s. Photo: collection of the author, gift of Elizabeth Cornell Benton
66 Raoul Ubac, *Mannequin*, 1937, photograph. Photo: © ADAGP, Paris and DACS, London 1998
67 *Untitled (called 'Sequestered Bower')*, 1948 (painted, paper-covered, glazed wooden box for an assemblage of amber glass, wood, bark, plastic doll, twine, wire, dried plants, mirrors, and sawdust-like substance). Art Institute of Chicago (Lindy and Edwin Bergman Joseph Cornell Collection). Photo: © Art Institute of Chicago 1996; all rights reserved

68 Hans Bellmer, *Doll (La Poupée)*, 1936/1949. Photo: © ADAGP, Paris and DACS, London 1998
69 *Untitled*, c. 1960s, collage. Private collection. Photo: Pace Gallery
70 *Fountain of Youth*, 1959, collage. Dr and Mrs Joseph Roshe Collection, courtesy Donald Morris Gallery Inc., Birmingham, MI.
71 *Untitled*, 1959, verso of illus 70. Dr and Mrs Joseph Roshe Collection, courtesy Donald Morris Gallery Inc., Birmingham, MI.
72 *Nymphlight*, 1957, a still of Gwen Thomas in Bryant Park. Photo: Anthology Film Archives, New York
73 Robert being swung in his mother's arms ('Cherubino'), *c.* 1911. Photo: Joseph Cornell Study Centre (Gift of Mr and Mrs John A. Benton)/National Museum of American Art (Smithsonian Institution), Washington, D.C.
74 *Untitled* (*Cherub with Kitten*), an undated collage.Private collection. Photo: Richard L. Feigen & Company
75 *Untitled (Ondine)*, *c.* 1944–6, box construction with electric light. Private collection. Photo: Richard L. Feigen & Company
76 *Untitled*, *c.* mid–1950s, box construction. Private collection. Photo: Pace Gallery/© Ellen Page Wilson 1969
77 'The Crystal Cage: Portrait of Bérénice', *c.* 1943, valise containing documents. Collection of Richard L. Feigen & Company
78 Calligram of the Pagode de Chanteloup in 'The Crystal Cage', 1943. Collection of Richard L. Feigen & Company
79 Collage from 'The Crystal Cage', 1943. Collection of Richard L. Feigen & Company
80 Bérénice gazing into her own past and future, from 'The Crystal Cage', published in *View* magazine, January 1943. Collection of Richard L. Feigen & Company
81 *Untitled (Mélisande)*, *c.* 1948–50, construction. Private collection
82 The 'Penny Arcade Portrait' dossier for the Lauren Bacall box, 1945–6, (paperboard folder containing photographs and various paper materials). Art Institute of Chicago, loaned by Lindy Bergman. Photo: © Art Institute of Chicago 1996; all rights reserved
83 *Untitled (Penny Arcade Portrait of Lauren Bacall)*, 1945–6, mixed-media construction. Lindy Bergman Collection, Chicago. Photo: © Art Institute of Chicago 1996; all rights reserved
84 *Swiss Shoot-the-Chutes*, 1944, construction. The Solomon R. Guggenheim Museum, New York, Peggy Guggenheim Collection
85 *The Caliph of Bagdad*, *c.* 1954, box construction. Collection Mrs Lindy Bergman, Chicago
86 *The Ellipsian*, 1966, collage of reproduction, illustration and paper, with pencil, crayon and stain. Private collection. Photo: Richard L. Feigen & Company
87 *Le Tournesol de Minuit*, *c.* 1966, collage. Susan Sontag collection
88 *Untitled*, *c.* 1966, collage, verso of illus. Susan Sontag collection
89 *Untitled (Hôtel de l'Etoile, Grand Hôtel Bon Port, Apollinaris)*, *c.* 1966, collage. Susan Sontag collection
90 *Untitled (Susan Sontag, Veilleuse)*, *c.* 1966, collage, verso of illus. 89. Susan Sontag collection
91 *The Uncertainty Principle*, 1966, collage. Private collection. Photo: Pace Gallery
92 *Portrait*, *c.* 1955, box construction. Private collection. Photo: Pace Gallery
93 *Untitled (Leila Hadley with Haiti stamp)*, *c.* 1960s, collage. Collection of Leila Hadley. Photo: N. L. Roberts
94 *Untitled*, *c.* 1964, mixed-media construction. Private collection
95 *Untitled*, *c.* 1964, construction. Private collection
96 The automat photo of Leila Hadley seen in illus. 95. Collection of Leila Hadley

97 The three automat photos of Leila Hadley aged twelve. Collection of Leila Hadley

98 Cornell and Leila Hadley having tea at the kitchen table, Utopia Parkway, 1971.Collection of Leila Hadley. Photo: Courtesy of Leila Hadley

99 *Untitled (after La Pression Atmosphérique)*, *c.* 1932–9, collage of engravings and photomechanical reproductions on paper and cardboard

100 *Soap Bubble Set (Lunar Rainbow) (Space Object)*, an undated box construction. Private collection. Photo: Pace Gallery/Bill Jacobsen Studio

101 Odilon Redon, *The Eye like a Strange Balloon wafts itself towards the Infinite*, 1882, lithograph.

102 Illustration from C. V. Boys, *Soap-Bubbles, and the Forces which Mould Them*, London, 1902.

103 Illustration from C. V. Boys, *Soap-Bubbles, and the Forces which Mould Them*, London, 1902.

104 *Untitled*, an undated box construction. Private collection. Photo: Pace Gallery/Phillips/Schwab

105 *Untitled*, an undated box construction. Private collection. Photo: Pace Gallery

106 *Untitled (Hote)*, an undated construction. Private collection. Photo: courtesy of Dore Ashton

107 Source materials for the collage *Eine Kleine Schnee-Musik* including landscape illustration from *Arizona Highways* and cutout of a Mozart automaton, *c.* 1962. From the Archives of American Art, Smithsonian Institution (Joseph Cornell Papers), sheet music and gramaphone record from the Joseph Cornell Study Centre, National Museum of American Art, gift of Mr and Mrs John A. Benton. Photo: Joseph Cornell Study Centre, National Museum of American Art, Smithsonian Institution (gift of Mr and Mrs John A. Benton)

108 *Eine Kleine Schnee-Musik*, *c.* 1962, collage. Private collection. Photo: Otto Nelson/reverse of print return to Margery Byers/NMAA Smithsonian Institution Washington D.C.

109 *Soap Bubble Set*, 1936, box construction. Wadsworth Athenaeum, Hartford, CT. Gift of Henry and Walter Keney. Photo: ©Wadsworth Athenaeum/Joseph Szaszfai

110 Installation view of *Elements of Natural Philosophy* and *Soap Bubble Set*, shown as part of the exhibition 'Fantastic Art, Dada, Surrealism' at the Museum of Modern Art, New York, 7 December 1936 – 17 January 1937. Photo: © 1997 Museum of Modern Art, New York

111 George Platt Lynes's re–arrangement of Cornell's installation: *Soap Bubble Set, Composition of Objects*, 1936

112 *Spirit Level*, 1940s, box construction. Private collection. Photo: courtesy of Dore Ashton

113 *Soap Bubble Set*, 1942, box construction. Solomon R. Guggenheim Museum, New York

114 *An Analemna, Shewing by Inspection the Time of Sun Rising and Sun Setting, the Length of Days and Nights*, 1948–50, box construction. Private collection. Photo: Pace Gallery/Bill Jacobsen Studio

115 *Untitled*, 1950, box construction. Private collection. Photo: Pace Gallery /Bill Jacobsen Studio

116 *Soap Bubble Set*, 1947, box construction. Private collection. Photo: courtesy Shigeru Yokota Inc., Tokyo

117 *Rose des Vents*, *c.* 1966, box construction. Collection of Mr and Mrs Robert Lehrman, Washington, D.C.

118 *Soap Bubble Set*, 1939, construction of wood, glass, fibreboard, clay, velvet and photomechanical reproductions. Collection of Mr and Mrs E. A. Bergman.

119 *L'Humeur Vagabonde*, late 1950s, box construction. Private collection. Photo: Pace Gallery/Ellen Page Wilson 1969
120 The lid from a can of *Il Sole Antipasto*, 1964. Collection of John Willenbacher. Photo: courtesy of the author
121 *Dieppe*, an undated box construction. Private collection. Photo: courtesy of Dore Ashton
122 *The Magnetism of the Sun*, an undated box construction. Photo: courtesy of Dore Ashton
123 *'Sono un caro, e riverito foglio di . . . illustris'*, an undated box construction. Private collection. Photo: courtesy of Dore Ashton
124 *Untitled (Hôtel du Nord)*, c. 1950–51, box construction. Private collection. Photo: Pace Gallery
125 *An Image for 2 Emilies*, c. 1954, box construction. Collection of Mr and Mrs Robert Lehrman, Washington, D.C.